SURVIVING THE *Essex*

AMERICA AND THE SEA

Richard J. King, Williams College at Mystic Seaport, Editor

AMERICA AND THE SEA is a series of original and classic works
of fiction, nonfiction, poetry, and drama bearing on the history of
America's engagement with our oceans and coastlines. Spanning
diverse eras, populations, and geographical settings, the series strives
to introduce, revive, and aggregate a wide range of exemplary and
seminal stories about our American maritime heritage, including the
accounts of First Peoples, explorers, voluntary and forced immigrants,
fishermen, whalers, captains, common sailors, members of the navy
and coast guard, marine biologists, and the crews of vessels ranging
from lifeboats, riverboats, and tugboats to recreational yachts. As a
sailor's library, America and the Sea introduces new stories of maritime
interest and reprints books that have fallen out of circulation and
deserve reappraisal, and publishes selections from well-known works
that reward reconsideration because of the lessons they offer about
our relationship with the ocean.

For a complete list of books available in this series, see www.upne.com

Surviving the Essex: The Afterlife of America's Most Storied Shipwreck
David O. Dowling

David O. Dowling

~~~~~~

SURVIVING THE *Essex*

~~~~~~

The Afterlife of America's Most Storied Shipwreck

~~~~~~

ForeEdge

ForeEdge
An imprint of University Press of New England
www.upne.com
© 2016 David O. Dowling
Manufactured in the United States of America
Designed by Mindy Basinger Hill
Typeset in Adobe Caslon Pro

Library of Congress Cataloging-in-Publication Data

Names: Dowling, David Oakey, 1967– author.
Title: Surviving the Essex : the afterlife of America's
most storied shipwreck / David O. Dowling.

Description: Hanover, NH : ForeEdge,
An imprint of University Press of New England, [2016] |
Includes bibliographical references and index.

Identifiers: LCCN 2015034637 (print) | LCCN 2015047432
(ebook) | ISBN 9781611689419 (cloth) | ISBN 9781611689075
(pbk.) | ISBN 9781611689426 (ebook) | ISBN 9781611689426
(epub, pdf & mobi)

Subjects: LCSH: Essex (Whaleship) | Shipwrecks—
Pacific Ocean. | Shipwreck survival—Pacific Ocean.

Classification: LCC G530. E77 D68 2016 (print) |
LCC G530. E77 (ebook) | DCC 910.9164/9—dc23
LC record available at http://lccn.loc.gov/2015034637

5 4 3 2 1

FOR *Julie*, A SURVIVOR

CONTENTS

ACKNOWLEDGMENTS

Among the many people who made this book possible, Nathaniel Philbrick deserves special recognition for initially inspiring it with his stellar history *In the Heart of the Sea: The Tragedy of the Whaleship* Essex. Much of the primary research for this project took place at the Nantucket Historical Association (NHA), where Elizabeth Oldham of the Research and Collections Department guided my exploration of the vast archive. Marie Henke and the staff were particularly accommodating in allowing me access to rare materials vital to this project. I would like to thank William J. Tramposch, Gosnell Executive Director of the NHA, for his enthusiasm and insights into the nature of whaling culture on Nantucket. Mark H. Procknik, librarian at the New Bedford Whaling Museum, was extremely helpful in providing access to materials for this project. Dr. Kelly Gleason Keogh, the archaeologist at the Papahanaumokuakea Marine National Monument (PMNM) who led the *Two Brothers* shipwreck project, deserves recognition for her encouragement and vital contribution to this research. The University of Iowa College of Liberal Arts and Sciences supplied essential travel funds. I am deeply indebted to all these individuals and institutions.

The development of the manuscript depended on the encouragement of the following people. My longtime friend Scott Baxter, Navy veteran and Melville aficionado, contributed ideas and materials that shaped this project. His passion is truly contagious, like that of Melville Society colleagues Timothy Marr, Daniel Goske, Peter Riley, A. Robert Lee, and Michael Jonik. Kind words regarding my Melville research from Hershel Parker and Sam Otter have been especially encouraging. I am particularly grateful for the generous support of John Bryant for my earlier work for the journal *Leviathan*, and Wyn Kelley for *Chasing the White Whale*. Thanks go to my former neighbor Louie Psihoyos, an Academy Award–winning director (*The Cove*), for lending his wisdom on cetacean behavior for both the coda on the *Essex* whale, and a related work of digital journalism for Narrative.ly on *Jaws* author Peter Benchley. The conversation and collegiality of Martin Bickman and Jarad Krywicki enriched this book; Jarad and I were fortunate to present our papers in May 2014 on the same Melville Society panel at the American Literature Association Conference in Washington, D.C. I am indebted to my University of Iowa colleagues Ed Folsom, Brooks Landon, and Travis Vogan for their loyalty and camaraderie. George Cotkin and Elisabeth Chretien provided crucial feedback based on their perceptive readings of the manuscript. I appreciate the expertise and professional care of my editor, Richard Pult, and the staff at UPNE, who made this dream become a reality.

I would finally like to thank my wife, Caroline, and our children, Jacqueline, Eveline, and Edward, for their love and sympathy. Like the sea, the vitality they radiate is immeasurable.

SURVIVING THE *Essex*

PROLOGUE

Although she was an old ship, the *Essex* gleamed with opportunity in the July sun as she rested moored in the dock of Nantucket harbor. Her former captain, Daniel Russell, had commanded the vessel on four consecutive whaling voyages with great success, and now looked forward to manning the helm of the *Aurora*, a ship of more recent construction with a much larger hold. Russell's former first mate, George Pollard Jr., would become the new captain of the *Essex*, and boatsteerer Owen Chase would assume the position of first mate for her next voyage, planned for summer of 1819. Chase knew this was a pivotal step in his career, an opportunity to prove his competence as an expert navigator and leader of the youthful whaling crew. Pollard had his sights on a propitious debut, stepping gingerly aboard the *Essex* with the spring of a man meeting his bright future. His great expectations for a long and successful career were buoyed by the ideal circumstances—a fortuitous privilege he would never forsake—of launching his career as a captain hailing from Nantucket, home of the world's oldest and most lucrative whaling port.

With a full complement of men aboard, the *Essex* eased out of the harbor on August 5, 1819, beyond the shallow waters of the infamous Nantucket bar and dropped anchor. Here the crew and workers heaved the heaviest of the cargo onboard from light craft scurrying around the old ship's periphery, displacing her bulk ever deeper beneath the water's surface with each new load. The eagerly awaited departure for the South Pacific, home to the world's richest whaling waters, was nearly upon them. The crew thirsted for the first hunt, with Pollard seeking to set the keynote for his career and Chase yearning to prove himself worthy of rising to the rank of captain for his next voyage. Young Thomas Nickerson, the ship's cabin boy, would venture to sea for the first time. Amid the stowing down, the crisscrossing of decks, and the incessant comings and goings of boats delivering ever more provisions, the crew could hardly appreciate how precious their food stores would become. Instead, they could only recognize the growing tedium of a process heading into its sixth day. At last, their moment arrived and dawn liberated the *Essex* into the open ocean with the Nantucket shore receding behind her.

Captain Pollard's speech to the crew on the first day at sea, like all such orations on whaling vessels, was met with great anticipation, for it would set the tone for the entire voyage. The crew was particularly attentive to the character expressed in the grain of his voice, from which they might measure the manner of his command. In inaugurating the voyage, Pollard's bearing was not that of a spitfire or martinet; he would deliver no hortatory invective maligning the whale as a devilish species, nor would he condescend to the penniless common sailors as some captains with genteel pretentions could from above on the quarterdeck. Instead, Pollard was frank and direct, a seaman's captain with no airs or ulterior motive, no revenge to exact from a former loss or injury. His message was clear: success depended on the cooperation of crew and officers, who in turn were expected to obey the word of their captain. If the address bore no note of originality—captains typically made such admonitions—its delivery distinguished Pollard as a democratic leader more interested in weaving a strong social bond among the crew than subduing them with fear, or worse, transfixing them with supernatural mortal terrors intrinsic to the perilous enterprise before them.

After just three days at sea, the *Essex* was on course for the Azores, cruising full sail for a gam, a meeting of captains and crew, with the whale-ship *Midas*. Now Pollard brimmed with confidence, aggressively opening his studding sails, the canvas rectangles fitted to the far extremity of the fore-topsail yardarm. Pollard's haste was not entirely unreasonable. The voyage had begun relatively late in the whaling season and there was no time to lose. After exchanging pleasantries with the *Midas*, the *Essex* now carried up to eight knots of careening momentum as the clouds darkened and thunder rolled. With the main topgallant and studding sails still flying into the approaching tempest, the *Essex* heaved as Pollard barked the command to come about and face the opposite direction of the incoming gale. During the maneuver, the uppermost sails violently yanked the ship over while the crew desperately clung to her decks. The old whaler keeled over in the gale, leaning almost forty-five degrees until her beam-ends were completely submerged. The storm soon abated, however, and like a phoenix from the ashes, the *Essex* rose again, her mainmast reaching heavenward in what to officers and crew was an unmistakable harbinger of good fortune for the duration of their journey.

Weeks later, darkness loomed over the *Essex* again as she emerged from the Gulf Stream to face the formidable obstacle of Cape Horn. The crew looked on in horror as yet another massive weather front spread across the horizon, making the already challenging passing appear nearly impossible. Sailing as close to shore as possible without running aground on the Horn's jagged coastline, Pollard pressed on through the tempest for days. The days dragged on into weeks, draining the men's endurance and morale until an entire month had passed under such profound strain. Ultimately, to the crew's delight, the *Essex* emerged from the pounding passage without taking in so much as a gallon of water, incurring no damage on the treacherous shoals. But another force of nature awaited them, of which they were blissfully unaware during their cruise along the coast of Chile north to Peru. In these whale-rich seas they would reap the rewards of their herculean effort around the Horn, hauling in eleven whales for 450 barrels of precious oil, the gold of this watery Wild West.

Sailing westward into the Pacific after a brief stop on Charles Island for provisions on October 23, 1819, the *Essex* crew happily found itself surrounded by a shoal of whales. The men lowered their boats and waited with harpoons poised for what appeared to be an easy take of oil-rich sperm whales. First mate Owen Chase stood ready to hurl his lance when suddenly a whale swam directly under his boat, unleashing its formidable tail like a giant whip against the boat's bottom with the force of a cannonball, catapulting its occupants skyward. The whalemen splashed about, scrambling to gain a handhold on the shattered wreckage and pull their heads above the rolling sea. Clinging to the sinking boat, they screamed to their mates in the other chase boat for aid. So another narrow escape and another fortuitous turn, this time with a rambunctious whale, left the whalemen once again unscathed.

One month after their violent introduction to the concussive force of the sperm whale's tale, the *Essex* crew lowered its boats in pursuit of a pod of whales, this time swimming swiftly away from the ship. Captain Pollard was to lead the hunt with a team of harpooners, leaving first mate Chase in command of the crew left behind on the ship. Chase welcomed this relatively secure role away from the front lines. The trauma of his earlier clash that upended his boat was fresh in his mind, so the mother ship seemed a haven while Pollard marshaled his forces at a considerable distance. Any illusion of safety, however, was soon shattered when an eighty-five-foot bull seeking revenge for the attack on his predominantly female companions assumed the knightly role and bolted from the pod, whose members Pollard and company were butchering with their darts and lances. Flushed with fury, the leviathan rushed directly back at the ship, as the unsuspecting crew helplessly watched. Turning his full vengeance on the *Essex*, the bull accelerated to top speed, pumping its tail vigorously and ramming the hull with brute force as the men recoiled. But the creature was not through. Now circling back to gather momentum for the final blow while Chase stood frozen on deck, the whale blasted a fresh gaping hole in the ship's hull. In minutes the old whaler keeled over, disappearing into the sea, with men scrambling onto open boats desperately salvaging provisions from her hold. His vengeance complete for the time being, the whale glided off into the vast Pacific in search of his next victims.[1]

So reads the accepted story of events leading to the *Essex* wreck, primarily as handed down from first mate Owen Chase. Accounts of the crew's struggle for survival in the aftermath also bear his stamp. After the *Essex* was lost on November 20, 1820, Captain Pollard suggested seeking the closest refuge available, on the Society Islands to the West. But Chase objected, along with Matthew Joy, who feared cannibals and instead insisted on rowing for South America—some three thousand miles away—despite the triple vulnerability of navigating tiny open boats in unfavorable winds with dangerously low provisions. After yielding to the headstrong first mate's will, Pollard and the crew set off for the long journey, first landing on Henderson Island, where they stayed for a week before departing for the coast of Chile on December 27. The crew, desperate and now dying, launched themselves into the vast expanse of the sea, hopeful that the current and their strength would somehow bring them safely ashore. In the nearly two-month period after they left Henderson Island, they would experience horrors that forever changed their lives. In March of 1821, a month after their rescue, the press was still reporting on the harrowing ordeal, reprinting a letter Pollard had left in a tin box on the island. Not knowing if he would survive the journey to the mainland, Pollard accounted for the events on one page, and on another he poured out a wrenching farewell: "I shall leave with this a letter for my wife, and whoever finds, and has the good will and has the goodness to forward it, will oblige an unfortunate man and receive his sincerest wishes."[2]

As the most storied and horrifying shipwreck in whaling history, the *Essex* disaster is astonishing for both the way the ship was sunk—rammed by a massive sperm whale—and the grisly scenes of starvation and cannibalism that thinned the original crew of twenty men down to eight. Three of the survivors stayed behind on Henderson Island and were later rescued by the *Surry*, an English vessel. Of the three boats carrying the seventeen crewmen who attempted to row to Chile—while subsisting on the meager supply of bread, water, and Galápagos tortoises they salvaged from the sinking *Essex*—only two boats arrived, with five survivors.[3] But more shocking in many ways was the ensuing struggle to survive the stigma of cannibalism, and the more improbable challenge for crew members of salvaging their professional reputations and careers at sea. At stake was the story of the wreck itself, as seen in the inconsistent and highly contested survivors' accounts, and the race to print it.

News coverage of the ordeal inspired a flurry of sensationalized shipwreck narratives in the popular press, soon followed by the 1821 publication of Chase's *Narrative of the Most Extraordinary and Distressing Shipwreck of the Whale-Ship Essex.*[4] Chase's narrative, which Nathaniel and Thomas Philbrick call "an excellent work of self-promotion," casts the writer as a hero who overturned the allegedly misguided and ill-conceived instincts of Captain Pollard, and calmed and encouraged his hysterical crew, particularly the young cabin boy, Thomas Nickerson.[5] For Pollard's part, rather than racing to print his account, the captain sought redemption in another whaling expedition, aboard the *Two Brothers*, buoyed by the confidence of his Nantucket community and the good faith of his cabin boy, Nickerson, who signed on for the venture. This time Nickerson elevated his practice of keeping a standard log by immortalizing in verse the propitious journey of the *Two Brothers*.[6] Despite lofty expectations for Pollard's return to whaling—one worthy of epic poetry—the journey proved disastrous, as the ship crashed on craggy shoals northwest of Hawaii. His spirit crushed, Pollard retreated into exile on Nantucket. Having saved his manuscript from the *Essex* voyage, Nickerson retrieved it from storage decades later to revise for publication with Leon Lewis, a staff writer for the *New York Ledger*, the widest circulating story paper of the nineteenth century.[7] But, in a detail nearly lost to history, Lewis agreed to work on but eventually abandoned what was then the most coveted manuscript of America's most notorious shipwreck.

This book unearths the stories behind the survivors' accounts of the *Essex* voyage, the Nantucket whaler that captured Herman Melville's imagination after colliding with a massive sperm whale in November 1820. The story lay with the few men who finally returned to Nantucket under the scrutiny of a clamoring public. Although Chase was the first to print his account, others would provide their own unique perspectives. *Surviving the "Essex"* seeks to give a richer, more contextualized portrait than what is already available, looking closely at the survivors' lives, ambitions, and motives, their pivotal actions during the wreck itself, and their will to reconcile themselves to those actions in both the short and the long term. This book also seeks to identify as-yet-identified villains and unsung heroes.

Penned by a ghostwriter, Chase's account reflects his objective to preempt questions about his competence as a seaman by heaping the blame on the whale, as well as to question Captain Pollard's leadership. For him, and each survivor who offered his particular story, the retelling uniquely shaped his public and private life, cementing his place in maritime Nantucket history as well as showing his particular form of psychological reconciliation. For Chase, the traumatic event became an opportunity to enter the ranks of the most successful captains in whaling history. After the *Essex*, Pollard's loss of the *Two Brothers* meant a kind of personal exile and highly modest work as a night watchman. Then there was Nickerson, who years later attempted to publish his account. The whale itself, especially its behavior and purported motives, also factors into profiles of the event. As for the thumbnail portraits ultimately associated with these men (and the beast), they go roughly as follows: Chase brimmed with ambition but ultimately went mad in old age; Pollard, in Nantucket, came to embody suffering with dignity; Nickerson was cast as the aging seaman who tried but ultimately failed to communicate his story to a wider audience; and the whale, speechless and maligned, was the scapegoat for a civilization determined to justify a ruthless industry.

Tracking down lost clues not only helps expose the exaggerations and inaccuracies of Chase's account, but also pieces the story back together for a richer, more detailed view of the event's impact. In profiling Chase, Pollard, and Nickerson, this book explores how these survivors shaped their own respective versions of the tale in order to preserve their dignity and names for posterity, and to conceal their liability for the lost lives of the other crew members.

The most mythologized elements in the *Essex* narratives are the death of crewman Owen Coffin and the whale's strike. This book begins with the former and ends with the latter. Chapter 1 thus takes up the question of who shot Coffin as a means of exploring the ambiguities regarding this messianic figure at the heart of the crew's deadly survival ritual. What Coffin means—whether he died in vain, or gave his life meaningfully based on the fairest and most reasonable intentions and procedure, as directed by Pollard—was a crucial consideration for all the narratives. His life was framed as the most sacred and telling of those lost at sea. Many facts are unclear. Did Pollard refuse, in a fit of cowardice, to execute the youth himself for the crew's sustenance? How does the ritual consumption of Coffin's body compare to that of the black sailors, who all died unusually soon in the scope of the event?

Chapter 2 concerns Chase's ghostwritten *Narrative* as an attempt to not only live down the event but also defend himself from allegations of negligence and incompetence. It details Chase's efforts to rid himself of associations with savage cannibalism and cast himself as an icon of civility and productive industry. Why were other options for survival not mentioned or considered in his *Narrative*, especially the prospect of seeking aid from one of the many ships near Henderson Island, or the use of the first deceased crewman, Matthew Joy, as shark and porpoise bait?

Chapter 3 considers Nickerson's use of his personal experience aboard the *Essex* as a source of fame and profit, as well as an opportunity to place himself more admirably in the tale for posterity. He attempted to publish his story immediately after Chase's decline into madness and death, precisely when a power vacuum opened in the competition for the *Essex*'s master narrative.

Moving from Owen Coffin's iconic death (chapter 1) and assessments of the respective motives behind Chase's and Nickerson's narratives (chapters 2 and 3), chapter 4 explores the conditions of Pollard's return to sea. There I suggest an alternative to the commonly held view that the disaster was a consequence of his Ahab-like obsessive pursuit of whales, and that its demise, like that of the *Pequod*, in *Moby-Dick*, provides a cautionary tale stressing the need for personal restraint and humility. Such readings run counter not only to Pollard's humble, self-effacing temperament but also to his optimistic attempt at seafaring redemption so soon after the *Essex* debacle. He was seemingly compelled not by a drive for vengeance but instead by a sincere desire to support his community and crew.

Pollard's unselfish, community-driven life is the subject of chapter 5, covering his final years, as Nantucket's night watchman. Chapter 6 finally settles the question of which among the *Essex* survivors was the "real Captain Ahab." The associative and creative work Melville did with the *Essex*, both in *Moby-Dick* and *Clarel*, his epic poem set in the Holy Land and partly inspired by the author's meeting with Pollard, is far more complicated and disorderly than we might have assumed. But what Melville made of the actual man Pollard when he met him is far less ambiguous. Equally telling is the manner in which Pollard and Chase played out their twilight years.

The coda examines the role of the whale itself. Given what we now know about the behavioral tendencies of sperm whales, to what extent could the animal in question be accused of perpetrating a malicious attack? Could such a creature even be capable of malice of forethought in addition to intent to harm? Or was the contact merely incidental, making any character assassination against the whale as preposterous as blaming the coral reef for sinking the *Two Brothers*? Ascertaining the nature of the whale leads back to Melville, in that Ishmael dedicates inordinate time and energy to puzzling over precisely this enigma in *Moby-Dick*. Is the whale the embodiment of all good or evil? Do the whale's legendary status and the string of fantastic stories that follow him across the globe have any grounding in reality? And, if so, what might this say about the whale's captors, who understand it as a malevolent natural force that must be destroyed to keep the world safe for the perpetuation of commercial and industrial progress? Pollard never ascribed malicious intent to the whale, unlike Chase. Pollard, however, was not oblivious to how whales, like all large animals, can become highly dangerous when aroused. Ascribing blame to a force of nature seemed absurd to Pollard, who could only weigh his circumstances and trust in the confidence of his surviving crew (besides Chase)—and that of the island of Nantucket for his follow-up voyage.

This book recovers and humanizes the real people who fired Melville's imagination for a novel whose celebrated status has made it one of the most reproduced and adapted in literary history. Word of the *Essex* was so inescapable for the three decades prior to the publication of *Moby-Dick* that, as early as 1834, Ralph Waldo Emerson overheard a tale on a stagecoach so moving he felt compelled to record it in his journal. A young seaman had stunned Emerson with "the story of an old sperm whale which he called a white whale. The creature was known for many years as Old Tom and would rush upon the boats which attacked him and crushed the boats to small chips in his jaws, the men generally escaping by jumping overboard and being picked up." As in Melville's "The Affidavit," it would appear perfectly reasonable to hunt a single whale in the oceans because "a vessel was fitted out at New Bedford, he said, to take him. And he was finally taken somewhere off Payta Head by the *Winslow* or the *Essex*."[8] Seventeen years after recording this entry, Emerson would journey to Nantucket, meet Pollard, and record his thoughts on the incident, especially the significance of Owen Coffin's ultimate sacrifice. The crew of the *Winslow*, of course, had destroyed the whale, since the *Essex* had sunk fourteen years prior. But in a telling twist, the *Winslow* captain who avenged Old Tom was none other than Owen Chase.

With the *Essex* in many ways functioning as the mother of all whale tales, the ur-saga of a destructive whale that spawned an industry of nautical narratives, *Moby-Dick* had already been written and rewritten thousands of times before it got to Melville, who of course transformed it in the most enduring way.[9] But the book's colossal presence in our world and culture has obscured Pollard's dignity while polishing Chase's image. This light into the whaling industry's darkest chapter will reveal a Captain Pollard whom Nantucket can be proud of, and to whom much more than the industry of whaling should look for inspiration. In the context of nearly two centuries of retellings of the *Essex*, his proper place in history has been occluded by the murkiness of memory. It is to that sea of memory associated with the *Essex*, and the event's most sentimentalized and sensationalized scene, that we now turn.

Chapter 1

~~~~~~

WHO SHOT OWEN COFFIN?

After the *Essex* collided with a whale on November 20, 1820, in the South
Pacific west of the Galápagos Islands, most of the stunned crew determined to row their tiny open boats some three thousand miles east to
the South American coast. Their decision was based in part on a fear of
cannibals on nearby islands to the West. Covering such a vast distance
into a formidable trade wind without restocking provisions along the way,
however, seemed suicidal. Ducie Island, located due south, appeared an
ideal spot to restock. After landing on Henderson Island, seventy miles
west of Ducie, they soon found their resources depleted and abandoned
their quest for the Chilean coast. Instead, they resolved to make the more
reasonable journey to Easter Island, a third of the way to South America.
Such a decision apparently reflected the crew's diminished fear of cannibals and a corresponding willingness to employ their diplomatic skills
to avert any danger. With acute starvation and malnutrition setting in,
they felt they had no choice but to travel for the aptly named isle, site of
their potential rebirth and resurrection.[1]

But undoing their original plan to sail for South America proved more
difficult than anticipated. This was because following that plan, and the
journey to Henderson Island, had set them on a more difficult trajectory
for Easter Island, which was a tantalizing several hundred miles due east
of the wreckage site. In their ill-equipped open boats with makeshift
canvas sails, which had been frantically slashed from the masts of the
sinking *Essex*, the sailors were helpless against the stiff gales that tossed
them about. The best trajectory they could muster was a derelict south-
eastern stagger.[2] The elements played havoc with their eastbound tack, as

if controlled by a vengeful Poseidon bearing down on Odysseus. As in the ancient Greek depiction of Odysseus's seafaring struggles, the sufferings of the *Essex* seamen against the elements can be traced to one rash action.[3]

That decision, at the wreckage site more than a thousand miles to the North, was engineered by the first mate, Owen Chase, who had roused the crew's support to sail for the mainland, overturning Captain George Pollard Jr.'s plan to cover one-third that distance, following a favorable southwesterly wind for the Marquesas Islands or Tahiti. The decision instead to sail due south placed them virtually out of reach of Easter Island, apparently dooming them to a slow journey toward South America. Like Sophocles's Oedipus, who inadvertently kills his father and then does all he can to avoid the horrifying prospect of wedding his mother, the sailors may have tried to escape their fate, only to realize its grim inevitability. As is widely known, the Oedipus story centering on unintended consequences borne of good intentions seized the imagination of Sigmund Freud; likewise, the saga of the *Essex*, including its rich psychological elements, riveted antebellum readers.[4]

The *Essex* trauma would feature its own archetypical taboos rivaling those of *Oedipus Rex*. Namely, Oedipus kills his own father, and Pollard issues the order to kill his own teenage cousin. As if randomly choosing a crew member to execute for sustenance were not weighty enough, Owen Coffin was the beloved son of Pollard's aunt and uncle, with whom he had been close on Nantucket. On February 2, 1821, the day Coffin died, he was eighteen and Pollard was twenty-nine, making the captain something between a father and a brother figure to the youth, with whom he shared a family resemblance.[5] In the innumerable retellings of the *Essex* tragedy, this killing of one's kin becomes the iconic moment of terror, the men's darkest hour. Oedipus's moment of terror lies in his realization that he was his father's killer; like Oedipus, Pollard would have preferred to die than consume the flesh of his own relative.[6] And murder, in this instance, preceded cannibalism, adding to the realization of the crew's, and Pollard's, darkest nightmare.

The most conspicuous scene separating one *Essex* account from another is the shooting of Owen Coffin. No other detail is more contested, or retold with such ritual significance, as the drawing of lots that eventuated in his execution. With four men left in Pollard's open boat and all provisions depleted, including the flesh and blood of their dead shipmates, they resolved to draw straws. After Coffin drew the fatal straw, Pollard offered to take his place. Refusing, Coffin accepted his fate, which was solemnly delivered in a single gunshot.[7]

Many retellings of the lottery exaggerated and sensationalized the facts for dramatic effect.[8] "The Shipwreck of the Essex," a ballad published in Cornwall, England, offers a remarkable measure of the distance traveled by the *Essex* story, the speed at which it traveled, and the liberties taken with Chase's *Narrative*. The ballad distorts the deadly lottery by sentimentalizing Coffin, who "was to die, / For his wife and poor children most bitterly did cry." Of course the teenage Coffin had neither wife nor children. Nor does the poet miss the full dramatic import of the parricide suggested in Pollard's complicity in the killing of his cousin: "the captain and cabin boy . . . cast lots who should die, / But it happened to fall on the poor cabin boy." The ballad also, in attempting to portray the selection process as exceedingly fair and democratic, reports falsely that, instead of once, "eight different times lots amongst them were drawn."[9] Such rhetoric presumably reflected an attempt to divert attention from the savagery to follow. Thus the event and the actions of the sailors are characterized simultaneously as murderous and empathetic. In turn, this tableau of seeming contradiction resonated more than any other with those who encountered the story.

The sacrifice of Owen Coffin tapped for audiences a powerful realization that they, too, might draw the short straw in their personal lotteries. They also sympathized more basically with Coffin's death. For Melville himself, the first reading of Chase's narrative was moving precisely because he, sailing on the *Acushnet*, had recently passed the site of the tragedy. Even more powerful than geographic proximity was a sense of shared mortal risk linked with traveling aboard a whaling vessel. *This could happen to me*, Melville apparently understood while at the gam. *Could I take the bullet if so selected?* Alternatively, could he pull trigger against his best friend and coconspirator, Toby, who had defected from the *Acushnet* while on Nuku Hiva, in the Marquesas Islands? The ghost of Owen Coffin undoubtedly haunted Melville in 1841, as he recalled how "the reading of this wondrous story upon the landless sea, and close to the very latitude of the shipwreck had a surprising effect upon me."[10] That surprising effect for those encountering the story merged a palpable sense of mortality with the more complicated moral conundrum associated with killing a shipmate to survive. Melville, along with twenty years of readers and tale tellers before him, acutely felt this human vulnerability.[11]

The shooting of Owen Coffin was the signal event of both Chase's *Narrative* and the journal that the cabin boy Thomas Nickerson ultimately sought to publish decades later. Coffin's death, as intimated already, signified a blood ritual not unlike that spurred by Ahab, when he exhorts the crew to pledge death to Moby Dick in the "Quarter-Deck" chapter. The communal embrace of cannibalism brought about the galling realization among the crew that the practice would continue as long as provisions were inadequate and the men were starving. The civilized method of the lottery, indeed, would give way to the most primitive acts imaginable.

Not only does the killing of Coffin symbolize the transformation of the civilized ambassadors of American whaling into savage brutes. It also raises questions about the leadership errors that might have prompted this outcome. Such questions more pointedly challenge the fairness with which the lottery itself was carried out. The familial relationship between Coffin and Pollard, furthermore, casts doubt on the captain's concern for a relative. Such concern was highly valued by the culture. Questions include the following: Was Coffin's killing unnecessary? Was Pollard to blame? Did Pollard sin unpardonably by failing to intervene and take the bullet himself? Or was Chase to blame for his own earlier errors of preemptive leadership? Other rudimentary questions, such as who shot Owen Coffin and what event followed another, are difficult to answer, given the wild variance in the documentary evidence.

This question of who shot Coffin renders our otherwise respectable *Essex* seamen at their moment of deepest crisis. As the sensational detail that helped sell so many books, the corresponding scene captures the transformation of the men at the journey's breaking point. The rawest component of their experience may have been the "whisper of necessity" that likely crept upon them.[12]

Chase's *Narrative*, the ur-text of the *Essex* tragedy, states clearly, "On the 1st of February, having consumed the last morsel, the captain and the three other men that remained with him, were reduced to the necessity of casting lots. It fell upon Owen Coffin to die, who with great fortitude and resignation submitted to his fate." Chase, through his ghostwriter, then relates that "they drew lots to see who would shoot him: he placed himself firmly to receive his death, and was immediately shot by Charles Ramsdale [*sic*]" and not Captain Pollard. The narrator sympathizes with Ramsdell, as his name was correctly spelled, for suffering the "hard fortune it was to become his executioner."[13]

Although long considered authoritative, Chase's account contains huge omissions designed to grant credit to the writer at Pollard's expense. In particular, Chase did not include Pollard's offer to take Coffin's lot for him. In Nickerson's rendition, moreover, it was Pollard and not Ramsdell who shot Coffin. His account states that when "they were compelled again to cast lots," identifying "who should draw the fatal trigger," destiny rather than ill-luck pointed to the captain. "As if fate would have it, the awful die turned upon Captain Pollard[.] For a long time [he] declared that he could never do it, but finally had to submit." At stake in determining who shot Coffin was Pollard's reputation as hero or coward. A hero would have not permitted the killing of his own kinsman eleven years his junior, but instead would have taken the bullet for him. Nickerson clearly suggests that Pollard had precisely this inclination, given that the captain insisted "that he would take the lot himself, but to this Coffin would not listen for a moment."[14]

Indeed, for failing to follow through on his purported offer to Coffin, Pollard was later maligned on Nantucket. This detail was so unsettling to most locals that they twisted the facts further to vilify Pollard, as Cyrus Townsend Brady reported in an early twentieth-century study on Nantucket lore surrounding the incident. Even as late as 1904, Brady writes, "a tradition still current in Nantucket has it that the lot fell to the captain, whereupon his cousin, already near death, feeling that he could not survive the afternoon, offered and insisted upon taking his [cousin's] place."[15] Here, then, it hadn't been Coffin who drew the fatal straw but Pollard, who was portrayed as both an unforgivable coward and even a swindler of his own relative.

Like the Nantucket rumor suggesting that Pollard had drawn the lot himself, however, Nickerson's narrative of the critical moment represents a callous lie. Both, of course, seize on the implication that Pollard missed an opportunity to show loyalty to his crew by sacrificing his life for them. More subtly, Nickerson's account, written in 1876, more than a half-century after the event, shares with the Nantucket rumor a desire to punish Pollard for allowing the situation to unfold to begin with.[16] The willingness of the Nantucket community to alter details to blame Pollard suggests a deeper cathartic function in finding a scapegoat, for reasons moral and practical, after tragedy strikes. The effect is not only to cleanse the survivors of any sense of guilt or shame for partaking in cannibalism, but also to exonerate Nantucket for supporting the perilous commercial whaling enterprise altogether. Placing the smoking gun in Pollard's hand indeed exculpates the surviving crew and the entire whaling industry, while reinforcing the reasonableness of the dangers of the trade so as to encourage and perpetuate its continuation as usual.[17]

When Pollard returned to Nantucket after his rescue, he brought news of Coffin's death to the youth's mother, who herself turned on Pollard, blaming him for failing to save her son. As for Nickerson, in his 1876 letter pitching his story to the pulp journalist Leon Lewis, he offers a token defense of Pollard's honor but more prominently portrays the captain as an object of scorn. In the hands of a sensationalist like Lewis, such an introduction would have been sure to lead to Pollard's ruined reputation. In Nickerson's perfunctory defense, "Captain Pollard was not nor could he be thought to have dealt unfairly with this trying matter." But the very next sentence shifts to Coffin's mother's reaction: "On [Pollard's] arrival he bore the awful message to the mother as her son desired, but she became almost frantic with the thought, and I have heared [sic] that she never could become reconciled to the captain's presence." Thereafter, Nickerson again limply defends the captain, writing that he "lived on the island, greatly respected by all whose business or pleasure brought

them in contact with and died lamented by a large circle of friends."
But this circle obviously did not include Coffin's mother, or the rumor-
mongers responsible for the claim that Pollard had handed the lot to his
vulnerable cousin. In Nickerson's alteration of the narrative, wherein the
captain, rather than Ramsdell, "pulls the fatal trigger," the former cabin
boy is playing into the deceptive narrative inaugurated by his shipmate
Owen Chase.[18]

As a tavern owner on Nantucket in his final decades, Nickerson was
positioned at the heart of the small island's gossip mill. Despite having
participated in the event himself, he undoubtedly had been exposed to
its myriad narratives, and apparently believed the hard angle on Pollard
would capture Lewis's imagination and ultimately prove most salable.
Oddly, the compendium of notes he had furnished for Lewis contradicts
his version of the event described in the letter. In the notes he alleges that
Coffin "was immediately shot by Charles Ramsdell who became his executioner by fair lot." Was this simply an error accountable to Nickerson's
advancing age and shaky memory? Or was this an intentional alteration of
the facts designed to spice up the tale, which he anticipated would bring
handsome profits through installments in the *New York Ledger*, Lewis's
home paper? Further, had Nickerson, deciding to embellish the event in
the letter, simply neglected to go back to his memoir, labeled "Desultory
Sketches from a Seaman's Log," to revise this key detail? Most likely,
Nickerson would not have enjoyed the onerous task of searching through
the fair copy of 105 leaves written in his own hand to make the change,
especially since he had already invested considerable time penciling in
revisions and additions to the manuscript near the time he transferred
it to Lewis.

Such controversy over the drawing of the lots was no trivial matter,
but in fact determined Pollard's ungenerous and unjust reception by
Coffin's mother and the Nantucket community. Pollard's recovery from
the trauma, seen in his surprisingly stable mental condition and will to
survive literally in darkness as a night watchman, suggests that his former actions were unassailable. The historical revisionism at his expense
suggested not only a classic example of scapegoating but also a morally
unambiguous way of understanding an extremely complex set of circum-

stances. Perhaps Coffin's mother and the Nantucket community were seeking somehow to define ideal behavior by delineating its opposite in the invented actions and behaviors of the captain.

According to Nickerson's original account, Pollard actually advised against using the lottery in the first place, preferring to simply await the first death, evidence that further exonerates him from the claim that he pursued the lottery with the malicious goal of sacrificing his cousin. For their parts, both Chase and Nickerson confirm that Coffin insisted on going through with the lottery, perhaps with the intention of sacrificing himself. For all antebellum versions of the narrative, the larger Christian context would suggest Coffin as the self-sacrificial messiah. One survivor, Thomas Chappel, even published his account in 1824 under the imprint of London's Religious Tract Society. Although Chappel's evangelical strains are the most thorough and strident of all—he makes the tale into a Christian object lesson on how prayers will be answered by a benevolent God—Chase does not neglect the opportunity to appeal to pious readers by liberally applying theological dogma to his tale.

MERCIES OF OUR CREATOR?

Interestingly, Melville himself could see through these strained attempts at creating a religious allegory, especially one that illustrates the presence of a divine and loving providence. In *Moby-Dick*, particularly in "The Whiteness of the Whale," a prevailing nihilism reveals Melville's deep skepticism toward naïve trust in a caring and protecting God. The deity is repeatedly portrayed instead as a weaver alternately deaf to the prayers of humans, as in the chapter "A Bower in Arsicades," or too busy weaving time in His tapestry to notice, let alone aid, the drowning Pip, whose cowardice during a whale chase nearly kills him. Pip does not receive the comforting hand of consolation that, in "The Counterpane," soothes a youthful Ishmael when he has spent a disorienting sixteen hours isolated in his bedroom as punishment for a misdeed. The "supernatural hand seemed placed in mine" appears only in this separate childhood memory, whereas most of the novel locates a deity in natural convergences, energies, and rhythms—as in weaving a mat with Queequeg in

"The Mat-Maker" chapter, beholding the stunning beauty of the whale's brow, tail, and skeleton.[19]

Indeed, instances in the novel of an anthropomorphized God usually feature characters like Ahab and Pip totally disillusioned with His indifference and the meaningless universe He has created, or conversely, zealots like Gabriel of "The Jeroboam's Story," who scream prophecies of doom to those who violate God's will. Indeed, through the whale's agency, God's righteous retribution corrects the disobedience of Jonah in Father Mapple's sermon, just as the killing of Radney the instant he is to punish Steelkilt in "The Town-Ho's Story" comes by way of a deus ex machina whale blasting the sadistic captain into the sea. God's sharpshooting is also on display when Harry Macey, despite Gabriel's archangelic warnings to desist, presses on after the White Whale and is miraculously plucked from a crowded whaleboat and sent to his watery death, leaving the remaining crew totally unharmed. Gabriel's shrieking "prophecies of the speedy doom to the sacrilegious assailants of his divinity" foretell the divine retribution exacted on the sinner Macey, just as Jonah and Radney are punished by a just intervening God in the form of a whale. God is unambiguous in meting out justice, as Macey, at the height of his profane frenzy, "was smitten bodily into the air, and making a long arc in his descent, fell into the sea at the distance of about fifty yards. Not a chip of the boat was harmed, nor a hair of any oarsman's head; but the mate for ever sank."[20]

In using the *Essex* story to support his argument that a whale can plausibly attack a ship, and that a captain can find a specific whale in the ocean, Melville thus portrays the whale's swift destructive power: "Dashing his forehead against her hull, he so stove her in, that in less than 'ten minutes' she settled down and fell over." Strikingly, Melville points to divine agency in determining the fate of Pollard's next command, when he "once more sailed for the Pacific . . . but the gods shipwrecked him again upon unknown rocks and breakers."[21] The reference here is to pagan Greek gods rather than the Judeo-Christian biblical God of mercy in Radney and Jonah's examples, both of which Melville himself treats with skeptical irony, thereby questioning the credible existence of such a consistent and reliable God.

In Chappel's Religious Tract Society rendition of the *Essex* tale, he seeks rhetorically to illustrate the power of prayer and divine providence, unlike Melville, who in "The Affidavit" uses the event to illustrate how an aggressive whale, with one swift blow, can sink an entire ship. To bear such "severe trials," Chappel asserts, "belief in God and trust in him" is "absolutely necessary." He continues: "It is particularly important that seamen whose troubles and dangers are so numerous should bear this in mind." And he insists that "the soul that is led by the teaching of the Holy Spirit to draw near to the Savior will find support under all the troubles of life. It will find that peace which the world cannot give."

For Chappel and his two shipmates, attributing their good fortune to a benevolent deity makes sense, given that their rescue by Captain Raine of the *Surry*—correlating to the "devious cruising *Rachel*," which saves Ishmael as he bobs above the wreckage on Queequeg's sealed coffin— seemed fated. Rather than sail for South America with Chase and Pollard, they had elected to stay on Henderson Island, only to deplete their provisions and stand at the brink of death. In ascribing his group's rescue to providence, true to his Christian orientation, he focuses especially on one mate who zealously summons the strength to swim out to the *Surry*, nearly drowning in the process. Here, yet again, "the same Providence which had hitherto protected, now preserved him" quite actively.[22]

As for Chase and Pollard, Chappel can only lament their "deplorable and painful history," in which they were "sustained by the dead bodies of their companions." He meanwhile omits mention of their willingness to shoot one of their own. Troubling Chappel's formulation here is his inability to account for Chase and Pollard's ill-fortune. Was it that they, unlike Chappel and his mates, had failed to trust enough in God, or to "pray earnestly to God for the knowledge of his truth"? Although they indeed survived, and in large part due to cannibalism, they did not benefit from the protective divine powers that aided "these men [who] prayed earnestly for deliverance from their sufferings." Chappel thus offers a model for the reader to emulate, asking rhetorically, "Can you be less earnest respecting your soul?"[23]

On display in Chappel's account is a search for moral structure and guidance in a chaotic universe. Thus, the question emerges whether Christianity holds up under circumstances such as those seen with the *Essex*. As the next chapter explores, Chase invokes providence to explain his experience, a proposition Melville found patently absurd. In Melville's copy of the *Narrative*, a telling annotation appears in the following passage: "There was not a hope now remaining to us but that which was derived from a sense of the mercies of our Creator. The night of the 18th was a despairing era in our sufferings." The phrase *mercies of our Creator* in the context of such brutal misfortune struck the novelist as bizarre and incongruous.[24] How could a Creator subjecting these men to such torture be construed as merciful? Given what they had been through, and how often their prayers had seemingly been ignored, how could they hold out belief in a deity? Melville underlined the phrase, and set a question mark in parentheses at the end of the sentence.

COFFIN'S LAST WORDS

In his account, Nickerson clearly wished to cast Coffin as a Christ figure nobly accepting his sacrificial role. With the Christ position occupied, Pollard is cast as something of a tragic figure, although with a compromised dignity that contrasted with Melville's own admiring sense of the real-life captain. As for Coffin, his insistence on the lottery's fairness and his self-possessed articulation of his desire to whisper "a parting message to his dear mother and family" ultimately uphold *Pollard's* unassailable stature in his cousin's eyes. Coffin's mother, as we have seen, could never share her son's apparent reverence for Pollard, whether or not she believed it was he or Ramsdell who pulled the trigger. Avoiding him for the rest of her life, despite living on the same small island, she considered Pollard's insufficient will to resist the lottery's outcome to be his unforgivable crime. Only following through on Pollard's original suggestion—that the crew members nourish themselves on whoever should die first, with the implication being that this person might be Pollard—would have marked an acceptable outcome, in Coffin's mother's view. Pollard's instinct, for its part, issued from his Quaker worldview, which Philbrick reminds us opposed killing and games of chance, both of which the cannibalistic lottery entailed.[25]

Coffin's exoneration of his cousin would seem to put to rest any question about the captain's negligence. All the same, the perception of Coffin as a messiah figure, with the consumption of his remains directly echoing the Christian Communion, easily slips Pollard into the role of a misunderstood leader caught in a moral quagmire. Coffin's mother likely felt that Pollard should have insisted on his initial suggestion, resisting the lottery to the end and realizing the protective paternal role she expected him to embody. However unjust the interpretive errors of Nickerson or Coffin's mother, Pollard does emerge as a possible tragic hero displaying a distinct shortcoming.

If a flaw can be found in Pollard, it is his exceeding flexibility and broader support for democracy, attributes that under different circumstances could have garnered sympathy. Indeed, agreeing to the lottery demonstrated his belief in untainted democracy—with an equal risk for each man, regardless of age or rank. The more consequential display of Pollard's "fatal flaw," however, may have occurred some 1,500 miles to the Northwest, when perhaps he was too conciliatory in dispensing with his suggestion to sail west toward the Marquesas or Tahiti. An alternative explanation is that he was simply avoiding a potential subversion of his authority that might lead to mutiny, especially given how few provisions the crew had salvaged from the sinking *Essex*. His responsiveness to the crew's pleas to head for a civilized port may indeed have arisen from the ascendance of Chase, the second-in-command, who was actually present during the whale's assault on the ship.

Nickerson, in his account, exploits such perceptions of Pollard's tragic qualities, and their consequences for the crew, by also placing the gun in the captain's hand. Not only would Pollard here be forced to eat his cousin, but he would also kill him, a titillating irony, given his resistance to the lottery from the outset. Fascinatingly, Nickerson so manipulates the text for dramatic value but does not reckon, in his letter to Lewis, with the contradiction between Coffin's forgiveness of his uncle and Coffin's mother's inability to forgive. Yet the story of Pollard's relaying of the message invariably shows his humanity. Through an act of principle and courage, he has intended to console and pacify his relative, only to inflame her. Here, a sort of "flaw" of sensitivity emerges again, with the captain possibly unable to predict Coffin's mother's reaction. She likely could not, or did not wish to, empathize with the impossibly complex moral conundrum faced by the *Essex* captain and his crew. In her grief, she likely had no patience for psychological vagaries or contending with the base need to survive.

Some readers may hear an echo between Coffin's parting message and Kurtz's last words—"The horror! The horror!"—in Joseph Conrad's *Heart of Darkness* (1899). But unlike Conrad's narrator Marlow, who lies to Kurtz's beloved back in Europe to mollify her, Pollard does not alter Coffin's message for the boy's mother. Whatever comparisons may be made, the evidence shows that Pollard's message was too painful for Coffin's mother, and she lashed out at the messenger. This was her over-arching response regardless of which detail she fixed on: the possibility that Pollard had drawn the lot, according to Nantucket legend; his lack of insistence on rejecting the lottery; or his insufficient resolve to take the bullet himself. Most fundamentally, she would have preferred right then to be talking to her own son rather than to her nephew.

In his letter to Lewis, Nickerson seizes on this "truly trying moment [in which] the son of a beloved sister [was] to fall by their hands."[26] Falsely sympathetic to Pollard, Nickerson was eager to cull full dramatic impact, with its dramatic irony, from Pollard's delivery and Coffin's mother's furious reaction—and he manipulated other details of the story, as submitted to Leon Lewis, with his audience similarly in mind. Nickerson took a similar approach to Pollard's implication in cannibalism. The author, for example, excludes himself from the consuming of crew member Isaac Cole. Instead he describes himself surviving "by means of the small pittance meted out for the share" of bread made available upon the death of Cole and another crew member, Richard Peterson. He likewise cast himself as following Pollard's suggestion, later overturned, that "let whatever would come, we would never draw lots after our food had quite gone for each other's death, but leave all with God."

But the mere invocation of drawing lots indicated that this path might ultimately be taken. The step toward cannibalism represented a crucial breaching of all civilized taboos, a burst into survivalist necessity, and just one trigger pull from the next source of sustenance. Writes Chase:

"We consented, however at this time," in the agreement to commit contingency cannibalism, "in case one should die first the others could if they thought proper subsist upon our remains with the hope that some one might carry the news to our friends." In a stroke of divine mercy—interpreted alternatively as a punishment for forcing them to kill their own crew—"God designed it should be otherwise and again gave his protecting arm and saved us from the very jaws of death."[27]

Omitted conspicuously from Nickerson's account, alongside his participation in cannibalism, is his descent into temporary madness, recorded by Chase. His will broken late in the surviving crew's voyage on the open boats, Nickerson sank into a passive despondency so profound that Chase himself feared being "unexpectedly overtaken by a like weakness, or dizziness of nature, that would bereave me at once of both reason and life." Were Nickerson to have died in this state, he hardly would be remembered as meeting death with dignity. With seeming high drama, the fourteen-year-old cabin boy "laid down, drew a piece of canvass over him, and cried out, that he had wished to die immediately." Chase describes his own futile efforts to rally Nickerson's spirit and, in the process, reveals a perception of the boy's particular cowardice: "I saw that he had given up, and I attempted to speak a few words of comfort and encouragement to him, and endeavored to persuade him that it was a great weakness and even wickedness to abandon a reliance upon the Almighty, while the least hope, and a breath of life remained." Nickerson emerges from this description as the antithesis of Chappel's model of pious endurance. Even worse, the cabin boy did not even respond to the prospect that the sailors "would be gaining the land before the end of two days more." He had clearly convinced himself, without reason, that he would die, given that he was physically stronger, if not psychologically so, than he thought. However dispiriting the journey, Nickerson emerges as a childish, stubborn believer in his own demise: "A fixed look of settled and forsaken despondency came over his face: he lay for some time silent, sullen and sorrowful" locked in "unaccountable earnestness."[28]

We see, then, how offering his own version of events allowed Nickerson to preserve, even rescue, his reputation. This applied to both cannibalism and a perceived irrational childishness, with the latter quality reappearing in Melville's Pip, who jumps overboard when approaching a whale. We can further understand why Nickerson would want to redirect attention to Pollard, who was dead by the time the former cabin boy tried to publish his account, as a purported coward, however "sympathetic" Nickerson's superficial narrative. Maligned in Chase's account for giving up—and just on the verge of being saved—Nickerson seeks to create an alternative to Chase's portrayal of him as the antithesis of Christian virtue. While absenting himself from the narrative for obvious reasons, Nickerson readily construes Pollard as a captivating figure mixing a lack of foresight with all-too-human intentions.

EXCELLENT SUGGESTION

In Chase's *Narrative*, as well as Edgar Allan Poe's *Narrative of Arthur Gordon Pym*, a novel portraying a ship on which cannibalism occurs, the first to suggest the drawing of lots for cannibalism is the first chosen. After suggesting the crew randomly select the executioner, Ramsdell himself draws the undesirable lot. Nickerson represents an exception here, in choosing Pollard as the assigned killer for dramatic impact—as well as perhaps to downplay the democratic nature of the exercise by casting Pollard, the authority figure, as the shooter. Poe, by sharp contrast, portrays the Ramsdell figure suggesting the lottery as a paragon of fair-minded idealism.

In Poe's novel, Pym's resistance to a lottery for cannibalism, much like Pollard's, reflects an earnest attempt to avoid "the most horrible alternative which could enter into the mind of man." But given the circumstances, according to crewman Richard Parker, since they "had now held out as long as human nature could be sustained; that it was unnecessary for all to perish, when, by the death of one, it was possible, and even probable, that the rest might be finally preserved." Further, the other two mates, Augustus and Peters, had agreed to the lottery, placing Pym in the minority. Like Pollard, Pym eventually succumbs to the collective will. But even in Poe's narrative, the surface sympathy is absent, replaced by a stewing animosity that explodes into a knife brawl pitting Pym against Parker. Again echoing Pollard, Pym's vow to never allow the lottery includes the fiery oath that "if [Parker] attempted in any manner to acquaint the others with his bloody and cannibal designs, I would not hesitate to throw him into the sea."[29] Little did he know, but Parker had already convinced the others to partake of his plan.

Pym later confesses no democratic kinship and Christlike self-sacrificial love for Parker. Instead, as he puts it, "the fierceness of a tiger possessed my bosom, and I felt towards my fellow creature, Parker, the most intense, the most diabolical hatred." Rather than submitting to a horrific necessity, Poe's characters dispense with their inhibitions in a primal frenzy. This is the case once Parker himself chooses the lot initiating "the consummation of the tragedy in the death of him who had been chiefly instrumental in bringing it about." Once the controlled process of selection has ended, Pym and his mates become savages themselves, never once pausing to deliberate over drawing again to determine a killer, as Ramsdell had done with the *Essex* crew. Parker's death is immediate; he is "stabbed in the back by Peters"; his remains "appeased the raging thirst which consumed us by the blood of the victim." The men then proceed to take off "the hands, feet, and head, throwing them, together with the entrails, into the sea," and unceremoniously "devoured the rest of the body" like the brutes they had now become.[30]

Writing in the 1830s, Poe was well aware of Chase's *Narrative*, given that he had been close friends with Jeremiah N. Reynolds, author of *Mocha Dick: White Whale of the Pacific* (1832) and a lecturer on scientific sea expeditions, and was steeped in the era's nautical narrative culture. Further, Poe seems to pick up on a tendency of politicians, who as candidates call for broader self-sacrifice, whether regarding taxes or liberties, only to promote their own personal interests in the long run. Unlike Chase and Nickerson, Poe makes no appeal to the patriotic and pious, but rather mocks the spokesperson for such, Parker, by having him endure the sacrifice he had extolled for the good of the group. The unsentimental devouring of Parker reveals the ultimate baseness of human nature, versus the wispiness of oratory.

Long before Charles Olson wrote *Call Me Ishmael* (1947), his seminal work of Melville criticism, Pollard's reputation on Nantucket had evolved from the rumor-tinged calumny of the days following the *Essex* wreck. Olson begins his work by emphatically citing the *Essex* ordeal as not just one source but the "first fact" of *Moby-Dick*. Olson then lays out carefully selected details to illustrate his book's overarching design. In Olson's telling, Coffin's death appears as an almost organic outcome of the situation, initiated by a joint decision, all but erasing any controversy or innuendo regarding Pollard's role. Later in the volume, Olson makes liberal use of Melville's notes on Chase's *Narrative*, especially those indicating his sympathy for the stricken captain. When it comes to Pollard's possible role in a parricide, Olson establishes distance, impartially narrating the events that would lead to *Moby-Dick*'s genesis. "Within three days," he writes, "these four men, calculating the miles they had to go," and thus executing a consensual resolution, "decided to draw two lots, one to choose who should die that the others might live, and one to choose who should kill him."[31]

In this account Pollard goes unmentioned and no man—namely Ramsdell—is identified as the one to suggest drawing lots to determine the shooter. Human agency and free will are virtually removed as drivers of the event, and "the youngest, Owen Coffin, serving on his first voyage as a cabin boy" with the wholesome objective "to learn his family trade, lost," becoming the object of a dark but necessary act. Olson interestingly highlights the ritual quality of the human sacrifice to extract its full significance. It is not Coffin's body, but that of Isaac Cole, a common seaman from Barnstable, that becomes the body of Christ in Olson's narration. The ritual process seems to occur spontaneously, given that it "happened to them this once, in this way: they separated the limbs from the body, and cut all the flesh from the bones, after which they opened the body, took out the heart, closed the body again, sewed it up as well as they could and committed it to the sea. They drank of the heart and ate it. They ate a few pieces of the flesh and hung the rest." Cole is the focus here, but Olson also highlights the consumption of the ship's African American crewmen, who were the first to die. The disposal of the crew's black members, Olson observes, mirrors the elite devouring the laboring classes through exploitation and economic domination.

Aboard Chase's boat, Cole "was forced," in one of the many passive constructions Olson employs to signify the fated nature of the ordeal, "to propose to his two men, Benjamin Lawrence and Thomas Nickerson, that they should partake of their own flesh." Crucially, these men had lived on the bodies of the first to die, the African American crewmen. No emphasis on the dread of eating of one's "own flesh" appears in this narration. Instead, the writer rather mechanically reports that "Lawson Thomas, Negro, died and was eaten. Again two days and Isaac Shepherd, Negro, died and was eaten."[32] In Olson's telling, eating blacks for the white crewmen is not nearly as appalling as devouring fellow whites, or one's kin such as Coffin. The black crew dies early and quickly, likely owing to malnutrition perhaps resulting from unequal access to provisions on the open boats. Indeed, Chase reports of one particular black crewman whom he apprehends for raiding the rations.[33] Blacks are never once considered in any *Essex* accounts to assume the Christ role, yet they indeed provide for the crew's first sustenance in the form of human flesh. The lack of consensus on the fitness of African Americans for heaven may have played into their omission from Christ narratives, as the question of whether blacks could be Christianized was hotly debated even among New Englanders, who were by no means exclusively abolitionists. Indeed, from the Northern perspective, blacks were considered to be of a wholly distinct racial category or "species of mankind" than whites, according to many popular pseudoscientific studies. As such, the racial "other" was removed enough from whiteness that its members might have been considered to be comparatively more suitable as nourishment.[34] Nathaniel Philbrick notes that "a disturbing racial aspect to the rumors of cannibalism that sailors swapped" was confirmed by a Maori chief, who claimed that "black men had a much more agreeable flavor than white." Captain Benjamin Worth, whose command led him to New Zealand's shores in 1805, insisted that this view was accepted as fact among Nantucket whalemen. Blacks begged him not to land on remote islands inhabited by cannibals because "natives preferred Negro flesh to that of the white man."[35] Indeed, the logic of cannibalism here suggests that, alongside "taste," racial difference may have helped lift the taboo when it came to whites consuming blacks. Homogeneity, conversely, highlighted the act as an extension of self-consumption, epitomized by Pollard's partaking of his own kin's body.

Thus one can perceive a continuum marked at one end by flesh closest to one's own genetics and race—here coded "white," according to conventional antebellum racial ideology—and at the other by animal flesh. African American flesh, somewhere in between, was associated with moral dilemmas tied to the slaveholder-slave dynamic. In a sense, white slaveholders had been long been "consuming" their black slaves in the South. As the examples thus far have shown, consuming black flesh was less of a taboo than consuming white flesh. Moreover, the practice was typically not treated with the same ritual or symbolic significance as that applied to white-on-white cannibalism, or cannibalism associated with one's kin. In a lengthy section on "workers," Olson elaborates on this exploitation of blacks, particularly the culture's valuing of their bodies without heed to their spirits.[36] He describes them as the bone and muscle driving the whaling industry, with, I would add, the black sailor the most exploited member of this class. He writes: "The money and the glory" of the whaling venture "came later, on top with the exploiters. And the force went down, stayed where it always does," according to his neo-Marxist formulation, "at the underpaid bottom." This situation was marked by maintenance of the "lowest wages and miserable working conditions," making these 1840s crews "the bottom dogs of all nations and all races."[37]

Echoing the broader U.S. economic system, the men resolved to starve the black sailors and eat them first. As the evidence shows, their deaths were almost routinely grouped together and treated without ceremony.[38] This was the case even though, for the *Essex* crew, it was a first foray into cannibalism. Because blacks were then considered, at best, less than fully human, they could evidently be consumed without either ritual or psychological burden. In one sense, Olson's account perpetuates the belittling of the black sailor's life, in his indifferent rattling off of the names of black sailors killed and then consumed—a tendency also apparent in Chase's *Narrative*. But in another sense, his emphasis on the exploitation of workers across ethnic and national boundaries represents a distinctly progressive strain in his account.

As implied thus far, Olson is careful not to scapegoat any of the *Essex* crew members for bringing about their regrettable circumstances. Such a tactic would have obscured his emphasis on a fated event playing out for a contingent of men who seemed to act as one rather than as warring factions. Indeed, his desire to write the mythological and literary history of *Moby-Dick* as a work of prose poetry naturally leads him to eschew a focus on the minute details and debates that captivated nineteenth-century audiences. Yet scapegoating had its purpose both for the survivors and Nantucket islanders—that all could maintain their collective dignity and cleanse themselves of the taint of cannibalism. Cannibalism came to stand for a maddening and highly visible display of human sin and vulnerability, a flaw like that in Nathaniel Hawthorne's "The Birth-Mark." Eradicating all its traces was paramount after the *Essex* disaster, explaining the rush to vilify Pollard. According to the timeless practice of collective scapegoating, his flaws and sins were magnified so that they came to define his identity, exonerating all others who might be implicated. Indeed, the lottery system itself was designed to *pre*-exonerate those involved in the sea murder and cannibalism. One is reminded of the black box at the heart of Shirley Jackson's 1948 short story "The Lottery," which functions as an icon for democracy that inadvertently has become a vehicle for such scapegoating and social cleansing through human sacrifice.

In *The Jonah Man*, a 1984 novelized version of the *Essex* tragedy, Henry Carlisle depicts an imagined yet telling scene in which Chase meets Pollard on Nantucket. In it, the fictional Chase says nothing of his own participation in cannibalism. The scene points not only to how the *Essex* tale has moved into the twentieth century but also to the particular enduring desire to hear the human story behind these whalemen. Carlisle craftily captures Chase's dodging of the subject, an evasion that Nickerson would likewise attempt. After Chase tells of the whale's assault, Pollard poses the critical question: "And that's all?" This stuns Chase, who, still unwilling to divulge his own participation in the unspeakable, "reflected a moment . . . then said, 'Even if there was anything more to it we'd never fathom it, so what's the use of thinking about it?'"[39] As the chapter to follow will show, this exchange epitomizes Chase's character. His method, unlike Pollard's, was to live down the event through aggressive dissociation from both the taboo of cannibalism and the liabilities attendant to his fatal decisions—decisions that would ultimately force the crew to mull their alternatives to starvation.

Chapter 2

~~~~~~~~~~~~~~~~~~~~~~~~~~~~~~~~~~~~~~~

DAMAGE CONTROL

In the wake of the *Essex* tragedy, Owen Chase behaved with the urgency of a man drowning. In order to preserve his career, he rushed into print with his version of the story, casting himself as the consummate survivor. Most curious of all was that he had virtually emblazoned his tale of suffering and survival—a testament to the human spirit—with a giant "For Sale" sign. By seeking to avert any suspicion of cowardice, with his heroic story steeped in the entrepreneurial and Christian values tightly held in antebellum culture, Chase harnessed the era's commercial rhetoric in his *Narrative* as part of his elaborate plan for damage control.

Reading Chase's *Narrative*, one is struck by his desire to survive with the greatest dignity possible. But his efforts, at every turn, also seem trained on his release from any blame, as couched in his ghostwriter's suave prose. In *The Jonah Man*, Henry Carlisle's novel of the *Essex* saga, Chase appears exactly in this character, refusing to accept his part in the ordeal. As detailed toward the close of chapter 1, Chase demurs at Pollard's question regarding the wreck's aftermath: "And that's all?" Chase, ever smooth and superficial, "smiled and said, 'We just had a little bad luck.'" Pollard, in response, is flush with emotion as "fever swept through me."[1] Although Chase would enjoy a lucrative and lengthy whaling career and set the blueprint for nearly all subsequent retellings of the *Essex* tragedy with his *Narrative*, he would pay dearly for his unwillingness to reckon with his demons. Unlike Pollard, who directly addressed the horrors of the *Essex* experience, Chase repressed the truth—and ultimately descended into madness.

In beginning to understand Chase's approach, one must note that the drawing of lots that led to Owen Coffin's death was but one episode in a lengthy history of killing at sea for survival. More generally, even as the custom had been accepted to some extent, killing one's shipmate could be very much like murdering a beloved relative. Shipmates frequently forged intense bonds over years and looked out for one another's safety. Toby of Melville's *Typee* (1846) and the majestic Jack Chase of his *Redburn* (1849) are two such fictional companions who correspond to real shipmates the author deeply revered. Killing such companions, although this occurs in *Billy Budd*, would have been wildly intolerable even in Melville's imagination. As for Charles Ramsdell, who pulled the trigger against Owen Coffin only after expressing his reluctance to do so, the question indeed arises whether he had committed a murder—in his own perception, that of his mates, and that of the public.

Pollard's all-too-human wail of regret in 1823, two months after the sinking of the *Two Brothers*, was simultaneously a lament for the dead and a confession of a captain's complicity in the event. Daniel Tyerman, a well-traveled agent of the London Missionary Society responsible for surveying Pacific and Far Eastern missions, reported that Pollard delivered his tale "in a tone of despondency never to be forgotten by him who heard it," with the captain wincing in agony as he spoke. "My head is on fire at the recollection," he confessed, in telling how he "cried out, 'My lad, my lad, *if you don't like your lot*, I'll shoot the first man that touches you.' The poor emaciated boy hesitated a moment or two; then, quietly laying his head down upon the gunnel of the boat, he said, '*I like my lot as well as any other*.'"[2] Coffin's hesitation here indicates he might very well have taken up Pollard's offer. Should Pollard, then have exploited that slight hesitation to show himself as a true hero and protective paternal figure? The recollection indeed was too much for Pollard to bear.

Even as Chase projected full composure in his print rendering of the tale, this doesn't mean he could speak of it without breaking down. Nantucketer Jethro Macy wrote in 1821 that though of "firm mind and strong constitution of body," Chase's "sufferings have been such that it is impossible for him to talk much about it; even the parts most distant from the worst start the tears, his voice falters." Macy's next observation is telling of Chase's trajectory, particularly his parlaying of the *Essex* disaster into a successful career: "strong efforts mixed with smiles mark his disjointed sentences."[3] Those disjointed sentences would be transformed by his hired writer. Given Chase's emerging reputation for dissembling self-promotion, it is little wonder why Melville and Emerson did not visit him, instead gravitating toward Pollard, who, better than any survivor, embodied the tremors of the experience.

CHASING AWAY GHOSTS:
THE FIRST MATE'S GHOSTWRITER

Whereas Chase donned a forced smile in his *Narrative* and, when he could, in his personal demeanor, Pollard never comported himself in this way. Melville accordingly describes Pollard's traits in his epic poem *Clarel*: "Never he smiled; / Call him, and he would come; not sour / In spirit, but meek and reconciled; / Patient he was, he none withstood." But he was not without his scars, for "Oft on some secret thing would brood."[4] Melville initially felt Chase "to have been the fittest person to narrate the thing" in print, likely because he was on another boat during its most intense moment—the shooting of Owen Coffin. That distance, along with the fact that he was not captain, may have allowed Chase greater objectivity. But what Melville found in Chase's *Narrative* was not reportorial objectivity but instead a veneer of completeness despite its glaring omission of an explanation for the pivotal decision to sail for South America.

For Chase's narrative Melville detected a ghostwriter, seeing how he served as a kind of defense attorney and character witness in one. "There seems no reason to suppose that Owen himself wrote the *Narrative*," Melville concluded. "It bears obvious tokens of having been written for him; but at the same time, its whole air plainly evinces that it was carefully and conscientiously written to Owen's dictation of the facts—It is almost as good as tho' Owen wrote it himself." This last qualification, it would seem, might indicate a surprising fidelity to the facts, given its "whole air." Yet by that phrase Melville means something entirely different. *Whole* alludes to the narrative's seamless coherence, including its succession of events and unmistakable attention to details—from catching flying fish by sail and devouring them whole to Nickerson's delirium—that only a survivor could recall. But the causal connections crafted to tie together the events, particularly those that turned fatal such as the decision to sail for the mainland—an error Melville had recorded with astonishment—struck Melville as the work of a ghostwriter under Chase's close surveillance. Melville knew also that employing a ghostwriter would help whitewash complicity in a terrible strategic decision that "*might have been avoided*," particularly obvious in how they, "*strange to tell*, knew not that for more than twenty years the English missionaries had been resident in Tahiti."[5]

Historians have variously conjectured three different identities for Chase's ghostwriter, who so deftly helped him hide truths ascertainable only by readers as astute as Melville. Samuel Jenks, the easiest to rule out, was editor of the *Nantucket Inquirer*, first published in June 1821. Between fielding submissions, soliciting contributions, scribbling editorials, and setting type to meet his paper's first deadlines, he likely would not have been able to compose the *Narrative* by the following month. Yet his "self-important, inflated rhetoric," contrary to Thomas Heffernan's speculation, was actually consonant with that of the *Narrative*, which openly aggrandizes Chase's heroism far more than it achieves a "sensitive, imaginative, and timelessly literary" finish.[6] Heffernan, writing in 1981, has also proposed that Jenks's father-in-law, William Coffin, had written the *Narrative*. This was based on Coffin's skilled prose in a pamphlet seeking to exonerate himself from involvement in a 1795 Nantucket bank robbery. Coffin was an older man with ample time to write Chase's *Narrative*, but the age discrepancy between the two probably would not have allowed for the intimacy necessary to produce such a nuanced work. The ghostwriter was more likely a young man at the beginning of his career, and who thus could sympathize more deeply with Chase's plight.

William Coffin's *son*, meanwhile, William Jr., had a freshly minted Harvard degree and would later ghostwrite William Lay and Cyrus Hussey's *Mutiny on Board the Whaleship* Globe (1828) and Obed Macy's *History of Nantucket* (1834). Besides the *Essex*, the *Globe* would become the period's most spectacular nautical disaster in American print culture; Coffin Jr.'s original account profoundly shaped innumerable retellings including that featured in Poe's *Narrative of Arthur Gordon Pym*. The eventual author of such a powerful and highly publicized seafaring disaster is likely to have also penned Chase's account. Although it was his first time writing in such a genre, Coffin Jr. had experience authoring pamphlets for the temperance movement, and thus was skilled in the art of rhetorical persuasion. Such experience meant that he was even more qualified than an attorney to "defend" Chase, given his access to the potent literary devices of sentimentality and sensationalism. He understood the earliest forms of what we would now call a mass audience, and could strike a sympathetic chord with great success, according to Nantucket historian Helen Winslow Chase.[7] Likewise his own father, accused of a crime he did not commit, had used the literary market as his means of self-defense. For Chase's objective, then, Coffin Jr. was a perfect match.

Poe registers his appreciation, and perhaps disdain, for the prevalence of ghostwriters in contemporary nautical tales by prefacing his *Narrative of Arthur Gordon Pym* under the name of his fictional narrator and protagonist, who alludes to "Mr. Poe" as his ghostwriter. The challenge of solving the mystery of the "real" author's identity fascinated audiences well into the nineteenth century, just as the question of authorship and autobiography fueled much interest in Charlotte Brontë's *Jane Eyre*.[8] Poe's fictional narrator Pym claims in his preface to have originally considered throwing his imperfect, yet totally authentic, account of his voyage before the public. He continues, "Its very uncouthness, if there were any, would give it all the better chance of being received as truth" but that such a move would have demanded exceptional bravery and "trust in the shrewdness and common sense of the public." Out of modesty he turns the manuscript of his "factual account" over to Poe, who then resolves to work it into a "pretended fiction." Pym nonetheless contends that the resulting version will convey his authentic experience: "I thence concluded that the facts of my narrative" were strong enough to throw off any "score of popular incredulity." A ruse in itself, this claim called attention to the common inclusion of fabricated material in seafaring narratives, a tendency largely facilitated by fluid ideas about authorship. Just as it is difficult to parse Chase's particular influence on his *Narrative*—an issue that perplexed Melville to no end—Poe as Pym also sounds this note in his preface: "Even to those readers who have not seen the Messenger, it will be unnecessary to point out where his portion ends and my own commences; the difference in point of style will be readily perceived"—which of course it is not.[9] I hereby confess to falling prey to exactly the folly Poe parodies here—who can resist it?—of parsing a sea story to discern its "true" author, and thus join the ranks of other historians who bear this dubious distinction. It is not so much a frivolous foible to pursue this question for Chase, however, given the utter necessity of weighing the relative veracity of his versus subsequent narratives of the *Essex* story. I also consider this act essential for deducing the various motives of the storytellers.

Relentless self-promotion has likewise followed the nautical genre. Chase begins with a confession of writing for financial gain, a gesture also made by Poe in *Pym*. This is not as tawdry an admission as it may at first appear, but like Walt Whitman's poem, "To Rich Givers," frankly acknowledges self-advertisement for the sake of finding a donor. "Why should I be ashamed," Whitman asks, "to advertise for" and "to cheerfully accept" the various forms of patronage that keep him solvent, such as "a little sustenance, a hut and garden, a little money." Whitman's proud embrace of his human impulse, no doubt, would have appeared indiscreet, or taboo, in antebellum culture.[10] In *Pym*, in a scene describing the protagonist's attempt to turn a countermutiny by frightening the tyrants into submission, Poe similarly confesses his profit motive in offering his writings to the public: "I made up my mind, however, to sell my life as dearly as possible, and not to suffer myself to be overcome by any feelings of trepidation."[11] Indeed, Chase, whether he admitted it or not, was also selling his life "as dearly as possible" to live down his error at sea.

Chase's *Narrative* helped safeguard his reputation from scrutiny. Selling it aggressively was the best way he knew of to achieve this objective, as he announces in "To the Reader." Here, he demonstrates an awareness of the literary marketplace and, in particular, of "the private stories of individuals . . . and the injuries which have resulted from the promulgation of fictitious histories, and in many instances, of journals entirely fabricated for the purpose."[12] The "injuries" referred to here are those to reputation, not body, and the faked sea tales he notes, designed to impugn character, were the very sort he most feared. Chase knew that by printing his story first, he could preempt and discredit any subsequent renderings that might cast him in an unflattering light. Chase acts much in the same spirit as his ghostwriter's father, William Coffin, who had eloquently defended himself from the slanderous bank robbery allegations. His expressed worry that falsified nautical accounts could "undervalue the general cause of truth" reflects both a rhetorical ploy to invest himself with steady authenticity and an admission of his own paranoia that his negligence in the tragedy be might disclosed by rumor or the press.[13]

Chase dubiously situates the *Narrative* in the scholarly genre of "any department of the arts or sciences . . . founded in fact." With an eye to entertainment value, he promises "new and astonishing traits of human character" for both the serious "philanthropist and philosopher" and, democratically, for "every description of readers." He continues this self-advertisement by claiming his descriptions are intrinsically interesting and thus not in the least amplified for sensationalistic effect. He ends the note in the spirit of Whitman by expressing "the hope of obtaining something of remuneration" for his tale. He justifies his plea based on the financial hit he incurred from the destruction of the *Essex*, claiming to have "lost all the little I had ventured, but my situation and the prospects of bettering it."[14] Describing his *Narrative* as an entrepreneurial venture, notably, could ally him with other industrious readers who might have had to reinvent themselves professionally for survival in the turbulent, surging economy of the 1820s, when all trades felt the beginnings of the market revolution.[15]

Once a man of considerable means, whose prospects "seemed to smile upon me," Chase now finds it "all in one short moment destroyed. . . ."[16] As for the financial effect of the shipwreck, he certainly lost less money than the boat's owners had, but as first mate, he likely invested at least modestly in the voyage's search for profitable whale oil. A study for the National Bureau of Economic Research confirms that "from 1820 onward, 39 percent of captains had shares in the voyages in which they participated." Further, "these shares were not negligible" since "they averaged from about 10 to almost 30 percent."[17] Chase's purported economic ruin from the sinking of the *Essex* is therefore grossly exaggerated; Pollard, meanwhile, given these data, would likely have suffered the worst financial loss of all the survivors. If anyone were justified in selling "a short history of my sufferings" in exchange for "something of remuneration," it was Pollard.

Rather than modestly recover his losses, Chase aimed to cash in on demand in a surging free-market economy. His humility was a sure ruse. Among noncaptains, the losses incurred on failed voyages consisted of "bonus payments that depended upon the amount of oil or bone (or both) taken. Like the performance bonuses written into the contracts of major-league baseball players, these bonuses were designed to spur employees on to high levels of performance." Chase may be more accurately understood as grousing about extra earnings lost through "a slush fund made from the sale of goods brought along to trade with South Sea islanders, Africans, or Inuit." The crew, like the captain in this case, "probably supplemented their incomes nicely in this way"; however, "it is unlikely that trade represented a major part of their total earnings," as economic historians Lance Davis and Charles Nordhoff report.[18]

Like in Harriet Wilson's preface to her now famous autobiographical novel, *Our Nig: Sketches from the Life of a Free Black* (1859), among the first ever written by an African American, Chase claims in his note to readers to be writing hungry and out of economic necessity. But far from the situation experienced by Wilson, who was near starvation and needed funds to save her ill child's life, Chase, like most whalemen, was something of a gambler, who in truth was lamenting the earnings that might have been.[19] Sebastian Junger, in his stellar profile of 1990s New England swordfishermen, observes the popularity for these seamen of Dick Francis horse racing novels, "which [seem] to appeal" to them "because it's another way to win or lose huge amounts of money." So popular that they "get passed around the fleet 'at about four hundred miles per hour,'" according to one fisherman, Junger speculates "they've probably been to the Grand Banks [of New Foundland] more times than the men themselves."[20] Indeed, for Chase, writing about the *Essex* was a kind of high-stakes gamble, like whaling itself. Along with material rewards, the payoff promised fame.

Upon Chase's return to Nantucket on June 11, 1820, time was of the essence to craft his *Narrative*. The whaling community had been well aware that Nuku Hiva and the islands around Tahiti were inhabited by peaceful indigenous people who had communed near an expansive royal chapel that housed a large contingent of missionaries. These peaceful natives, reported on in the *New Bedford Mercury* as early as April 28, 1819, meant that at least some portion of the broader public might begin to question the *Essex* sailors' decision not to tack West, as Pollard had advocated. They in turn might deduce that Chase's thwarting of this move was the real cause of the disaster, and not a murderous whale, as Chase argued. This was why the urgency of the situation must have struck the first mate like a blow to the head.

If all New England learned, based on survivors' testimony, that Chase had led the resistance against Pollard's argument for sailing west, then the first mate could face permanent ignominy in a region known for its puritanical intolerance of sinners. He did not, therefore, savor public gratitude for his survival. As would John Proctor in Arthur Miller's *Crucible*, Chase set forth to defend his name with the very best resources available.

The quest for a ghostwriter began, and once he secured the services of Coffin Jr., he initiated a highly impressive rhetorical defense of his reputation. Chase's method of constructing his own defense, which bleeds into an appeal for celebrity, points to how, according to literary scholar Leo Braudy, writers seeking fame exhibit a larger sense of "the nature of commercial civilization, [and] the expansion of . . . media, as much as they are about the special nature or the special self-consciousness of an individual."[21] As implied thus far, Chase's special self-consciousness derived from his pivotal role in an event so traumatic and brutal that it called into question whether the perils of the trade were worth such profound costs.

As important as securing an effective ghostwriter was Chase's match with the New York publisher and bookseller William B. Gilley. Although running a small shop, Gilley specialized, based on a 1819 source, "in a varied selection of current and popular books—Thomson, Southey, Watts, and Smollett, along with a large number of moralistic and didactic works," with the latter resonating well with the role of providence in Chase's *Narrative*.[22] But more crucially, Gilley was known for tales of shipwrecks on the South Seas, and worked closely with Matthew Carey of Philadelphia, the most powerful publisher of the day with the broadest distribution network. Heffernan speculates that Chase may indeed have gone with his manuscript to Carey, who redirected him to Gilley. Exemplifying the cooperation between the two firms, arrangements were made for Gilley to print William Parry's *Voyages of Discovery* on the condition that he would send Carey forty copies. Despite having an ostensibly modest publisher, Chase was actually engaging the largest print market available, reaching the expanding literate audiences of New York and Philadelphia. Here, one must remember that this was an era of starkly limited publishing options, before mass-circulation outlets such as the *New York Ledger*, later used by Nickerson, emerged for such narratives. Whether or not Chase first approached Carey, he was likely more than satisfied to have the New York publisher of nautical tales, celebrity writers, and didactic moral tracts publish his story.[23]

Despite conducting himself with a self-seriousness that suggested a desire for long-term renown, Chase's fame would prove ephemeral. As Braudy writes, "If fame includes such an element of turning away from us, celebrity stares us right in the face, flaunting its performance and trying desperately to keep our attention."[24] Chase does both by self-consciously courting his audience and by turning his head away, insisting he is telling modest unvarnished truth alone.

For the sake of comparison, the contemporary fictional film *Anonymous* (2011) centers on ghostwriting as it pertains to Shakespeare. The politics of playwriting during the Elizabethan era were such that an influential and well-to-do gentleman like the Earl of Oxford, whom the filmmakers conjecture to be the real author of the plays, could not afford to subject himself to the political controversy most plays attracted. Many playwrights at the time were executed for staging content with treasonous views; Oxford may have wanted to avoid the glare of political scrutiny that could draw such violence against him and thus may have conscripted a young actor named William Shakespeare to conceal his identity. For Chase, the temporal circumstances were reversed. Unlike the plays of Oxford, Chase's story, nonfiction in this case, was yet to be told. So he sought, with the help of a ghostwriter, to *construct* a personal narrative that could ward off would-be critics, transforming them into backers or perhaps even adorers. Oxford, for his part, had already written his plays when he solicited a plausible creature of the theatre, Shakespeare, as his stand-in to conceal his identity. In both cases, whatever the sequence, we witness authors managing their works and themselves into the market.

"COMMERCIAL EXCITEMENT"

As the market for literature developed, authors increasingly "fed and nurtured some aspect of the audience's narcissism."[25] In this fashion Chase reinforced his audience members' best image of themselves, kowtowing to both their Christian moral sentimentality and free-market capitalism. His first order of business after appealing for "remuneration" in exchange for his tale was to render a robust defense of the whaling industry, which Melville would echo in bombastic legalistic rhetoric in *Moby-Dick*'s "The Advocate" chapter. Yet unlike Chase, Melville peppers his appeal with intentionally facetious, outlandish claims conflating Queequeg with George Washington. Chase's discussion of whaling, meanwhile, is pure "commercial excitement," not unlike the *Narrative* he is weaving before our eyes. His emphasis on the whaling industry's rise to power, which is "as important and general a branch of commerce as any belonging to our country," evades the inevitable issue of internal competition among neighboring whaling firms, and thus skirts the inconvenient truth of economic "cannibalism." Just as Chase elides human cannibalism in converting the *Essex* tale into one of providential resurrection, he avoids the unpleasant difficulties of the broader whaling industry. He also finds a useful enemy in the British—and an opportunity for mercantile triumph. In particular, he cites the "extensive and powerful competition" from the British, whose whalers benefited from subsidies and tax breaks; he then implores the U.S. government to aid its own commercial whaling firms through similar measures. British whalers, he contends, "are enabled to realize a greater profit from the demand and price of oil in their markets," and thus put the American whaling industry at a distinct disadvantage.[26]

Chase asks in "To the Reader" and the "Preface," as we have seen, for personal aid from potential buyers of his book as well as U.S. government aid for the industry. Given that Chase planned to spend his career as a whaling captain, the appeal for favorable industry treatment has the outward look of patriotism but could ultimately boost his own career—and profits. His future survival, he postulates, calls "for the want of a deserved government patronage."[27] Whaling is "a most hazardous business; involving many incidental and unavoidable sacrifices," he explains in a thinly veiled allusion to the killing of Owen Coffin, "the severity of which it seems cruel to increase by neglect or refusal of a proper protection." Thus starved of proper financial support, he reasons, an already struggling trade sinks deeper into brutish, even cannibalistic means for survival. The U.S. government, he clearly implies, is the real culprit behind the practice of cannibalism by American sailors, and the failure to support their increasingly competitive circumstances is tantamount to causing cannibalism itself. The claim fits Chase's larger plan in the *Narrative* to shift scrutiny away from his negligence. The American government receives the blame here, just as another large, unwieldy force capable of great destruction—an eighty-five-foot sperm whale—does later in his tale.

Chase's desire to exculpate himself did not preclude his equally powerful desire to entertain. His *Narrative* works from the assumption that for readers of gothic fiction, according to Poe's formulation, "the appalling horror . . . where most suffering has been experienced" is attributed more to "a kind of anticipative horror, lest the apparition *might possibly be* real, than to an unwavering belief in its reality."[28] The suspension of disbelief, therefore, actually intensifies the reader's fright, according to Poe's theory. In *The Narrative of Arthur Gordon Pym*, exemplifying this theme, the protagonist, Pym, stages a countermutiny by playing on the crew's superstition and guilt and dressing up as a recently deceased shipmate, whose bloated and discolored body has been conspicuously visible to the crew for days. At the sight of the dressed-up Pym, one unsuspecting crew member drops dead of fear, killed by "anticipative horror." Poe's commentary on the gothic nautical tale draws upon the conventional standard set by Chase's own *Narrative*, which, although nonfiction, sought the same effect on readers. Commercial excitement by way of anticipative horror was an objective shared by both Poe and Chase.[29]

Like the sensational narrative effect Chase seeks to achieve in the literary market through his grisly tale, a whaleman's work is characterized by the "commercial excitement" of vigorous ambition, according to Chase. Situating Nantucket fishermen among the professions, unlike those who "labour only for their temporary existence," Chase argues that whalemen like himself "have an ambition and pride among them which seeks after distinguishment and promotion." This is not so much an appeal to dignify the common sailor's experience as it is a defense of his own professional ambition, one uncommon to most whalemen yet to command their first voyage. But on his open boat, Chase tasted what it was like to captain his own ship, albeit under extremely compromised conditions. Much of the *Narrative* therefore is Chase's justification of his own skills and qualifications with an eye toward securing a career as a whale captain. His assertion that "almost all" seamen in the whaling industry "enter the service with views of their own command" is very much self-reflexive, if not entirely true.[30] Indeed, a relatively high rate of turnover occurred among common whalemen, as two-thirds of original crews never returned to their home port, but instead deserted, were discharged, or died on the voyage.

Many common sailors, therefore, may have initially approached the trade with the ambition to eventually become captain, only to succumb to the temptations of shore, thereby showing a lack of discipline precisely contrary to what was needed to reach their stated goal. Given multiple desertions, discharges, reenlistments, and a practice of island-hopping, many sailors engaged in something akin to global hitchhiking. Further, most whaleboat laborers had a disincentive to stay with a crew. In particular, according to one study that looked at crew members, a laborer's "wage entitled him, as time went on, to a smaller fractional share of the voyages for which he shipped." In other words, common sailors saw their wages decrease as productivity dropped off toward the latter portions of long voyages. Their economic exploitation derived from the "gradually deteriorating character and efficiency of the crews," especially after a voyage's first six months, which by then usually saw an accumulation of injuries, illnesses, and even fatalities, most often by drowning or falls from the masthead or yardarm onto the deck. Captains were also tempted "to exploit . . . inferior crews" as they accumulated oil, freely substituting such capital gains by paying in kind rather than dollars for labor.[31]

Whereas Chase may have accurately depicted himself as a mate seeking advancement, his insinuation that professional ambition characterized entire whale crews down to boatsteerers and cabin boys is less convincing. The industry did not allow the necessary avenues for advancement into the position of mate, captain, and owner. These were positions occupied by individuals with special privileges or connections that moved them up the hierarchy more rapidly. Sailors grinding out voyages at lowly ranks tended to stay in those positions, with the exception of the extraordinarily dedicated and fortuitous. The nineteenth-century New England intellectual Orestes Brownson's assessment of pre–Civil War Northern wage laborers, and their regrettable conditions, applies to the era's nautical workers. "The employer has him at his mercy," he observes. "No man born poor has ever risen to the class of the wealthy." This reflected a sobering recognition of the hurdles standing in the way of true socioeconomic progress. Class mobility and permeability may in fact have characterized American society during the prewar market revolution, but wage labor was too often a recipe for stasis. "Rich he may become, but it has not been by his own manual labor," Brownson astutely notes.[32] Indeed, as the wages of unskilled sea laborers steadily declined, those of officers rose. "It is difficult to see how, given these wage differentials, the whaling industry could have continued to recruit trained Americans for enlisted jobs over the two antebellum decades," the social scientist Lance E. Davis observes, noting that the whaling industry instead relied heavily on unskilled Americans and foreigners alike. "The presence of both professional and amateur gamblers" among the era's typical crewmen "may indicate something about the degree of risk aversion shared by at least the American component of that crew," whose members were lured by the prospect of a lucky voyage, with an impressive haul, which would convert to profits that would overshadow otherwise meager wages.[33] It is telling indeed that, as Hester Blum observes, "the definition of a strike as a labor action came into use after Royal Naval sailors struck their sails—in the nautical meaning of 'strike,' to take down or put away—in protest of poor conditions and low wages in the Spithead and Nore mutinies of 1797."[34]

Surviving a voyage—at least 50 out of 754 commanders whose careers were limited to a single voyage perished at sea—often encouraged this gambling mentality among officers as well as common crewmen. According to Davis, "a successful first voyage might convince a captain to get out [on the open sea] while there was still time."[35] Experience and access to data about the richest whaling waters of course mitigated that risk. Yet unlike most land-based industries, whaling lacked access to a reliable and transparent set of data. "Informational asymmetries in whaling," as Davis describes it, abounded.[36] The *Essex* crew's reliance on the seriously flawed *New American Practical Navigator*, by Nathaniel Bowditch, was a prime example.

Cannibalism can be a metaphor for a type of economic failure, with the savage free market mocking the very notion of building civilization through profitable enterprise. For the whaling industry, this principle was epitomized by the skillful manipulation of an ever dynamic and elusive body of nautical knowledge. The race for knowledge preceded the race for whales. Thus "agents tried to gain advantages over their competitors by restricting access to knowledge of the routes and timing of whale migrations."[37] Captains who transferred between firms, of course, had little reason to keep these secrets, standing to profit by sharing knowledge on matters such as migration patterns, currents, and the seasonal movement of whales. Chase did this expertly as part of the quintessential Yankee enterprise, fueled by an uncommon drive for mastery and control, seemingly a compensatory psychological response to his literal and emotional lack of direction as a decision maker during the *Essex* journey.

And Chase's later success as a whaleman was unparalleled. Of more than a half-century of captains on the *Winslow*, which sailed under dozens of commands from 1802 to 1858, no one matched his feats. Between 1828 and 1830, he had the top two richest outings in the vessel's history, boasting 1,906 and 1,800 barrels of sperm oil landed or sent home on back-to-back ventures hailing from New Bedford. After manning the helm for three of the five most profitable voyages of the *Winslow*'s history, his two outings on the *Charles Carroll* totaled an ungodly eight years at sea, with but one three-month layover in Nantucket from March to August 1836. Just as he did for the *Winslow*, Chase set the record for the most profitable run of the *Charles Carroll*'s existence. In that time his relentless pursuit of whales would net 5,288 barrels of oil, a sum unparalleled in the industry. With profits dwarfing those of other captains sailing at the time—Thomas S. Andrews would garner just more than 3,300 units in the *Charles Carroll*'s next two ventures—Chase's productivity strongly indicates his total immersion in the profession, an obsession just as extraordinary and unprecedented as the traumatic *Essex* disaster itself.[38]

If Chase's post-*Essex* career was marked by these attributes, it was likely only because he knew too well the horror of disorientation at sea. Melville would seize upon this nightmare of being lost with an unreliable guidebook in both *Redburn* and *Clarel*. Chase's copy of the *New American Practical Navigator* was hardly new. His edition while on the *Essex*, and the latest to be published, was probably dated to 1817, or three years old, but contained data virtually identical to its previous 1802 version. It would erroneously indicate that the *Essex* had landed on Ducie rather than Henderson Island. Nevertheless, Chase's guidebook was hardly useless, unlike those depicted in Melville's *Pierre* and *Redburn*. Pierre, Melville's protagonist, finds an engrossing pamphlet on the compromise between idealistic vision and earthly ambition that promises to unlock the mystery of his life only to discover that its conclusion is torn off. Redburn, meanwhile, is thrown into Liverpool after a transatlantic voyage with his father's antiquated guidebook, which promises him the England of his dreams. Instead, he confronts a glaring gap between book and reality, concluding that "guidebooks are the least reliable in all literature . . . old ones tell us the ways our fathers went, through the thoroughfares and courts of old, but how few of those former places can their posterity trace amid avenues of modern erections."[39] He had naïvely assumed the book would navigate him through the crookedest streets, enabling him "to march through them in the darkest night, and even run for the most distant dock on a pressing emergency." Like the life buoy on the *Pequod* in *Moby-Dick* that sinks like a stone when thrown to one drowning mate, Redburn's guidebook fails to serve its function and instead is a "miserable cicerone to the modern."[40] Tellingly, the book bears a copyright of 1802, the same year data were compiled and remaining unchanged in the later 1817 edition of the *Practical Navigator*.

Judging from the massive success of his four voyages on the *Winslow* and *Charles Carroll*, Chase appears to have been armed with an abundance of accurate information regarding the location of whales. After sailing with the *Florida* just eighteen months on the heels of the *Essex* voyage, Chase took the helm of the *Winslow* in August 1825 for his first command. The voyage garnered 1,440 barrels of oil, a rich reward for having reached the prized Japanese cruising grounds. By 1832 Chase had established his reputation as one of the most successful captains in the industry. Reflecting this stature, the *Charles Carroll* was built specifically for him by David Joy, the second cousin of Matthew Joy, one of the first *Essex* crewman to die of starvation. With Joy's blessing, and a freshly minted vessel boasting a 376-ton hold, Chase would return with an astonishing 2,610 barrels of oil. Not only would this be the largest single profit-earning voyage of his career, but Chase would also revisit the same waters that had claimed the *Essex*, and even land on Tahiti and the other islands he had convinced Pollard to avoid in 1820. The journey also brought him into contact with the world's most celebrated captain of the era, Charles Wilkes, who was then leading the United States Exploring Expedition. It would appear that Chase had lived down his previous catastrophic decisions by redoubling his efforts to master the sea—geographically, financially, and politically.

TOWARD NEAREST LAND

But the man who wrote the *Narrative* in 1820 was hardly so secure and accomplished. His language everywhere strains to defend his courage and deflect accusations of cowardice. In describing his "profession" as "one of great ambition and full of honorable excitement," he effectively casts himself as a representative and ambassador of this noble occupation. The more he defines the trade, the more he rhetorically defends his honor, since by nature "the coward is marked with that peculiar aversion" among whalers.[41] Melville would qualify this formulation through the fictional first mate of the *Pequod*: "'I will have no man in my boat,' said Starbuck, 'who is not afraid of a whale.' By this, he seems to mean not only that the most reliable and useful courage was that which arises from a fair estimation of the encountered peril, but that an utterly fearless man is a far more dangerous comrade than a coward."[42] Whereas Chase aligns whaling with the type of bravery that "distinguishes our public naval service," Melville here finds virtue in caution. Ironically, Chase would never advocate caution as a virtue in the early going of his *Narrative*.

In his description of the wreck's aftermath, Chase deliberately obscures his lead role in swaying Pollard from sailing to the relatively nearby Marquesas. One would never suspect he had so strenuously recruited the crew's support in this campaign, since he notes that his first suggestion to Pollard was that "no time should be lost in making the best of our way towards the nearest land." He makes it appear as though he never really resisted at all. Chase craftily evades the actual unfolding of the decision, as reported by historian Nathaniel Philbrick: "After the whale attack, Captain Pollard suggested that they sail for the Society Islands. Instead of sticking with his initial decision (which would have probably resulted in the deliverance of the entire crew)," Philbrick notes further, "Pollard yielded to the objections of Chase and second mate Matthew Joy, who advocated sailing for South America."[43] Far worse than Pollard's yielding to this pressure was the fact that he had faced resistance to his sensible decision to begin with. Chase hides his own major role in the deliberations by characterizing the decision-making body as "a council" consisting of "twenty men." The plural pronoun *we* is operative here; once out on the open boats, Chase reverts to the first-person voice in order to reestablish his heroism in the ordeal. Yet if indeed Chase had first proposed to sail to the nearest land, why had he not pressed for it? "We examined our navigators," he reports, "to ascertain the nearest land, and found it was the Marquesas." Absolutely no mention is made here of any dangers associated with the islands' indigenous peoples, making the Marquesas the obvious ideal destination, even according to the logic of Chase's account. Mention of the Society Islands, by contrast, raises the crew's fear that "if inhabited we presumed they were by savages, from whom we had as much to fear as from the elements or even death itself," all unalterable forces. The alarm about the Society Islands, but not the Marquesas, provides a key insight into the psychology behind the crew's fatal decision.

Chase does not mention his principal role in pushing the slippery-slope logic according to which the Marquesas would be too dangerous by sheer proximity to the Society Islands. "These islands we were entirely ignorant of," he confesses. Driven by ignorance and fear, the crew was also constrained by Pollard's "opinion that this was the season of the hurricanes which prevail in the vicinity of the Sandwich Islands [Hawaii], and that consequently it would be unsafe to steer for them."[44] So with only their navigation handbook, and advice from Pollard to avoid the Sandwich Islands (but no charts), we are led to believe that the decision to sail for South America came by default, a natural and virtually inevitable resolution to the dilemma.

The testimony even spuriously casts Chase as *desiring* to sail for the Marquesas, based on his claim that he had first insisted on sailing for the "nearest land." In fact Chase depicts himself speaking on his own behalf only once in this scene—to make this suggestion, which in retrospect would have saved all their lives. The only sense of his complicity with the decision to sail for South America surfaces in his rhetorical appeal for sympathy regarding the crew's ignorance of the Society Islands, which fueled their fear of savages. As we saw, he casts the native threat as being as insurmountable as "the elements and even death itself." But in all this he is hardly confessing so much as appearing to sympathize with the error. His claim, further, is that the crew was ignorant of and fearful *specifically* of the Society Islands rather than the Marquesas, which suggests that the latter were a plausible destination. One can imagine the crew's wild and persistent screams of desperation led by Chase, who irrationally vetoed going for the thoroughly civilized Marquesas, just two days away with favorable winds. Pollard, as noted earlier, knew his refusal might very well have triggered a mutiny.

Once the remaining crew took to their boats and set sail for South America, a killer whale struck Pollard's boat, making "a considerable breach in the bows . . . through which the water had begun to pour fast." Pollard could not afford to underreact, given the recent loss of the main ship, and thus he "immediately took measures to remove his provisions into the second mate's boat and mine, in order to lighten his own." Such action may have appeared totally appropriate, yet Chase nonetheless condemns it by alleging Pollard was "imagining matters to be considerably worse than they were."[45] Such a characterization, however, would have better applied to Chase himself during the decision-making tussle. Pollard here was not overreacting so much as wisely protecting provisions from an alarming gush of water into the boat's hull.

Chase not only unfairly faults Pollard for excessive alarm—he also blames the crew's slow progress on the wait for his open boats. He complains of having to "heave to immediately and set a light, by which the missing boat might be directed to us." These lagging boats indeed wasted precious time. But Chase also insinuates that if his boat were sailing alone, his superior navigational skills would have brought the crew to shore in time to avert starvation. The *Narrative* makes an argument for Chase's fitness for future command even beyond this show of superior nautical skill. The crew, for example, was in possession of two large turtles, and Chase gives himself outsize credit for proposing to kill one for sustenance. "I need to say that the proposition was hailed with the utmost enthusiasm," writes Chase, the apparent benevolent provider and caretaker of his men. He imagines himself the host of this, "I may say[,] exquisite banquet."[46] Later in the journey, after landing on Henderson Island, Chase presents a moment of near perfect harmony between his private will and that of the crew. "I made a silent determination in my own mind," he recalls, "to remain [on the island] at least four or five days," regardless of any dissenting views. But, according to Chase, "I found no difference in the views of any of us as to this matter," a finding that may have pointed to his skills of persuasion, already displayed in his earlier argument to head toward South America.[47]

The issue of dissenting views and misconduct among the men loomed large as the weeks wore on aboard their open boats. The situation had all the ingredients of mutiny—starving men vying for a dwindling supply of food presented a powder keg that threatened to burst into a wild raid on the provisions and overthrow of Chase. In the *Narrative*, Chase builds this tension toward such a scene, which erupts when he apprehends a black sailor in the process of filching bread. In his account Chase heroically springs to action and forces a trembling gunpoint confession out of the thief. Although the sailor's crime "loudly called for a prompt and signal punishment," Chase credits himself for exercising restraint, assuming the role of caring patriarch driven by sympathy, for "every humane feeling of nature plead in his behalf."[48] In Nickerson's account Chase is hardly the brave, gun-wielding disciplinarian stopping a black scoundrel, according to the first mate's racist portrayal of the sailor. We discover, in Nickerson, that the sailor is but a harmless "good old man," more pathetic than sinister.[49] Was Chase's the "fresh eyewitness account" and objective, authoritative text of the *Essex* disaster? Thomas Heffernan defends it as such, claiming that "the story of the *Essex* is Chase's story," one not only boasting reportorial accuracy, but—as noted before—merit worthy of canonization for its "sensitive, timeless, imaginative, and literary" attributes.[50] Heffernan is far too reverent, and even worshipful, of Chase, seemingly because of the *Narrative*'s status as the *Moby-Dick* original.

Heffernan argues that "the biggest single 'if only' of the whole *Essex* story" was the group's failure to head west from Henderson Island for about a hundred miles to Pitcairn Island. Relatedly, one 1847 captain's log laments, "What a pity that they did not know of Pitcairn Island for they might [have] been to it in a few days or even one day with a good breeze."[51] Upon their rescue the survivors on Henderson, as Heffernan notes, were taken directly to Pitcairn in only a day, appearing to confirm the speculation that this was the crew's best chance for survival. Nevertheless, similar fortune likely would have been found in the Marquesas or Tahiti, where there were plenty of provisions and connections to homeward-bound vessels, as Melville had pointed out in his notes.

In truth, the biggest "if only" had already occurred upon the crew's eastward departure from the wreckage site. There had been the known coast of South America, providing some psychological ease, versus the unknowns of the westward islands. In this regard, the blow from the vessel's loss must have had the crew scrambling for any possible sense of certainty and protection. If they could not exactly retrace their steps to the South American mainland, then they could attempt a shortcut toward a port such as Valparaiso, Saint Mary's, or Decamas—or die trying. Decamas, on the coast of Peru, was the last mainland port the crew had visited prior to the sinking of the *Essex*, and thus a place they associated with replenishing stocks of food, wood, and water.[52] This stop had impressed them, particularly Chase, as one of comfort and utility, a very portal to civilization apart from hostile natives and attacking whales.

But necessity ultimately forced the crew to land on an unknown island after all, at precisely the wrong time. Easter Island, alas, might have been exactly the threatening environment the sailors had envisioned in the Marquesas or Tahiti. A few years later, in 1825, records show natives looting the *Surry* after receiving gifts from Captain F. W. Beechey. When Beechey ordered the natives to retreat at once, they responded by bloodying the crew with heavy stones, drawing warning gunfire that became deadly when one chief failed to outrun the bullets. Previously, it is worth noting, voyages headed by Jean-François La Pérouse (1786) and Thomas Raine (1821) went ashore on Easter Island without experiencing any such turmoil.

In the 1820s shipping out of Nantucket, as Nickerson recalls, took "three weeks [of] labor . . . in getting the ship rigged and over the bar, there to await her loading and that too to be accomplished by the assistance of lighters."[53] New Bedford, by contrast, was a deepwater port, both navigable and safe, which thus gradually became the industry's preferred point of origin. Seasoned crew and officers like Chase were at a premium in this new commercial hub; no stigma attached itself to Chase in this cosmopolitan whaling center, which was decidedly rougher, more diverse, and bent on profit than close-knit Nantucket, an island that carefully guarded its prestigious status as the cradle of the whaling industry. Indeed, New Bedford was where Chase would begin his quest to make up for the harpoon he had *failed* to throw at Old Tom (a failure discussed in later chapters). Indeed, had that notorious whale been killed, the *Essex* crew likely would have survived. For the next two decades Chase would effectively loose his anguish on all the whales of the oceans, killing as many of them as any ship captain alive at the time. Clearing his name of any liability in the *Essex* disaster was the crucial first step toward beginning his illustrious career, and his *Narrative* was designed to serve that purpose. Some saw through him, and understood the full weight of his actions. Decades later, Nickerson, then the owner of a Nantucket tavern and boardinghouse, would seek profit and honor by telling his version of events.

Chapter 3

~~~~~~

NICKERSON AND LEWIS

~~~~~~

Selling the Tale

What did Thomas Nickerson, the cabin boy and youngest *Essex* sailor at age fourteen, know that Chase had carefully concealed from his *Narrative*? What secrets did he divulge, and what incorrect details did he introduce, when he finally decided to write his own narrative? And what finally drove him to attempt to publish his tale after living in the shadow of Chase's publication, the de facto authority on the event, for fifty-four years?

One catalyst for committing to publish the story was the discovery by Nickerson, as it had been for Chase, of a willing ghostwriter. This occurred in summer 1875, on Nantucket's windswept beaches, when Leon Lewis entered the scene. A writer of flashy fiction for Robert Bonner's *New York Ledger*, and a showy self-promoter, Lewis had enjoyed the privileges and prestige of occupying the inner circle of the most popular story paper since the early 1860s.[1] The gregarious Nickerson and the flamboyant Lewis seemed the perfect match to produce the book to end all books on the *Essex* tragedy.

This wedding between market-savvy ghostwriter and aging shipwreck survivor, however, would come eventually to resemble the Gilded Age's innumerable business scams. This was in part because Lewis, forty-two, had fallen out of favor with Bonner, owing to the declining health of the former's wife Harriet. Over many productive years, Lewis and Harriet had "coauthored" numerous stories. But the real writer, and conceiver of character, setting, and plot, had been Harriet, whereas Lewis had functioned mainly as her business agent and promoter during their most productive years. Lewis, while vacationing on Nantucket in 1875, sought to win back Bonner's favor. He saw in Nickerson's tale an opportunity to rescue his career, a back story of which the seventy-two-year-old Nickerson had no notion. Nickerson was also unaware that the seeming serendipity of their Nantucket encounter was really the first step of an elaborate plan to seize control of the century's most coveted sea narrative from the lone *Essex* survivor. The doddering Nickerson could not have known that he had entrusted his "Desultory Sketches from a Seaman's Log," the fullest account of the *Essex* tragedy ever written, to a charlatan bound for financial ruin.

As a boardinghouse and tavern proprietor, Nickerson had likely hosted Lewis at his establishment during the summer of 1875. One can imagine the interest Lewis had taken in Nickerson's repository of sensational nautical lore, which he freely shared with his guests as well as locals. As the last remaining *Essex* survivor, Nickerson served as an incomparable Nantucket ambassador to the island's tourists, including with respect to his personal seafaring experiences. It is highly probable, therefore, that Nickerson told the *Essex* story more than any other survivor. In committing the story to paper, he may well have hoped and expected that one of his cosmopolitan clients, especially one well connected to the publishing industry, would take an interest. These clients indeed represented the first generation of gentrified leisure travelers to Nantucket, and many were increasingly driven by profit in their business dealings. Alternatively, he may have planned on entrusting his manuscript to his family for posthumous publication. Whatever his intentions, Nickerson was painfully aware that his narrated version of events, while colorful and amusing, lacked the authority, continuity, and permanence of a print version. Undoubtedly, Nickerson relished the opportunity, likely spurred by the meeting with Lewis, to capitalize on his status as a living relic of the first mate's tale—and to move beyond being a kind of human footnote to the *Narrative*.

One senses that Nickerson ruminated not on whether he should come forward with his manuscript, but on when. Nantucket historian Edouard Stackpole has conjectured that Lewis urged Nickerson to write his memoir of the *Essex* tragedy, implying that without the popular author's encouragement, it would have remained unrecorded.[2] There is no question that Nickerson aggressively pursued publication subsequent to meeting Lewis. But would the old sailor have had the vigor and sheer power of memory necessary to record an experience from so many decades ago? Or did the tale, thanks to his countless retellings of it, simply flow from his pen as it had from his lips in his parlor?

The fund of detail and description in "Desultory Sketches," especially in the first eight chapters, which painstakingly recount the voyage prior to the whale encounter, suggests that Nickerson composed it well before the 1870s. This phase of the voyage would not have been fresh in Nickerson's memory during his old age; his fireside stories probably did not include this relatively dry material. I would thus argue that Nickerson possessed a rough draft of his memoir prior to his introduction to Lewis. Curiously, "Desultory Sketches" shifts in the middle of chapter 9 to a seaman's log with dates rather than chapter headings dividing the narrative, implying that Nickerson had transcribed his original log into chapter form in anticipation of Lewis's publication of it as a serializable narrative. After the whale-attack scene, out of either fatigue with transforming the original log into chapters or a desire for verisimilitude during the climatic moments, Nickerson switches to log form. Given his likely fatigue on at least some level, he must have been overjoyed to have an accomplished and popular author assemble his jagged and discontinuous narrative into a coherent whole.

MESSAGE IN A BOTTLE

After Nickerson's countless retellings, making a fair copy of his log likely seemed to him a natural way to confirm his point of view. Little did he know that his tale would travel like a message in a bottle, set aside by Lewis and utterly dependent on the care and comprehension of a random recipient. This discovery occurred in 1980, when the historian Ann Finch, a native New Englander, was rummaging through an attic in Penn Yan, New York, where Lewis had lived in the 1870s, and brushed off more than a hundred years of dust from a curious-looking volume. The cover bore the title "Desultory Sketches from a Seaman's Log," with no mention of an author. After consulting with the historian Stackpole, Finch learned that the penmanship on the 105 leaves, with inserted corrections, belonged to Nickerson. This was the fate of a story, ironically, entrusted to Lewis in faith that it would reach the nation's widest audience in the periodical press. This was the very belated answer to Chase's narrative, a forgotten tavern keeper's twilight rush at fame and fortune.

In "Desultory Sketches," one discovers a sanitized portrayal of Nickerson, who is not engaging in cannibalism or succumbing to his supposedly juvenile fears. Chase, for his part, comes off a lot worse than he does in the *Narrative*, with pivotal moments of paralysis and indecision included that were omitted from the first mate's account. Stackpole, examining the new evidence and feeling pressure to issue an opinion, could only allow that obvious discrepancies existed between the two documents, and that scholars would no doubt debate the vagaries therein.[3] But beyond the historical arcana, "Desultory Sketches," placed alongside Chase's *Narrative*, shows a survivor reaching full stride in the race for a popular audience. When it was discovered in the upstate New York attic, Nickerson's draft was still awaiting the ghostwriter's alchemy—with his precise desires for publication in the *New York Ledger* detailed in a letter to Lewis found with the manuscript—while Chase's *Narrative* stood as the published result of his collaboration with his own ghostwriter.

By the mid-1870s, when Nickerson met Lewis, the *New York Ledger* was well known even to the isolated community of Nantucket Island. Nickerson would have been exposed to the *Ledger*, given its massive advertising campaigns. When Bonner purchased the journal in 1855, he had made a point of revolutionizing authors' salaries, sparing no expense to acquire the brightest stars in the surging story-paper industry. Bonner did not grow talent so much as poach it, luring big-name writers away from rivals with lucrative contracts and liberal artistic license. By 1875 Nickerson would have therefore understood the privileged position Lewis occupied, and may have even read some of his work. His name typically appeared next to his wife's in the bylines of their stories, which ran serially, with each weekly installment earning the couple almost three times what they would have taken in for the daily newspapers. The Lewises had been writing for the *Ledger* and enjoying such an unheard of income for six years prior to the encounter between Leon and Nickerson.[4] The former cabin boy, for his part, hadn't missed out on speculation fever, profiting handsomely from the rising "demand for accommodations for visitors which marked the early years of the 1870s." And Nickerson "did not remain idle upon his retirement" but "bought a house on North Street (now Cliff Road) and opened a boarding house." Interestingly, Nickerson's work as an innkeeper famed for his seafaring yarns had at least two commercial components: his housing of paying guests and the draw of the story. Like Lewis, he became locally renowned and, by the time of his death in 1883, "among the most popular and best known of any here," according to the *Boston Traveller*.[5]

While Nickerson was busy entertaining guests with his stories, and thus attracting a greater clientele and realizing a respectable income, Lewis was employed with not only a periodical but the century's most powerful literary marketing machine. Bonner's colossal advertising campaigns involved annual sums routinely exceeding $100,000, reaching well over 400,000 subscribers and setting new records in the history of American journalism.[6] As noted, even Nickerson's post–Civil War location on remote Nantucket, along with other such locations, would have been privy to Bonner's production and distribution efforts. Indeed, as a storyteller and entrepreneur himself—despite his cluelessness regarding Lewis's mismanaged finances and penchant for speculation—Nickerson may very well have admired the enterprising spirit of the *Ledger* and its ability to win a national audience.

Serial fiction was the main selling point of the *Ledger* from its origins. But the outlet had been steadily building its nonfiction content, beginning with Fanny Fern's editorial column, which had initially fueled the paper's astonishing rise. The paper had expanded its reach into popular biography, garnering contributions on the lives of famous military generals from Robert E. Lee to Napoleon. Henry Ward Beecher, the most celebrated preacher of the day, also wrote for the *Ledger*, as did respected statesman and icon of American democratic diplomacy Edward Everett. Nautical fiction, which had enraptured the nation since the *Essex* disaster, had also been a staple. Echoes of the *Essex* are heard throughout Sylvanus

Cobb's racy high-seas adventures, with his "Forest Sketches," on the life of Colonel Walter B. Dunlap, and his subsequent "Forest Adventures," following Dunlap to distant locations to "fight elephants, lions, tigers, and cannibals." The triumphant return of Dunlap appeared in *The Cannibal's Necropolis! Home Again: Last of the Sketches of Adventure by Col. W. B. D.*[7] Cannibalism was a mainstay of *Ledger* fare, and global seafaring provided the setting and context.

The culture of the *Ledger* and its affiliation with the book trade were ideally suited to the *Essex* tale as told by Nickerson and Lewis. According to Nickerson's obituary, Lewis's proposal "to edit and publish [his manuscript] in book form" became the most significant pursuit of the final chapter of his life.[8] The most likely avenue for the manuscript would have been through serialization in the *Ledger*, and subsequent appearance in a printed volume published by Bonner himself or a press like G. W. Dillingham and Company. This was exactly the precedent established for Lewis's own work as well as some of the best-selling novels of the century, including Fanny Fern's *Ruth Hall*, E. D. E. N. Southworth's *The Hidden Hand*, and Sylvanus Cobb's *The Gunmaker of Moscow*, all of which were serially published in the *Ledger* and later released as books under Bonner's imprint or others. Southworth's most popular novel, *Ishmael*, was a *Ledger* serial before it became a novel and subsequently went through nineteen reprintings. Although not originally *Ledger* stories, Harriet Beecher Stowe's *Uncle Tom's Cabin* and James Fenimore Cooper's *Last of the Mohicans*, along with many notable works of the century, were serials before becoming bound novels. Lewis repeatedly exploited this pattern in his own career with novels like *Andrée at the Pole: With Details of His Fate*, which typically carried a notice after the introduction stating that the story "in almost its complete form, as now published, originally appeared in another paper, the *New York Evening World*."[9]

In the world of nonfiction, similar journal-to-book procedures were common. Henry David Thoreau, for example, was invited to write a series of biographical sketches, in the manner of his profile of Thomas Carlyle, for Horace Greeley's *New York Tribune*, which the editor had promised to collect and publish as a single volume to capitalize on both periodical and book markets. Though Thoreau demurred, thereby dealing a devastating blow to his professional career, the offer is illustrative of the wealth of such opportunities then available in print culture. Given the lofty status of the *Essex* saga as the blueprint for nautical narration, Nantucket's *Inquirer and Mirror* duly records that Nickerson had been robbed of his one opportunity at stardom by Lewis, the corrupt agent who effectively stole his intellectual property. By 1883, the year of Nickerson's death, Lewis had disappeared from the pages of the American popular press after squandering his fortune, losing his wife, and fleeing overseas to escape his creditors.

From 1876 to 1883 the fleecing of Nickerson had become common knowledge among Nantucketers. Islanders fostered great expectations for the publication of the new narrative, if only because the sole survivor of the *Essex* disaster had become a beloved fixture on Nantucket, a resident Rip Van Winkle and storytelling vestige now comfortably ensconced in his role as graying boardinghouse proprietor. One can imagine the intimate community rallying around the amiable host, rooting for the publication of his greatest tale as the just reward to commemorate his illustrious life. It is not surprising, therefore, that the tale of Lewis's scam receives a full paragraph in Nickerson's obituary, which functions not only as a lament for his lost magnum opus—the keynote for which he would most want to be remembered—but also as something of a wanted notice for Lewis's capture, the reward being the poetic justice Nickerson so obviously deserved. Thus maligned as an itinerant swindler, Lewis had become something like Mark Twain's traveling mesmerist in *Life on the Mississippi* or the huckster in "The Man That Corrupted Hadleyburg." The community's resentment toward Lewis was proportionate to its own anticipation of "the forthcoming volume" that they had even "announced in our advertising columns." The *Inquirer and Mirror*, and by extension the local islanders at large, voiced their disdain for Lewis because they too had naïvely trusted his proposal to edit and publish Nickerson's manuscript.

That sense of betrayal, interestingly, receives little attention in most histories of the Nickerson-Lewis relationship, which tend to emphasize the miraculous rediscovery of the manuscript after more than a century. Indeed, typical biographical profiles of Nickerson only mention Lewis's status as a professional author of popular tales, without noting his predilection for gambling and his financial straits. The reemergence of the dusty manuscript in 1980 speaks not only to the role of the uncanny in the life of the *Essex* story, it also raises the question of what motives drove Lewis in abandoning a manuscript he had obviously treasured and regarded as his financial life buoy, not to mention his relationship to the *New York Ledger*. Even considering his financial woes, and the death of his spouse, one wonders about the particular circumstances that caused Lewis to flee the North American continent for England.

A DUBIOUS DEAL

Unlike the Duke and Dauphin, the iconoclastic traveling literary hucksters of Twain's *Adventures of Huckleberry Finn*, Lewis never cashed in on his stolen goods. He could have easily stripped Nickerson's name from the manuscript and sold it to a willing publisher. Alternatively he could have written up the story himself in typical sensational *Ledger* style as derived from the "Desultory Sketches," only without Nickerson's consultation or any mention of his name. Less feloniously, he could have simply carried out Nickerson's wishes as planned, yet snubbed him at the eleventh hour by withholding his fair share of royalties. Given his financial track record, he may have seriously considered all these avenues. But he seems ultimately to have rejected them all. Meanwhile he could have pursued the virtuous option of returning the manuscript and confessing to Nickerson that he had fallen on hard times and could not arrange for its publication.

To arrive at the most plausible answer, one must retrace the conditions of the original deal. Nickerson, as we have seen, was attracted generally to the prestige of publication, but he was also aware, more specifically, of the steadily rising literary status of the *Ledger*. Henry Wadsworth Longfellow's "Hanging of the Crane," for example, appeared within its pages in 1874, the year before Nickerson and Lewis first met. Several years earlier, in 1857, Longfellow had refused an offer from Bonner on the general principle that he would not lower himself to writing for the newspapers. After hitting a rough financial patch, however, he felt compelled to accept Bonner's lucrative contract of $3,000 for a mere two hundred lines of poetry. Names like Longfellow's in the pages of the *Ledger* lent it an air of—if not an entirely legitimate claim to—literary seriousness.

Not only could an affiliation with a *Ledger* writer reflect credit upon Nickerson's work, but it might also help ensure the protection of his image. The popular press in general, and Robert Bonner in particular, made a concerted effort to appease any sense of moral discomfort in its audience for indulging in tales full of gore and lurid sensationalism. Indeed, Bonner's advertising for the paper insisted that its content was designed to appeal to the whole family. Bonner was famous for winning over celebrity authors, while also carefully shaping his own image for popular appeal. Reconciling morality and money was always a top priority for Bonner, and his staff writer Lewis clearly intended to take the same approach toward Nickerson and his story. Certainly in his manuscript and probably also in conversation, Nickerson had emphasized to Lewis his wish to be dissociated from cannibalism and to omit the display of cowardice described in Chase's *Narrative*. These desires seem even more understandable when one imagines the distinguished, aging Nickerson holding court with guests at his North Street boardinghouse overlooking the Nantucket shoreline and the Atlantic. As his popularity grew as an island personage, Nickerson inevitably was confronted with questions alluding to his own participation in cannibalism, as well as his cowardly lapse. He likely had heard unflattering rumors and innuendo spread among the less sympathetic boarders and among the island's growing numbers of tourists. Lewis, after decades of writing under Bonner, who peddled grisly tales of murder, abduction, mutiny, theft, and espionage as family entertainment, was an ideal recipient for Nickerson's demands. Lewis specialized in handling public reputations, just as Bonner had specialized in managing the *Ledger*'s popular image. The matter was not exactly one of lying but rather of skillful omission of critical facts and embellishment of others, precisely the ploy Chase himself had used.

The culture of ghostwriting in the 1860s and '70s enabled any writer to recreate himself in the smoke and mirrors of the literary marketplace. Anonymous authorship played a major role, with the exchange, invention, and circulation of pen names reflecting the importance attached to the branding and marketing of literature through author figures. Most of the reading public knew Lewis, for example, through several of his identities. Lewis's renown, if not his mercenary ambition, was prominently displayed in the *New York Weekly*'s announcement of his nautical adventure tale "The Silver Ship; or, The Bloodhound of the Caribbean." The editors credited themselves for securing rights to the pen "of one of the greatest of living romance writers." This author, "for reasons of his own, chooses to write for us, not under his own proper name, but under the nom de plume of Louis Leon. The fame of the gentleman is world-wide," the advertisement proclaims, "and it is safe to say that there is hardly a reader of romance on this continent who has not, at one time or another, been charmed by his genius."[10] This thinly veiled alias, of course, beckoned readers who otherwise associated Lewis with rival journals. Further, those "reasons of his own" for making such a deal could only be monetary, especially since his services had been secured "at great expense." Also appearing under the guise of "Illion Constellano . . . a citizen of the Mexican Republic [who] is actively employed in the commercial military service of his country," Lewis freely sold his work to several venues, including the *Weekly* and the *Ledger*, each of which boasted that "Señor Constellano, a Mexican, will be exclusively devoted to our journal" despite "some stories by him written under a previous contract."[11] If Lewis could don the identity of a Mexican national so convincingly as to create a bidding war among competing periodicals—while showing no loyalty whatsoever to any of them—then he could also assume the voice of the *Essex* cabin boy. His ventriloquism knew no bounds.

To Lewis, a pen name was not only a trick of authorship and means of self-promotion but also a process by which he came to perpetually reinvent himself, not unlike F. Scott Fitzgerald's James Gatz, who recreates himself as the Great Gatsby. Also a creature of the underground world of illegal trade, Lewis abandoned his given name of Julius Warren Lewis in his early twenties to serve his itinerant literary career. In the process he also built extensive experience publicizing and promoting the careers of his partners. Knowing that Lewis was essentially a publicist-and-editor for his wife, Harriet, helps explain why he would have taken to Nickerson. Insofar as he represented a *Ledger* author to Bonner, and Bonner had represented both Lewises through his advertising to the general public,

Lewis seemed to possess many of the same skills as Bonner. Indeed, Lewis's Bonneresque rhetorical bombast was on full display in his cover letters for his wife's weekly submissions, as he hawked their literary wares like a carnival barker. He ends one installment summary with the promise that "the interest of the tale has been deepening from the beginning, and it will continue to deepen from this point to the end, making it *The Greatest Story of the 19th Century!*"[12]

Bonner's signing of celebrity preachers like Henry Beecher was central to his effort to sanitize his paper's image. Some found respected statesman Edward Everett's agreement to write for the *Ledger* reprehensible, while others took it as a mutually beneficial partnership. Certainly Lewis felt he could benefit financially from Nickerson's story as much as Nickerson saw a golden opportunity to shape his image for posterity, and even spread his fame. The *Essex* and the *Ledger*, even at this late date, could be a union in the literary marketplace heretofore unseen, given that the survivors had only told their tales in local Nantucket papers or, in Chase's example, in book form. No *Essex* survivors had directly entered the pages of what was then the most popular journal in the periodical press, nor had any been promoted through a ghostwritten book by one of its staff writers. The *Daily Cleveland Herald*'s description of Everett's motives in accepting a contract from Bonner might also apply to Nickerson's interest in the Lewis deal. Publication with the *Ledger*, according to the *Herald*, was "a good thing for Mr. Everett. No other act of his life has been calculated to add so much to his popularity. Widely as he is known." Much like Nickerson's renown achieved through his association with the *Essex* disaster, "it will make his name a household word in many families where it is hardly known now." For Lewis and Bonner "it would add largely to [the *Ledger*'s] already immense number of readers." However, the claim of Everett enhancing the magazine's "pure moral tone and scrupulous regard to the nicest sense of propriety" could hardly apply to Nickerson.[13] The story, if anything, would have detracted from the magazine's larger aims in that regard, considering that Lewis undoubtedly would have played up the tale's already abundant intrigue and gore. Bonner, of course, was fully aware that Lewis was no moralizer, and was employed precisely because he could, both with Harriet and on his own, write a ripping adventure tale filled with violently bizarre and perverse details. Had Lewis written Nickerson's tale, Bonner in all likelihood would have embraced it openly, especially given its historical basis.

The death of Owen Coffin, the central episode in the *Essex* narrative, was exactly the sort of high drama on which Bonner's "family paper" thrived. Nickerson fully recognized that Lewis therefore would have a special interest in this scene, and thus used it as the main selling point in his cover letter. Just as Lewis had echoed Bonner's own self-aggrandizing tone in cover letters for his wife's stories, Nickerson, in his own voice, does not refrain from boasts. The letter, dated October 24, 1876, strains so intently to sell Lewis on the tale that it would seem all the assurance he had was a verbal promise and a handshake. Nickerson nonetheless felt confident enough to entrust the lone copy of his life story to Lewis, whose checkered past (and even shakier future) could not have been known to the former cabin boy. Such efforts to convince Lewis of the project's value are ironic, given that Lewis had likely first sought out Nickerson on Nantucket to begin with.

Nickerson's letter to Lewis was written with detail and formality rather than casually, and specifically replied to queries from Lewis about Ducie Island, the death of Owen Coffin, and other matters. Namely, Lewis had asked if Nickerson knew whether the missing boat from the *Essex* reached Ducie Island. Nickerson's reply confidently affirms that the mates rescued were instead on Elizabeth Island, according to *Surry* commander Thomas Raine. "Pollard was either mistaken or else the men had either died or were taken off," Raine concluded, before heading west on the off chance that the crew had instead landed on Elizabeth Island, seventy miles windward. Nickerson assures Lewis that the location of the rescued crew is "fully" and "plainly described in my manuscript."[14]

As in Chase's *Narrative*, "Desultory Sketches" focuses on Pollard's error in explaining why a portion of the crew remained on a given island. Lewis, for his part, had also pursued details on another supposed Pollard blunder, the sinking of the *Two Brothers*. In seeking such material, Lewis seems clearly to have been trying to portray Pollard according to his two signature failures, while hotly pursuing the moral implications of Pollard's decisions associated with each disaster. In his letter, then,

Nickerson cites Pollard's mistaken location of the remaining crew (not Ducie Island but Elizabeth Island) and where precisely his second ship had wrecked northwest of Hawaii.

Answering questions about Coffin's survivors, he notes that Owen's mother had been dead for years and that his brother died in the West Indies while commanding a voyage on the brig *Tom O'Shanter*. Most important of all is the casting of lots. This line of questioning, and indeed the answers, squarely focuses attention on the ever-salable moral circumstances surrounding Captain Pollard's role. From the evidence Lewis clearly wanted to paint Pollard as having no preexisting flaws or inclinations, no demons to battle or white whales to chase, yet whose virtue and democratic intentions are upended, leading to the horrifying casting of lots. Nickerson could not resist, therefore, making the beleaguered captain the executioner, according to the "awful die" that would make him pull "the fated trigger."[15] Nickerson's phrasing in the letter unmistakably signals to Lewis the melodramatic tone and tragic pitch he wishes to emphasize in the scene. As discussed in the previous chapter, this was not only a deviation from Chase's account but also one from Nickerson's own original manuscript, which depicts Ramsdell dispatching the youth. One then wonders why Nickerson would change the facts so egregiously, especially if Lewis would be reading the alternative version of the scene himself anyway.

Nickerson, always mindful of his reputation, intimated to Lewis that he wished for him to take extensive liberties with his outline. In his letter his language is too careful, too calculating, and indeed too like the sensational tales of the *Ledger* and the carnivalesque language of the popular print culture of which Lewis was a creature. Spotlighting Pollard, Nickerson believed, would draw attention away from his own participation in cannibalism and fit of cowardice. Placing himself more peripherally in the narrative would likewise grant him a detached third-person omniscience, that of a witness or reporter instead of a responsible actor. Pollard, the focal point of the letter, "was not nor could be thought to have dealt unfairly with this trying matter," but he is nonetheless described next as being excoriated by Coffin's mother.[16] Nickerson, accordingly, almost certainly wanted Lewis to end the tale with the captain's painful homecoming, rather than emphasizing his own experience—with his breakdown having occurred so relatively recently. The deal complete, Nickerson wrote, referring to his letter, that "for having parted with my manuscript I now have to write from memory only." The "parting," however, signaled to Lewis that he was free to season the tale for an audience hungry for an unforgettable adventure on the high seas.

THE BANDIT FLEES

"I have confined myself to facts," Nickerson wrote to Lewis, entrusting his precious "Desultory Sketches" for him "to handle as you think proper." In reality, of course, Nickerson had wantonly altered the facts for lurid effect, especially with regard to the killing of Owen Coffin. To make the story more salable, Nickerson surrendered full control to Lewis, even encouraging him to take creative departures, just as he himself had done in his recounting of Coffin's death. Now Nickerson had only to wait for a reply. In the missive's final sentence, one might sense Nickerson's suspicion that maybe there would be no reply, and that Lewis might in fact disappear with his manuscript. "I think I will not write to you again," he announces, "until I hear from you again or know if you are coming."[17] Their next meeting, Nickerson hoped, might confirm the method of publication, whether serially through the *Ledger* or in a small volume. The closing line feels oddly flat, evincing not a gracious invitation to visit again so much as a statement of his own intentions, which very much depended upon Lewis's availability. Nickerson's anxiety in the letter— from his strained sales pitch to this closing—may have arisen from a deeper dread over Lewis's commitment. Indeed, far from spurring Lewis to action, the letter, if he even read it at all, only hastened his escape from the scandal closing in on him.

The moment Nickerson sent the letter, he seems to have regretted doing so. He did not trust Lewis and would have preferred using another ghostwriter. He also knew that partnering with Lewis would compromise the veracity of the manuscript, which he had written "in a full tide of his recollections—later in life, with his memory reinforced by his former shipmates."[18] But Nickerson, as we have seen, was aware of the risks associated with publication, and knew he had ceded control of his story; moreover, he was prepared to blame any factual errors on his failing memory. So the facts weren't what worried Nickerson. What worried him was Lewis's follow-through on publication plans. Nickerson's suspicions would be validated.

Nickerson's manuscript, however, was the least of Lewis's worries. The ghostwriter's original plan had been to prove himself worthy of Bonner's lucrative salary without the partnership of his wife, Harriet, who was already ill. The publication of Nickerson's manuscript would seemingly have erased any doubt about his productivity in Harriet's absence. On the surface the plan appeared more or less straightforward. But the ghost-writer's past offers hints of even worse possible consequences had Lewis not abandoned the project.

Lewis's rash behavior began in 1874, exactly when it became clear his wife would not survive her illness. More than the anguish he felt over losing his life's partner, Lewis feared for his financial security. While writing for the *Ledger*, the couple garnered steady combined weekly payments from Bonner of $300 for two separate story installments, presumably one written by each author. Harriet routinely wrote both installments herself, or had some cursory input from Leon. Historian Jan Cohn notes that "the Lewises made a good deal of money from the serialization and subsequent book publication of their stories," while allowing that their literary labor was shouldered primarily by Harriet. "Although they collaborated on much of their work, that collaboration took the form of Harriet's contributions to Leon's fiction; novels signed with Harriet's name were apparently entirely her own work."[19] Demonstrating his dependence on her, almost all Lewis's single-author titles appeared after his wife's death, the earliest of which were *The Demon Steer; or, Outlaws on the Abilene Cattle Trail* and *The Flying Glim; or, The Island Lure*, both 1887 Beadle & Adams dime novels. During their years on the *Ledger* staff, the couple lived extravagantly on an estate with a $1,500 stable, although Bonner's own world-class thoroughbreds trumped those of his writers.

The Lewises' opulent lifestyle, which included the finest cuisine and extravagant home furnishings, was—despite their generous salary—well beyond their means. When Harriet fell ill, only Bonner's routinely granted loans bailed them out of debt and saved them from utter ruin. At one point Lewis requested that Bonner send $1,500 for expenses. This amount, however, far exceeded the couple's usual requests, so Bonner asked for details. In a tone of confession, if not outright shame, Leon offered a litany of his declining assets, including his library, purchased for $5,000 and now worth half as much; three houses, which had fallen in value from $8,000 to $6,000; outstanding insurance bills amounting to $4,400; and even his furniture, acquired for $1,800 and now worth only $1,200. Leon acknowledged the scale of this particular request, noting, "The above are the principal parts of the information demanded. Personal enough to open my outside debts."[20]

All evidence suggests that Leon, not Harriet, was the source of such reckless habits. In a letter to Bonner written after the $1,500 loan request, and thus breaking a pattern whereby Leon was Bonner's sole correspondent, Harriet told the publisher of the couple's troubles. Her aim was to ensure steady work for her husband after her death. "He has wild ideas that seem to him to promise wealth or fame," she wrote of Leon. "I have tried to be his balance wheel. What will he do when I am gone?" She ends with a plea "to continue your friendship with him, and be patient with him," invoking the state of her own soul upon her imminent death. "If I could think that you would keep him on with the *Ledger* and see him now and then and keep him busy, I would not dread death for his sake as I do now."[21] Written only nineteen days before her death on May 20, 1878, at age thirty-seven in Rochester, New York, Harriet's missive reads like an installment of one of the couple's sensational tales. Bonner recognized this. He published it in the *Ledger* days after Harriet passed away.

Two decades would pass before Leon's next extant letter to Bonner, dated 1898. In an arthritic scrawl, the letter shows the wisdom of Harriet's dire prophecy, with Leon pathetically begging Bonner for "10 dollars to make my connections." Again the writer emphasizes loss, but this time on a level much more intimate than furniture or library values. He writes that "my boy and I are all alone having lost my wife [Harriet] and daughter."[22] The implied recklessness of the intervening years again presents us with the question of whether and how Lewis might have ghostwritten and carried out the publication of Nickerson's "Desultory Sketches."

Kept carefully hidden from view was Lewis's lengthy history of corrupt dealings, tracing back to his twenties. Such activity took place in the publishing industry and involved high-risk speculative schemes featuring a cocktail of coercion and graft that careened toward assault and, at least once, attempted murder. Thus Lewis made his first foray into publishing with the flash paper *Life in Boston*, which he launched with $300 coaxed from the financier Enoch Train. The flash press consisted of small weeklies bearing bold titles such as the *Whip*, the *Rake*, and the *Libertine*, journals aimed at entertaining and informing "literate sporting men about leisure-time activities and erotic entertainments" available in their city.[23] When the paper lost its market foothold, Lewis promptly requested another $300 loan from Train. But with little incentive to reinvest in a failed venture, Train rebuffed Lewis, whose subsequent erratic and stealthy behavior drew the attention of police. The emerging writer had taken to lurking in alleys, haunting train stations after hours, and consorting with Boston and New York's criminal element. Eventually he began stalking Train and menacing him with death threats. Then, in the dead of night, Lewis stormed onto the elderly gentleman's estate and headed straight for the mansion's main entrance, determined to forcibly extract the needed sum. As artfully intimidating as he had been in the weeks prior, Lewis's patience had clearly run out. Train's servant and groundskeeper, having espied his approach, waited poised behind the door. According to a police report, these employees "suddenly opened it and pitched him headlong down the steps, and instantly jumped on him, thus finally securing him. He was then firmly bound with a bed cord and kept until police officers took him into custody." After being charged with armed robbery and attempted murder, he likely served time in the Boston penitentiary for his crimes. Similar tactics made the April 23, 1853, headlines of the *Hartford Weekly Times*, when "two ruffians in the employ of the Boston Gamblers" hired by Lewis "beat and bruised the publisher of 'Life in Boston.'. . . A sling shot was employed, and there is no doubt they intended to kill him."[24] Although he did not habitually resort to such ruthless methods, his engagement in them at all suggests the ethics and practice that would shape the rest of his career.[25] Luckily for Nickerson, unlike Enoch Train, he never invested any money in Lewis.

Just prior to soliciting Nickerson's manuscript, Lewis had turned his attention toward a new journal he would launch shortly after his wife's death. The *Penn Yan Mystery* story paper borrowed heavily from the format and style used for the *Ledger*, and even exploited Harriet's memory to draw readers, just as his old employer had done. He would routinely allude to her as his "spirit wife" in an effort to heighten the supernatural intrigue of the tales set in their hometown.[26] Strikingly he had married Harriet when she was only fifteen years old, and began immediately employing her as his author, hawking her services up and down publishers' row in New York. Not coincidentally, Lewis also married his second wife, Julia Wheelock, when she was just fifteen, with the marriage occurring in Brazil, after Lewis had fled Penn Yan in 1879 and before arriving in England. Local media reported the event as a scandal in which Lewis, then forty-seven, "went missing" with the girl, who was also his niece— the daughter of his sister-in-law—whom Leon and Harriet had adopted and raised as their own daughter.[27] Perhaps only one cultural taboo is greater in Western culture than incest—cannibalism. Lewis wanted to air these in all their glory through Nickerson's tale.

Lewis's *Penn Yan Mystery* paper collapsed after its first issue, released in a startling print run of 480,000. Like his much earlier *Life in Boston* gambit, Lewis had overreached. Now, following Harriet's death and a failed attempt at fashioning his publishing career after Bonner's, Lewis reached a breaking point. His debts were insurmountable, and his desperation hit a fever pitch. A steadier-minded criminal might have simply focused on recouping through the Nickerson project, but a veritable lynch mob was now on his trail. This was because the bogus stock in the Mexican Pacific and Central American railroad companies he had sold to unwitting investors, along with other debts, totaled more than $50,000. He could only elude his inevitable pursuers—who had been subjected to his trademark elaborate rhetoric and bombastic claims—for so long. With word of his schemes spreading, the manhunt for Lewis officially began when the *Penn Yan Express* ran a half-column listing of his offenses under the heading "Shams." After packing his trunk, he sped for the coast with Julia in tow. The next ship, a steamer, was bound for Brazil and eventually the safety of England, where he might begin his life over again as a romance writer. By January 1879 Lewis had escaped the upstate New York chill, his debts, and his dead-end literary career—and was now wedded to his young niece.

Paradise was soon lost, however. Five years later, in 1884, Lewis returned to America with his resources depleted, having once again squandered a steady writing salary on various schemes. His handsome income from contributions to Ralph Rollington's *Our Boys' Paper* and *Boys' World* apparently did not satisfy his outsize ambition and desire to match his former U.S. standard of living. Rollington recalled one telling incident "when paying him a cheque for ten numbers." The publisher remarked, "'Why, Lewis, old boy, you must be making a fortune.' 'Not out of *Boys' Stories*,' he replied laconically, with a slight American accent." In one sense Rollington may have associated such expressions with Lewis's wholesome audience and plucky, pure-hearted protagonists, concluding that "he always looked on the bright side of life." But something darker may have lurked beneath his observation that Lewis "was certain he would eventually make a big fortune in the newspaper world," which he pursued with characteristic nerve and trickery.[28]

Lewis was operating at a historical moment when the story papers shared writers of moralistic tales, and a time when the three-volume novel yielded to the single-volume novel. In 1880 readers wanted their fiction and nonfiction fast and sharp, and Lewis trained his powers of imagination on meeting the demand. In addition, according to one study, "previously where the miscellany had sufficed for the family, a number of specialized periodicals targeted specific audiences," such as boys, girls, or women.[29] Lewis adapted to these developments, finding his niche with the boys' periodical and book markets. The *Essex* tale, not surprisingly, would be retold innumerable times in periodicals and books specializing in boys' fiction. Indeed, one of Melville's great career struggles was to shed an early association with boys' adventure stories. But for Lewis, as well as Nickerson, the increasing specialization of this genre was a welcome opportunity for profit.

The tale of Nickerson's lost *Essex* narrative embodies the corrupt business ethic of the Gilded Age. A useful contrast to Lewis's chicanery can be found in Chase's ghostwriter, William Coffin Jr., who worked thoroughly and meticulously. Whereas for Lewis ghostwriting was an opportunity to obfuscate for profit, with little conviction in his words, Coffin Jr. likely saw ghostwriting as something more like a legal defense, a tradition his own father had established through his self-exoneration. It is obvious that Lewis's objectives, all self-interested and self-aggrandizing, were not to represent his client and his aspirations—however self-serving they may have been—but rather to bolster his own career and wealth.

On his return to America, Lewis lived in Long Island, Dubuque, Iowa, and Chicago before settling in Connecticut, unbothered by his debtors and with Nickerson's manuscript a distant memory. During these years Lewis did befriend Clarence Darrow and advocate for wage laborers following the Haymarket Riot of 1886. Otherwise, like Nickerson, Lewis remained relatively aloof from politics.

But later, his thirst for the grandiose and his romance writer's imagination would come together in his most bizarre public appearance since his intimidation tactics of the 1850s. This effort, rooted in an elaborate crackpot theory, also spoke to whether any actual conviction lay beneath Lewis's devious plots. Bespectacled, portly, and with a giant walrus mustache draping his fleshy mouth and chin, Lewis in his later years appeared every bit the eccentric visionary implied by his new self-appointed role as president of the Deluge Publishing Company. His press, if it could be called such, specialized in spreading word of "The Great Deluge Which Is Now Due Again," the title of a speech he delivered on the subject. With his son as his "vice president," Lewis sought to voice without editorial censorship his ardent belief that a flood of biblical proportions threatened the planet. His language was indeed cataclysmic (leading one to imagine what this author would have done with Nickerson's tale): "All of the countries and continents of our globe are subject to this cataclysm, and very few of us can be safe in the vast regions reached by it. Only here and there on certain plateaus and table lands, which will remain emergent, can possibly save a mere remnant of our species."[30] Given earlier spurious theories from figures such as John Cleves Symmes, stipulating that giant holes existed in both the North and South Poles and could be entered via steamship to access the earth's interior, Lewis's mysticism could be located at the convergence of romantic sea fiction and scientific prophecy.

Lewis worked on his magnum opus throughout his final decades. Though he never published it, "The Great Glacial Deluge and Its Impending Recurrence" was intended to be a twelve-volume work. The magnitude of the project indicates that Lewis envisioned himself occupying the same sort of status and authority that Symmes had enjoyed in the 1820s, precisely when Chase's *Narrative* spawned an industry of sea tales. But Lewis had underestimated the growing power of scientific knowledge and ability to verify empirical data. Baseless assumptions, he argued ridiculously, "changed Geology from a science to a chatter."[31] Like Nickerson's "Desultory Sketches," "The Great Glacial Deluge" would remain unfinished mainly because it fell into the hands of (other) schemers.

Nickerson's memoir undoubtedly captured Lewis's imagination at first, but it had little chance of survival in the context of his chaotic life and underhanded dealings. His main goals had to have been economic, as they likely were with his Deluge Company. On the latter count the *New York Times* seized upon the inane quality of his proposal, gleefully highlighting the absurdity of his predictions. Integral to his rhetoric, as it had been from the start of his career, was a confidence game associated with luring stockholders. Instead of proclaiming himself "Projector, Builder, and Proprietor" of fictitious railroad companies, as he had done in earlier decades, he was now trafficking in biblical prophecy, lunging at much larger claims, boasting even bigger shareholders. Yet frighteningly Lewis seems to have convinced himself of his Deluge Company prophecy, whereas he never for a moment entertained the prospect that his imaginary railroads actually existed.

The language of the scam artist is unmistakable in the *Times* interview. Literary deals, anchored in his claims to publishing-industry credibility, mark the start of his pitch. "I have two or three offers from magazines for the publication of my work serially—in fact they offer me millions," he assures his interviewer. He then alleges that the "stockholders of the company number millions." Broad investment by the general public is thereby made to appear a natural outgrowth of validation by print culture. From publishers' row, he takes us to Wall Street: "The magnates interested in [the Deluge Company] run into the millions," he declares, arriving at the White House, as it were, and the preposterous assertion that "the rulers of the earth have subscribed millions." He goes on to say that his plan is predicated on awakening a new sensibility in a sensible human race. "I'll lay down principles for it," he trumpets, not surprisingly, "through a series of novels which solve all the problems now bothering the human race." As in all plots of Lewis's life, this too would lead to plots of his own imaginative writing, circling back to the publishing industry, which he had represented so promisingly in his proposal to publish Nickerson's narrative.

The man who wore his eccentricities on his sleeve, and who would eventually take his own life by lacerating his legs and throat with a rusty razor, mostly hid his demons from his *Ledger* audience while on staff from 1869 to 1878.[32] But this confidence man also failed to follow through for Nickerson, along with, presumably, the entire island community of Nantucket. Beneath the mantle of a "successful professional author" genuinely interested in ghostwriting an old seaman's life story was a scammer who ruthlessly pursued fame and fortune. Like his *Ledger* romances and boys' adventures, Nickerson's project represented but one of many pawns, the last of which finally seems to have won his own belief and consumed him. Filled with his dreams of a deluge, Lewis had missed an opportunity to bring new life, perhaps immortality, to the seminal sea tale of the century. Though spending a century of silence in a Penn Yan attic, Nickerson's "Desultory Sketches" helped tell another story: that of Lewis, a literary huckster and a new breed of bandit that would come to characterize publishing in the late 1800s. To Nickerson, Lewis seemed the ideal author to elegantly conceal his cannibalism and cowardice. Thus perhaps the deepest irony of the Lewis-Nickerson relationship was that the memoir Nickerson wanted to publish would have shimmered with the era's intrigues and deceptions, replete with self-promotion and wild entertainment.

Chapter 4

～～～～～～～～～～～～～～～～～～～～～～

LIGHTNING STRIKES TWICE

～～～～～～～～～～～～～～～～～～～～～～

The *Two Brothers*

On the ocean floor just off the French Frigate Shoals in the Northwestern Hawaiian Islands, the *Two Brothers*, a 217-ton Nantucket whaler, silently moldered for nearly two centuries. Then in August 2008, marine archaeologists with the National Oceanic and Atmospheric Administration discovered the remains of what Captain George Pollard Jr. had hoped would be a redemptive voyage with the dual purpose of reviving his career and exorcising the demons of the *Essex*.[1] The *Two Brothers* promised Pollard new life after his *Essex* experience two years earlier had nearly taken his life, while destabilizing his sense of professional competence as well as his sanity.

But the *Two Brothers* met its demise when Pollard temporarily lost his bearings while performing a dead-reckoning because of an overcast sky, with the ship crashing into the sprawling Hawaiian coral reef. Finding himself in another unfolding disaster, Pollard clung to the rail and resolved to go down with his ship. The captain could only stare grimly as his crew begged him to leave the sinking vessel. Then, "just as they were about to shove off from the ship," boatsteerer Thomas Nickerson recalls, "Captain Pollard reluctantly got into the boat."[2] To Pollard, the psychological effect must have been crushing. He must have perceived his future self as something of a walking corpse, a doubly cursed captain whose commands seemed fated to destruction.

In nautical culture, as Pollard quickly learned after the loss of the *Essex*, captains who do not go down with their ships can suffer severe public consequences. Here the contemporary case of Francesco Schettino, captain of the *Costa Concordia*—which crashed off the western coast of Italy in 2012—provides a sharp contrast to Pollard's integrity in the aftermath of a disaster. Whereas Pollard seemingly would have preferred to perish with his second sinking ship, Schettino brazenly flouted nautical decorum by preserving his own life and fleeing for the safety of shore while thirty-two crewmen and passengers died. A few more moments on the *Costa Concordia* will, by comparison, help demonstrate Pollard's noble seamanship aboard the *Two Brothers*.

It was a calm January night in the Tyrrhenian Sea, near the tiny Isola del Giglio, when the massive cruise ship *Costa Concordia*, which was carrying more than four thousand passengers and crew, suddenly steered off course. The diversion from the route programmed into the ship's GPS was intended to treat the islanders (and passengers) to a shoreline sail-by.[3] Such displays are not uncommon on cruise ships. The prior August, Costa Cruises management had approved a similar maneuver at the same location, also under Captain Schettino, who executed the stunt to the delight of Isola del Giglio's mayor and thousands of onlookers reveling in a summer festival. But just as cloud cover had obscured the stars that might have guided Pollard and the *Two Brothers* safely around the hazardous French Frigate Shoals in 1823, a dangerous reef near the island never materialized on Schettino's navigational charts. Like Pollard's night sky, Schettino's GPS had thus far done its job on the January cruise. But upon deviating from *Costa Concordia*'s course, Schettino had also inadvertently disarmed the elaborate alarm system that would have signaled the ship's approach to any worrisome underwater masses.

The collision rang out like a cannon, and in the ensuing panic those thirty-two trapped passengers lost their lives. (The vessel took up to twenty-four hours to sink, whereas Pollard's ship sank within an astonishing fifteen minutes.) Just as the ship's hull would be destroyed, so would the reputation of Schettino, who blamed the faulty GPS for the accident. Yet the public outcry against the captain, as it had been against Pollard, was merciless. Dubbed Captain Coward, the *Costa Concordia* captain was skewered across the internet for his failure to protect his crew and passengers. After the accident Schettino secured a lifeboat for himself and headed ashore. Even after the Italian Coast Guard urged him to return to the ship to save his passengers, overriding his childish complaints about darkness, cold, and fear, Schettino refused—and was spotted chatting with the ship's young translator, Domnica Cemortan. He even sought out the ship's chef to request a meal. Meanwhile, Schettino's move might have been backed by management, but his cocaine use, detected in hair samples after the crash, surely would not have been. Relatedly damning was Schettino's attempt during the sail-by to salute a prestigious retired seaman on shore in a display of nautical power. This move has since been condemned for breaching the ethics code for any ship captain.

The largest passenger ship ever to sink, the *Costa Concordia* was of a size commensurate with its profitability; the more rooms, the greater the revenue. Other vessels have suffered the consequences of carrying more bulk in search of increased financial return. The *Costa Concordia*'s bulk turned out to be a fatal weakness during its crash, with the numerous hallways and rooms flooding just two hundred meters from shore.[4] Even though most survivors were rescued on boats or helicopters, those two hundred meters were swimmable by even some of the weaker escapees.

In contrast to Schettino, who reacted with painful slowness to the crash and initially reported the trouble was a routine power outage to conceal the situation's urgency, Pollard was desperate to save the *Two Brothers* or die trying. Like Schettino, Pollard had once been pinned, by Nantucketers, with the label Captain Coward over the *Essex*-related rumors that he had saved his own life and sacrificed that of his young cousin Owen Coffin. This perception would dog him into his *Two Brothers* voyage. Upon inspection of Nickerson's account of the *Two Brothers* wreck, Pollard was anything but cowardly. Indeed, he had made every effort to save his crew. But more than this, Pollard's subsequent self-imposed exile from the whaling industry starkly contrasts with Schettino's shrill insistence upon his innocence and desire to return to the limelight. His trial ended with a sixteen-year prison sentence, sharply hindering any such aspirations. For his part, Pollard may have curtailed his career, as Nathaniel

Philbrick has observed, with the hope of becoming "strengthened by the surgery" of "cutting back his possibilities" and going on to lead a "happy, meaningful life for himself in his native town."[5]

The important question still remains as to how and when Pollard resolved to end his career at sea. This question can be explored by juxtaposing the prose account of the incident by *Two Brothers* first mate Eben Gardner and Nickerson's two-part poetic description of the voyage. These narratives help outline the decisions and directives made by the captain that imperiled his crew and for which he refused to forgive himself—decisions that precipitated Pollard's decision to never sail again. This chapter looks at these sources to determine the precise sequence of events that would derail the career of an otherwise promising captain.

TEMPTING FATE

Thomas Nickerson's October 1876 letter to his potential ghostwriter, Leon Lewis, confirming editorial changes to his account of the *Essex* disaster includes a paragraph detailing the location of the *Two Brothers* wreck. Indeed, Lewis would have had an interest in this mixed sequel— a shipwreck with no fatalities!—to the *Essex*, even if the earlier voyage was the planned subject of his project. To that end, Nickerson wished to confirm the "new discovery" of "Pollard's reef or shoal" made by Pollard and Captain John H. Pease of the rescuing ship, the *Martha*. Had Pollard not died six years earlier, in 1870, he would have been entirely accessible to Nickerson on cozy Nantucket, and likely would have thus provided his own testimony. Nickerson consulted the next best authority, the *Martha's* first mate, Thomas Derrick, who found Pollard in error regarding a discovery. "As well as myself," Nickerson writes, Derrick "believes that this was French Frigate Shoal notwithstanding [that] our two captains believed and reported that this was a new discovery." Nickerson accounts for the mistake by citing the unusually "thick weather," which had prevented "lunar observation for more than ten or twelve days."[6] Cloud cover was not the only factor contributing to their belief that they had discovered new territory; the captains also sought a shred of dignity in their explanation of the cause of the wreck, which they knew would so deeply shape the voyage's master narrative and their respective roles in it. Both captains would have preferred being known for hitting an uncharted shoal rather than the well-known and thoroughly documented French Frigate Shoals, scrupulously avoided by all whalers. In ascertaining the truth of the matter, the sensationalist Lewis was doing more than fact-checking. He was probing for telling details suggesting either a heroic discovery by Pollard or a fateful misapprehension in which the forces of sea and weather once again conspired against the captain.

Nickerson's log from aboard the *Essex* could not have been published as an integrated whole. While serving as Pollard's boatsteerer on the *Two Brothers*, however, Nickerson made certain to keep a proper log, stealing time on deck and in the forecastle to compose his impressions of the entire journey as it unfolded. In it he paid close attention to the myriad circumstances that affected the captain's command. To both distinguish his own account from Chase's *Essex* account and draw on the vogue of Samuel Taylor Coleridge's *Rime of the Ancient Mariner* (1797), Nickerson recorded his observations in rhyming A-A-B-B iambic pentameter. Poetry, the most self-consciously literary form he could have chosen, allowed for deeper aesthetic and philosophical reflection than prose. Interestingly, a lengthy prose account of the loss of the *Two Brothers* precedes the verse in his logbook, suggesting he may have planned to publish them together. Whereas Pollard's log of the *Two Brothers* no longer exists, the holograph of Nickerson's prose and poetry is held at the Nantucket Historical Association and has not been published in its entirety.

The only published nineteenth-century document recording the *Two Brothers* wreck is Obed Macy's *History of Nantucket* (1835). Macy is careful not to accuse Pollard of causing the wreck, and instead tactfully displaces agency from the captain, stating simply, "The ship struck on a reef of rocks." Pollard's association with the *Essex* Macy records in a respectful footnote praising his character: "Though singularly unfortunate as a sailor, he enjoys that which is more valuable than any other worldly consideration, a good name, and the esteem of his fellow citizens."[7] Sensitive to his responsibilities as the authority on Nantucket history, which would extend for nearly a century, Macy knew well that his portrait would indelibly set the unfortunate sailor's reputation. One sign of early belief in his dignity, despite the Captain Coward tag, can be found in the islanders' support of Pollard's *Two Brothers* command, confirmed by Nickerson and Charles Ramsdell's willingness to ship aboard with the *Essex* captain again. Nickerson's return to the sea—this time as a more self-aware and wily sixteen-year-old, as compared to the green cabin boy he was on the *Essex*—after the horrors he had faced less than two years prior demanded considerable courage. The decision would also be a romantic one, flush with themes of recovery, redemption, and a new lease on his nautical career.

The gambling impulse of most whalemen was confirmed in their return to sea after even the most calamitous voyages. By compulsively returning, as does Melville's Bulkington in *Moby-Dick*, whalemen embodied a belief that good fortune, the guiding hand of providence, or some combination of both would touch them. It was based on this curious blend of faith, a community's blessing, and Russian roulette that pre–Civil War captains typically continued their careers, if not cut short by death, for decades with little time ashore. But when does one stop tempting fate? Pollard presumably knew when to stop sailing, given the high odds of dying at sea and his self-perception as "unlucky." He was extraordinarily lucky, however, to have survived two shipwrecks. Chase, as we saw in chapter 2, was luckier, mainly to have been outfitted with superior crews out of New Bedford, drawing from an eclectic, experienced international pool of whalemen rather than the limited, somewhat inbred options on Nantucket. Chase took advantage of his situation, enjoying an astonishing career notable for being entirely free of whale collisions.

One appeal of a *Two Brothers* narrative, therefore, would be as a counterpoint to Chase's enormous success after the tragedy. Nickerson may not have been fully aware of this dynamic, but nonetheless in his "Loss of the Ship *Two Brothers* of Nantucket," Captain Pollard is the main attraction and protagonist. "As many people who are not familiar with Captain Pollard's history, would like to know something more of his after life," he writes, "I simply give a sketch of his succeeding voyage in which the writer formed one of his crew on the ill-fated *Two Brothers*."[8] Many indeed wanted to know more about him; about his biography and his reaction to his second failure. Nickerson's account has substantial implications that probe beneath a pat explanation offered by Nantucket historian and archivist Ben Simons: "Twice was too many for Captain George Pollard, Jr. He considered himself, and not his vessels, to be 'ill-fated.' In a superstitious industry, he chose to 'hang up his hat and retire' after captaining one merchant vessel successfully."[9] This approach to Pollard, though credible in historical context, fails to fully consider the role of reason. Aside from whatever sense of ill-fatedness Pollard may have harbored, much evidence in both Gardner's and Nickerson's accounts suggests that he felt unable to meet the almost impossible demands facing the era's whaling captains. More particularly, he found his ethic of safe leadership impossible to uphold against the cascade of variables, particularly the timing of decisions during a crisis.

Although Pollard's often-overlooked merchant voyage was less dangerous, it could be seen to rule out superstition as his sole motivation for ending his whaling career. Pollard must have felt that no such curse applied to this voyage, and that his skills were fully adequate. Moreover, his success on the voyage left open the option to continue sailing merchant ships, but this line of work did not suit him. It is possible that he would have continued whaling had it not been for his belief that "no owner will ever trust me with a whaler again, for all will say I am an *unlucky* man."[10] Important to note here is that Pollard is not declaring himself intrinsically unlucky but rather astutely acknowledging that whaleship owners would perceive him this way. This assessment reflected more savvy than superstition.

Aside from industry perception and superstition, the profound risks inherent in commanding a whaleship likely guided Pollard's exit from the profession. On the *Two Brothers*, two mates nearly died, events arguably brought about by the captain's own decisions. Specifically Gardner reports that Pollard commanded one of the two whaleboats, carrying the evacuated crew, to search out a fifty-foot mass in the distance. Pollard had hoped this mass was the *Martha*, their consort and sole means of survival in this remote, dangerous, and vast sprawl of reef and rock. The *Martha*, faster and newer than the *Two Brothers*, perhaps represented some version of the comfort for Pollard and his mates that the South American ports had represented for the *Essex* crew. The two captains, Pollard and

Pease, had made their plan to venture out into the Pacific together, for mutual safety, while on the west coast of South America. The captains had traveled together to port to gather food, wood, and water before making their way toward the rich whaling waters off Japan.

Once on the open ocean, Pollard stopped to gather water at a remote island with what Nickerson describes as "a beautiful fresh water pond" of "limpid waters clear as crystal [that] could easily be bailed into casks and rolled out onto the beach." The island's splendor and utility, however, were counterbalanced by its deadly predators, from which the natives sought protection by building their huts "upon stakes some ten or twelve feet high, which the natives said was to prevent the tigers and bears from paying them a nocturnal visit." The fear of animals attacking from the dark forest likely brought to mind at least indirectly the similar threats issuing from the sea, namely from whales like the one that had destroyed the *Essex*. After loading the ship, the seamen quickly "got out of the woods with only a slight scare or two from the dread of wild beasts." The seafarers' encounter with this tribe of "some half dozen natives" who were "miserable enough truly" thus seems to have darkened their attitude toward the open sea, informing the ominous tone of Nickerson's prose narrative from this point on.

On the open sea again, another token of ill fate emerged in their failure to find Fanning Island, slated as their next destination. Along with dealing a blow to morale, precisely such navigational miscalculation would eventually lead them into the rock and coral of the French Frigate Shoals. Nickerson describes how the *Two Brothers* and *Martha* sailed on "until we judged our ships to be in sight of the island and then hove the ships too [*sic*] to wait for daylight. But from a stronger current than expected or something else never accounted for," Nickerson writes, registering his disappointment, "we never saw Fannings Island, although we run [*sic*] for several hours in the supposed direction that it was to be in." Although Fanning offered no essential fuel and supplies that the sailors did not already have in their well-stocked hold, a successful landing would have helped the crew assess the island's relative safety, along with building confidence in Pollard's (and Pease's) navigational prowess. Although "it was not very important to us," failure to locate it shook everyone's faith. In an effort to appear undaunted—Had it been mismarked on the map? Did the captains heave to at a different location from where they assumed they were?—"our captains came to the conclusion to steer out to the North and search along for whales and then toward the Sandwich Islands." The final leg of the *Two Brothers'* journey thus began without knowledge either of Fanning Island's location or of whether hostile cannibals lived there, precisely the concerns that had diverted the *Essex* crew from Pollard's suggestion to go for the "nearest land" and instead sent them on a grueling three-thousand-mile quest for South America.

THE FOURTEEN-HOUR VIGIL

While sailing toward the Hawaiian Islands and on the lookout for whales, the *Two Brothers* was suddenly struck by a "very severe gale of wind" so furious that the crew was "obliged to reduce the sails" and ride out the ebbing "high sea running after us [and] causing the ship to steer badly." If navigation had been faulty under ideal conditions in the search for Fanning Island, now it was nearly impossible, as only "close reefed top sails and a reefed foresail" propelled the vessel.[11] The ship careened ahead at disconcerting speeds with minimal canvas aloft, as the turbulent sea rushed against the stern. The faster *Martha* had sped into the distance, unnerving Pollard and causing him to sacrifice steering for knots in a desperate attempt to regain sight of their companion ship. Likely fresh in his memory was how the *Essex* whaleboats had lost sight of each other, causing delays that would exacerbate the effects of starvation and disorientation.

With the *Martha* now all but vanished—"she could scarcely be seen from the masthead" since "it was raining and blowing hard at seven bells"—Pollard began to lose control of the ship as it gained momentum. Sea and wind tyrannized the *Two Brothers*, and soon, like a mountain river, the rushing deep waters began to show signs of becoming alarmingly shallow. The crew blanched when "one of the men remarked that the water alongside looked whiter than usual," grimly foreshadowing the breaking sea foaming on the jagged shoal ahead. Nickerson recalls "stepping into the cabin to get my watercoat" because the spindrift had begun showering the decks, while the virtually rudderless ship surfed the tide directly into the reef, before colliding with such "fearful" force that it "whirled me head foremost to the other side of the cabin."

With a tailwind of more than fifty miles per hour, a typical wind speed for the Pacific west of Hawaii during a February storm, the *Two Brothers* could have topped thirty-five knots, an extraordinarily fast pace for its size. The 217-ton ship struck the rocks with such violence that Nickerson assumed "we had run into some passing ship" that had returned the blow with its own momentum—a remark testifying to the *Two Brothers'* speed. The Revolutionary War sailor John Paul Jones had once expressed the brazen "wish to have no connection with any ship that does not sail fast, for I intend to go in harm's way"; such a sentiment could not have been further from Pollard's intention.[12] Yet tragically Pollard's quest to keep *out* of harm's way had drawn him directly into it. Had Pollard not felt the urgency to reach the *Martha*, he might have ordered the men to heave to and tack perpendicular to, or even against, the rushing sea in order to restore control. An experienced captain such as Pollard would have known that it is always best to sail directly into a storm, never away from it, especially with shallow water nearby. But in his haste to regain sight of the *Martha*, Pollard risked the ship's immediate safety for the long-term security of a companion vessel.

After the crash, the crew looked in "astonishment to find ourselves surrounded with breakers apparently mountains high." The men cut loose the whaleboats and scrambled into them, racing against the seawater tumbling into a giant gash in the port bow, with "our ship careening over onto her broadside" and being pulled relentlessly downward. After struggling to secure each and every man in a whaleboat, Pollard experienced a moment of paralysis. According to Nickerson, the captain "stood amazed at the scene before him, but under the swift management of the two mates Mr. Eben Gardner and Mr. Charles W. Riddell two boats were got clear of the wreck and all hands crowded into them saving nothing but what they stood in." In this striking scene, the captain then "reluctantly got into the boat just as they were about to shove off from the ship. I had taken hold of the steering oar to steer the boat through the breakers when a towering high sea struck the outer end of the oar throwing me the length of an oar away."[13] An alert mate hastily flung a rope to the thrashing Nickerson and drew him back in.

With the crew in two whaleboats carrying eleven men each, Nickerson rowed between breakers all night in heavy rain, his clothes soaking, surrounded by reefs and rocks rising above the water surface. This shallow, treacherous scene was made all the more chaotic by ebbing and shifting currents, pulling in unpredictable directions from below while breakers hammered from above. With still no sign of the *Martha*, Pollard's crew could only assume that their partner boat had also sunk. To the contrary, Pease's crew had spotted a high rock jutting out of the sea, which they had initially taken for a vessel and thus sailed for in earnest, nearly running aground in the process. Once Pease discovered his error, he frantically signaled back to the *Two Brothers* to warn its crew of the hazard, but this rock would be Pollard's boat's undoing. Here Pollard's dreaded scenario had come to pass—a loss of communication caused by physical separation. In one sense Pollard's instinct to sail as fast as possible despite reckless steering was the right one. Had he been just a hundred meters closer to the *Martha*, he and his crew might have picked up the signal and avoided the rock. In another sense, calling off the chase and instead tacking west at half the speed would have allowed for a more controlled approach toward the shoals, thus enabling the *Two Brothers* to circumnavigate the coral mass. Such independent sailing never crossed Nickerson's mind. He, like Pollard, may have been excessively attached to the *Martha*, given the trauma of the separated boats after the *Essex*'s sinking. "Being so far ahead of us we did not see her signal hence our disaster," as Nickerson puts it.[14]

As midnight approached, the poor visibility in the shoals led Pollard to believe that another jutting rock could be the remains of the *Two Brothers*. Taking the sea spray for its sail, Pollard wanted to check out the possibility, perhaps hoping to gather more provisions in the process. Here we encounter a crucial discrepancy between Nickerson's and Gardner's accounts. Nickerson describes *Pollard's and his boat* sailing for the rock only to realize it was not the ship, and depicts them instantly reversing course and hurrying back. Nickerson then simply cuts to the two whaleboats' rescue by the *Martha*. His use of the conjunction *and* in "Pollard's and his boat" leaves ambiguous the question of how much time elapsed before Gardner's boat arrived. "And to our great joy we saw our mates," he writes. "Mr. Eben Gardner's boat approaching the ship the first we had seen of them since leaving the wreck." Gardner's boat contained two suckling pigs, which had either swum from the sinking ship or were thrown by waves onto a sandy island. This account gives the impression that Gardner was rescued shortly after, or even simultaneous with, Pollard and Nickerson's rescue. But that was not necessarily the case, as Gardner's account makes clearer.

Not only were Nickerson and Pollard rescued first, but they were rescued long before Gardner was, suggesting Pollard had ample time on the *Martha* to contemplate how his directive to seek out the ship's mirage might have led to the deaths of the first mate and crew. Likely weighing heavily on Pollard's conscience was his decision, contrary to Nickerson's account, to assign pursuit of the sinking ship to Gardner's whaleboat, a decision that led the two boats to be separated for the night and well into the next day. Pollard and his men were rescued at 10 AM, whereas Gardner and crew did not climb aboard the *Martha* until 1 PM. So from 11PM the night before until 1 PM the next day, totaling at least fourteen hours, Pollard faced the very real possibility of never seeing Gardner's boat again and thus losing half his crew. The thought of more deaths on his watch would certainly have tortured him, given that he had only himself to blame for separating the men. According to Gardner, Pollard's order to pursue the ship was the direct cause of the boats' separation. His account forms the basis of my portrait of this fourteen-hour period as one of acute crisis for Pollard. Indeed, Gardner provides more time specificity than Nickerson on these crucial hours. Given the hasty, ungrammatical transcription of Gardner's oral telling by William Randall, a younger crew mate who served as Gardner's stenographer, it is clear that the two recorded the event at their first opportunity, vastly sooner than Nickerson, who polished his version some forty-seven years after the event.

Unlike his prose narration, Nickerson's poem was indeed written on the journey, yet it too skirts the separation of the whaleboats. Gardner, by contrast, writes with precision that they "saw a rock 50 feet high, it being verry [*sic*] dark. We took it to be the ship Capt. Pollard wished for me to Row up to see what it was as I had the best boat. It came on a verry hevy [*sic*] squall and I lost sight of Capt. Pollard." He then explains, "I saw no more of them for the knight [*sic*]" because visibility was severely limited by "thick and heavy squalls of rain" at the darkest time of the day (approaching midnight).[15]

The next morning at 10:00, soon after anchoring near the wreck to search for survivors, the *Martha* slipped her cable and drifted toward the treacherous reef. Then, an instant before the mighty vessel would have run aground with enough velocity to sink it, a "providential swell," in Nickerson's phrasing, lifted the hull clear from the reef.[16] Just minutes after righting itself, the *Martha* greeted Nickerson's boat. It was not for another three hours, then, at 1 PM, that the *Martha* met Gardner's boat, ending a period for Pollard of undoubtedly painful anxiety over his mates' whereabouts. So from 10 AM to 1 PM on February 11, 1823, Pollard may have experienced his darkest hours since the *Essex* tragedy. Whereas overnight he must have feared as well for his own rescue, aware from his *Essex* experience how unpredictable such attempts could be, in the morning he had only his lost mates to ruminate on. Indeed, in the earlier event, random ships had repeatedly passed the crew's whaleboats, and the crew reached safety only once on shore. Now, thinking of his potentially lost mates, mingled with the death of Owen Coffin and others from the *Essex* journey, the prospects of his future life under such a burden could well have been a torture. Likewise Pollard must have felt indescribable relief when Gardner's crew, moored beside an island overnight, burst into view. "At 1 PM we got onboard the *Martha* and found Captain Pollard safe with all his crew," Gardner reports, confirming "we had all men in each boat."[17] Had this reunion not occurred, Pollard would have had to suffer with the knowledge that his last words to his first mate were "to row up to see what it was" protruding from the water. In this new scenario of contingencies and decisions, like the death lottery that claimed Owen Coffin, "the awful die" seemed yet again "turned on Captain Pollard," as Nickerson would write decades later, reinventing and sensationalizing the scene for his prospective ghostwriter, Leon Lewis.[18] Only this time the outcome was happier.

Along with his mates, Pollard returned home on a ship called the *Pearl* and swore off whaling forever. He would lead the single voyage on a merchant ship, according to Nickerson, "but not liking that business, returned to his home in Nantucket and sought out a business which he continued until his death a few years since."[19] Gardner, as noted, had recited the incident to his shipmate Randall, whose transcription is distinguished by its shaky grammar, arbitrary use of commas and capitalization, poor spelling, and run-on sentences. Added consonants are found in "Coppy," "piggs," "boddy," and "verry," yet inexplicably omitted in terms such as "Sea Acount." His flamboyant signature, snaking its way down the page, also attests to his youth and perhaps his relief at completing an onerous transcription task. Randall did attempt some modest rhetorical flourishes. Overwhelming the decks of the *Two Brothers*, for example, "the sea made a road over us," he writes. Elsewhere he portrays dawn over the vast coral reef, and the whaleboat's isolation: "The Long Wished for Daylight at length appear[ing] and open[ing] to our view a dismal scene."[20]

These details suggest that, despite the jagged syntax, Gardner and Randall may have delivered a more faithful, if briefer, account of the shipwreck than does Nickerson, whose prose narrative was finalized almost a half-century after the fact. The omission of rescue details in Nickerson's record leaves readers without any sense of Pollard's apparently miserable state, with the timing of these details, in my opinion, so crucial in seeking to recreate his mind-set and the overall experience.[21] Perhaps, had the whole *Two Brothers* crew been with him through the night, he might have even reconsidered ending his whaling career. Yet Pollard's emotional vulnerability and noble humility were precisely the traits that Melville and Emerson admired. Pollard knew well that this trial, compounded by that of the *Essex*, threatened to plague him for the rest of his days. As it happens, morbid contemplation of "Death and Judgment," as Melville points out through the salty shipowner Peleg in *Moby-Dick*, is totally incompatible with a captain's job of urgently and constantly responding to a ship's needs. Moreover, the psychological anguish hits not when the ship is going down but in the aftermath: "With all three masts making such an everlasting thundering against the side; and every sea breaking over us, fore and aft. Think of Death and Judgment then? No! no time to think about Death then." Like Pollard rushing about as the *Two Brothers* keeled over, Peleg recalls being riveted in a crisis to the tasks of "how to save all hands—how to rig jury-masts—how to get into the nearest port; that was what I was thinking of."[22] As seemingly evidenced by his hesitation in boarding the whaleboat, Pollard would have preferred to die in the panic of saving a ship than to live out his years with the gnawing memory of being responsible for yet another catastrophe.

"THROWN INTO VERSE"

Nickerson planned his epic poem, "The Ship *Two Brothers*," as an ode to the redemption and triumphant return of Captain Pollard. Prior to the *Essex* disaster, Pollard seemed the epitome of what Melville describes in *Moby-Dick* as "scores of anonymous Captains [who] have sailed out of Nantucket, that were as great, and greater than your Cook and Krusenstern."[23] Nickerson anticipated that this second voyage would catapult Pollard to fame, while rescuing him from the ignominy of the *Essex* disaster. What better occasion to exalt a Nantucket captain to a worldwide audience? In the two years following the *Essex* disaster, Pollard had become pitied and even maligned, as we saw, and Nickerson thus resolved to craft a tribute, to borrow from Mary Shelley, to his captain's "Return, as heroes who have fought and conquered, and who know not what it is to turn their backs on the foe."[24] The former cabin boy could not have known that his poem would end up chronicling yet another disaster at sea.

Following Pollard's death in 1870, interest and demand spiked for writings on the former captain. Nickerson's privileged status as the lone survivor of the *Essex* and *Two Brothers* voyages, as the previous chapter detailed, prompted newspaper story writer Leon Lewis to approach him with an offer to ghostwrite and edit his works. In response an eager Nickerson promptly sent Lewis not only his notes toward an *Essex* manuscript, "Desultory Sketches from a Seaman's Log," but also his more finished tale of the *Two Brothers* told in prose and poetry. Sometime during the preparation of the poem's fair copy, after the voyage, Nickerson had decided to compose a full account of the event in prose as well, in part to create an accessible package for a wider audience. Composed on the same sheaf of papers and in the same hand, this finished product was clearly created with Pollard's passing and the readily available services of Lewis in mind.

Whereas "Desultory Sketches" was a scattered jumble of notes including excerpts from Chase's *Narrative*, essentially raw materials, Nickerson's prose and verse narratives of the *Two Brothers* journey would have required far less editorial work from Lewis. In a brief preface to the poem, Nickerson dramatizes its origin as a romantic sea tale in its own right. "The following lines were sketched and thrown into verse," he writes, very much in keeping with the Irvingesque preface, both self-effacing and careful to vouch for its own authenticity to eradicate any hint of being invented.[25] Linguistically he was striving for an unartful artfulness, which in the day's high-literary circles held considerable cachet. This was the era when Wordsworth's celebration of the common language of agrarians in "Preface to Lyrical Ballads" would have a profound influence on American authors such as Emerson, Thoreau, and Whitman, who championed unadorned speech that hews close to lived physical experience. As in Melville's immortal "Call Me Ishmael," which so deftly conjures his narrator's rough-hewn presence, Nickerson also wanted his lines to come directly out of the salt air and the jagged rocks of the voyage.

Alongside Nickerson's prose account, told from the distanced and resigned vantage point of a man older than seventy, the seventeen-year-old youth's poem is transformed into an artifact of immediate experience. Framed as poetic performance—however unscripted, improvised, and raw with imperfections—the verse draws both its prestige and thematic touchstones from Nickerson's association with the whaleship *Essex* and the intrigue surrounding Captain Pollard. For example, in footnoting an early line, he adheres to the nautical narrative convention Melville himself employs in the "His Mark" chapter of *Moby-Dick*, which dramatizes the recruitment of Ishmael and his mate, Queequeg, for service aboard the *Pequod*. "And thus [Pollard] mused while pacing to and fro / I'll see those lads perchance, they with me go," Nickerson writes, as Melville would of Peleg and Bildad's assessment of the sailors' fitness for service. Would Pollard dare tempt fate by conscripting these two lads, Nickerson and Ramsdell, who had survived the *Essex* disaster? The footnote Nickerson added a half-century after drafting the verse while preparing a copy of the original weathered holograph—which he had somehow saved from the flooding decks of the *Two Brothers*—is essential to the dramatic import of that decision. "Those lads" are later glossed as "the writer and Charles Ramsdell of the crew of the *Essex*" to emphasize the unique circumstance informing not only Pollard's decision to ship out again but Nickerson and Ramsdell's as well.[26]

In the poem this decision to sail again with Pollard—romantic, risky, and audacious—casts Nickerson and Ramsdell as figures drawn back into the fold by a stroke of fate. One could rightly question whether Pollard was courageous or reckless in his prompt return to whaling. This was a man, after all, venturing forth so soon after being rescued from his *Essex* whaleboat on February 23, 1820. He would set sail from Nantucket again on November 26, 1821, to face the dangers of the high seas after enduring starvation, cannibalism, and the death of more than half the *Essex* crew. As it happened, Pollard's poise struck Charles Wilkes, who met the captain at sea, off the coast of Ecuador, prior to the *Two Brothers* accident, as extraordinary. "I expressed myself how he could think of again putting his foot on board Ship to again pursue such a calling, or hazard another voyage," Wilkes recalled. "He simply remarked that it was an old adage that the lightning never struck twice in the same place."[27]

Such confidence from Pollard appears to have been magnetic, and thus irresistible to Nickerson. "Mine was the lot to plough with him," Nickerson writes, choosing his noun, *lot*, to invoke the memory of Owen Coffin's selection by lottery to be killed for the *Essex* crew's sustenance. Nickerson brings the *Essex* ordeal into clear view in the final line of the preface by stating that he "had also been one of his [i.e., Pollard's crew] in the ill-fated *Essex*."[28] The last phrase lends Nickerson unique authority as the poet/chronicler of the loss of the *Two Brothers*, since no one beside his mate Ramsdell had experienced both of Pollard's whaling commands. This self-disclosure also creates a sense of doomed prophecy, with Pollard's will interlocked with the hand of fate to which the youths are vulnerable. Interestingly Nickerson made the same rhetorical use of Pollard in his 1876 letter to Leon Lewis when he essentially blamed the captain for Owen Coffin's death. In both cases Nickerson isolated and scrutinized the captain's decisions to select youths for undertakings—the

Essex lottery and sailing aboard the *Two Brothers*—that would take them to the edge of death.

Nickerson chose to record his ship log in verse in part because he harbored literary aspirations in a culture in which "the sea," as the *North American Review* proclaimed in 1825, "with its thousand brilliant perils and accompaniments, is rich in materials for poetry."[29] Further, as a young sailor, Nickerson would have certainly been exposed to, and probably taken a keen interest in, Coleridge's *Rime of the Ancient Mariner*, which includes a prominent scene depicting a game of chance between Death, figured as a skeleton, and the "Night-mare Life-in-Death," embodied by a deathly pallid woman. A roll of the dice determines that Death wins the lives of the crew, while Life-in-Death wins the captain's life. His is considered a fate worse than death, as he is forced to live forever with the punishment for killing the albatross, which the crew took as a harbinger of salvation and new life. "As fate would have it, the awful die turned upon Captain Pollard," Nickerson wrote to Lewis, as cited earlier, in a clear echo of the death lottery in Coleridge's poem.[30] In his teens Nickerson may well have imagined Owen Coffin as the albatross around Pollard's neck while hoping for his own and the captain's resurrection through the capture of whales on their upcoming voyage aboard the *Two Brothers*. Coleridge's epic sea poem certainly may not only have inspired Nickerson's decision to express himself in verse but also, as the evidence suggests, informed the very tropes he deployed in depicting Pollard's command.

By Pollard's death in 1870, the story of the *Essex* was widely enough known that Nickerson could reasonably expect readers to find interest in an account of the sinking of Pollard's second ship. Relatedly, without any other evidence indicating why he never sought publication for his various texts until this point, one can plausibly point to the emergence of Lewis as spurring this decision. Yet, despite the seeming appeal of the *Two Brothers* narrative, and the far greater polish of his writings on this disaster, Nickerson still sensed that his story of the *Essex*, with its distinctions against Chase's version, offered his best prospects for success. All the same, Nickerson, as noted, did include the *Two Brothers* prose and poetry texts in his package to Lewis—even as he knew the sensational elements in the second voyage did not equal those of the first. Here, Nickerson likely recognized that the dual work of prose and poetry, perhaps to be packaged together as a short volume after appearing in the periodical press, could function as a sequel to Chase's *Narrative*.

Countless nineteenth-century narratives include an appendix with the author's poetry, a convention seen everywhere from Frederick Douglass's *Narrative of the Life of an American Slave* (1845), with its appended verse parody of Southern Christianity, to Melville's *Billy Budd*, which ends with the moving seaman's lyric "Billy in the Darbies." Echoing Melville's prose poetry chapter, "The Lee Shore," in *Moby-Dick*, Nickerson casts the fated captain as poetic subject: "Scarce had this worthy captain reached the strand / When once again appointed to command."[31] Nickerson darkens the mood with gothic portents: "faithless deep" in a "darksome night and cheerless day / Nonetheless doomed to pass, upon the way." The sea reigns supreme over any hope to master it, as "Dangers stand thick, the stoutest heart must quail / Nautic skill seemed scarcely to prevail" on the passage around Cape Horn.[32] Which particular danger those hearts fear, with the likely suspects whales and the threat of starvation in open boats associated with the *Essex*, remains veiled at this point in the poem.

Nickerson's poem then charts the *Two Brothers'* journey from the darkness of rounding Cape Horn to the visual ecstasy of "the lofty Cordilliers" on the coast of Chile, particularly their "wondrous height / Snowy tops their golden wealth concealed."[33] Here the poem's narrative rides the sort of buoyant optimism found in Chase's description of the *Essex*'s loading at several South American ports in preparation for the long whale hunt in the Pacific. When the *Two Brothers* meets the Nantucket ship *Martha* on the northwestern coast of Peru in the port of Payta, the poem reflects the distinct pleasures of outfitting and securing the vessel. Nickerson describes the *Martha* with noble language, honoring her as "Our gallant consort [that] bore us on our way." Gratitude fills the young tar, who regards the *Martha* as a protector from the risks inherent in braving waters alone. No such "gallant consort" accompanied the *Essex*, for which protective aid may indeed have warded off disaster. Safety and, given his limited experience, the novelty of partnership thus leaven the departure from Payta.

The poem then takes on nonseafaring themes, including critiquing ambitious generals in the Peruvian civil war: "How sadly here are nature's gifts destroyed / By demon agents artfully employed." And a lament over parting ways with a South American sweetheart: "Fairwell ye dark haired maid with eyes of fire, / Who could have known ye, yet could not admire." The sharp swing to criticism of "demon agents artfully employed" ends in a sweeping dismissal of Peru as a "benighted land," which Nickerson justifies with a footnote, "It is generally known that this country makes no improvements."[34] A clear sense of cultural supremacy emerges in such remarks. Surely Melville would find far more redeeming qualities in cultures of the Pacific, as compared with Nickerson in Peru. Yet Nickerson may very well be speaking more broadly for his Nantucket-based crew and its range of cultural assumptions.

Turning the focus back on Pollard, Nickerson attributes the sense of futility and depression in the crew once in the Pacific to a heartsickness in the captain: "Long men strove, yet nothing does repay / Our distant exile o'er this pathless way / Till worn and weary, Pollard sick at heart / Resolved from those dull seas soon to depart." Once in the Galápagos, the men begin to load wood, water, and terrapins (land tortoises) onto the ship. Here Pollard is cast as more the world-weary beast of burden than the fearless leader: "Three times each day he's driven through the woods / And like an ass he brings forth his laden goods" and "reloads the boat" with a "faint and weary" demeanor day and night.[35]

Such images of onerous labor set up Nickerson's meditation on the business of whaling, another convention of nineteenth-century nautical narratives. Nickerson was certainly familiar with Chase's prominent coverage of this topic in his *Narrative*, of which the entire preface is dedicated to the commercial circumstances of "the enterprise of whalemen" and their worthiness of the respect of "the active energies of capitalists." This is followed by the first chapter's portrayal of whalemen as "a very industrious and enterprising people" who labor under unusually dangerous circumstances.[36] "We seek a fortune o'er a distant sea," Nickerson writes, training his attention on the voyage's capitalist objective and on whaling in general as a profit-seeking venture to "mend broken fortunes."

He weighs how men "with fate contend" to chase their "flighty visions" of "where the treasure lies." This has fascinating implications for Nickerson, whose entrepreneurial guile distinguishes him (along with Chase) from the other crew members of the *Essex* and *Two Brothers*.

Even as a lowly teenage boatsteerer, Nickerson found solace in the prospect of financial reward while sailing on the otherwise alienating, risk-laden open Pacific. In the prose account he writes that the "hope for some better fortune" will "cheer us onward" trusting that "all may return without an empty hand."[37] This hope of course is extremely naïve, given that no boatsteerer ever obtained wealth from even the most lucrative of whaling voyages. Further, his attitude here contrasts sharply with that of Melville, voiced through Ishmael, who willingly accepts his scant earnings as a common sailor, and offers the gruff defense "Who ain't a slave?"[38] Following Nickerson's reflections on potential income comes "joyful news of friends and home" from an approaching sail.[39] Combined with visions of financial redemption following the *Essex* wreck, the prospect of the gam buoys Nickerson's spirit.

Thoughts of moneymaking naturally give way to an actual chase after the precious commodity of a whale. In hot pursuit Pollard is thus transformed and enlivened, presumably by the drive for profit. Herein, with Pollard fully engaged in the capitalist venture, Nickerson sees the potential for the former *Essex* commander's redemption. He rejoices to see his captain literally back in business, engrossed in capitalist behavior so widely accepted in early nineteenth-century New England that Emerson and his cadre of poet-seers dedicated their entire philosophy of transcendentalism to reimagining value as distinct from the industrialist standard. Far from the transcendentalists' view, Nickerson casts the whale chase as an invigorating and ennobling pursuit of wealth— and as neither sport nor revenge act. Nickerson here anticipates Starbuck's insistence that chasing all whales can drive away Ahab's demons and possibly cure him of his obsession with one particular whale. To Starbuck, furthermore, profit seeking represents God's will and thus the path to redemption. The blasphemy he decries is based on his perception of a sin against the almighty dollar: "How many barrels will thy vengeance yield thee even if thou gettest [the White Whale], Captain Ahab? It will not fetch thee much in our Nantucket market." Starbuck thus espouses the same ethos as Nickerson, who admires Pollard most when the chase, and indeed the deadly perils of the voyage at large, "fairly comes in the way of the business we follow."[40] Under such circumstances, death is not only tolerable but also sacred. Whereas Pollard was slow and depleted of energy before, now he is revived: "Swift as by magic on the deck now stands / The eager Captain—and he thus commands." Their "greasy spoil / By skill and care" is then "converted into oil," in this celebration of both capital and the defeat of the whale, which takes on the proportions of a "huge monster."[41]

Whereas the pursuit of capital clarifies and reassures the young Nickerson of the righteousness of the quest for redemption on the *Two Brothers*, the inscrutability of nature takes on a haunting ambiguity. Nickerson lifts two lines from Alexander Pope and waxes philosophical about an oncoming storm, beginning yet again with the keynote of the captain at the helm, this time solitary yet poised and self-possessed, eyeing the dark encroaching clouds. After his display of efficient energy during the whale chase scene, Pollard is now portrayed as pensive, silently mobilizing the full scale of his considerable nautical judgment: "He scans with anxious eye the gathering blast / And with a seaman's care surveys the mast." In this instance the captain is supremely under control, firmly steering the ship through the storm, though "the utmost skill could scarce control the bark." The captain and crew rise to the challenge, however, and survive the storm, as "nautic skill gainst elements prevail." This triumphant moment sharply contrasts with the poem's next section, "The Shipwreck."[42]

With breakers sighted ahead, indicating the approach to shallow rocks and reef, the crew surrounds the calming leader Pollard, hoping he will "ease their alarm." He asks them to "indulge me now, be all your fears allayed." But then the ship crashes upon the reef, whereupon first mate Gardner proposes to chop down the mast.[43] Pollard declines this suggestion for fear the mast might crush the boats. Here Pollard's narrative depiction moves from sure-handed authority to (almost) twice-defeated human being. And "when the boats prepared," Pollard "lingered yet" and "seemed his own salvation to forget." While the crewmen rush into the boats, Pollard hesitates because he "cared for others' safety not his own." Indeed, one clue, in addition to the footnote explaining that "the Captain when called upon could scarcely be prevailed on to embark," suggests that the captain's hesitation involved more than his preoccupation with securing the crew. In the poem Nickerson describes Pollard as "deep lost in thought, his reasoning powers had flown," indicating he may have been contemplating going down with the ship. His decision to board the boat reveals a revival in Pollard's sense of hope: "Through this trying hour / His buoyant spirit had sustained his power."[44] But this hope is short-lived, diminishing after he orders the second whaleboat to pursue the jutting rock. Mulling the possible loss of those eleven men at sea—especially given the ultimate folly of his instructions to Gardner—he faces his demons. The wait for the boat, as we saw, must have had profound effects on his thinking about the meaning, income, and risks associated with his chosen career.

As the survivors navigate between breakers and rock, Nickerson makes a clear allusion to the *Essex*, emphasizing that "we have no food our hunger to appease" and "how thirst steals over our parched lips" so that "Pale Death's stern pale visage threatens now again." Of course the men would have been frightened, but the likelihood that they had begun to starve after only one night at sea is far-fetched. Instead, these were probably symptoms of their excruciating anxiety about their lack of food and drink, rather than life-threatening hunger and thirst. Given Nickerson's affinity for invoking fate, it is fitting that he casts the *Martha* as the agent of divine providence, imagining God hearing, and responding to, "the hardy seaman's feeblest cry."[45]

The shoals, turbulent sea, and poor visibility were the natural forces seen to be conspiring to wreck the *Two Brothers*, evidently confirming to Pollard that lightning does strike twice. We already know something about Pollard's post–*Two Brothers* existence in the proud seafaring community of Nantucket. But what exactly would his second homecoming be like? And how would he be perceived, and carry on, after a wreck for which he held at least some responsibility? The next chapter considers Pollard's life after his career at sea, and the odd circumstance of finding a role on land that might serve the whaling industry and the island he called home.

Chapter 5

~~~~~~

NIGHT WATCHMAN

Somewhat like Oedipus after his fall, Captain George Pollard Jr. would transform himself, after the *Two Brothers* wreck, from a powerful leader into a humble figure bearing insights on the island of Nantucket. Of course he never intended to play the role of sage. Instead, it seems to have chosen him.

Pollard's decision to settle on Nantucket, where he was raised, rather than in a major urban center like New York City or Philadelphia relatively unconcerned with whaling, is worthy of mention. In the small community, he must have known he would be highly visible and thus the inevitable object of scorn and gossip. On the one hand, Melville's observation that "to the islanders, he was a nobody" accurately captures Pollard's withdrawal from the limelight as a ship captain, a vocation celebrated for strengthening the island's economy and embodying the virtues of bravery and fortitude.[1] On the other, Pollard was far from a "nobody." He would remain well known on the island, owing to his deep Nantucket Quaker lineage, his wife Mary's highly visible anticipation of his return from sea, and the community's profound awareness of both his failed voyages.

Upon his somber homecoming in February of 1823, having just wrecked the very ship that had brought him safely to shore after the *Essex* ordeal, Pollard was not afforded a hero's welcome, or a loser's chill reception, so much as folded back into the tribe. For his part, instead of wallowing in self-pity or claiming extra time to rehabilitate, Pollard set about to fill the island's immediate need for security by taking a job as a night watchman. The former captain could thus serve society's needs while also acting with integrity in a place where residents, for centuries, had shown little tolerance for self-righteousness following a public failing. As the last chapter made clear, Pollard knew that shipowners deemed him unfit for whaling. But the former captain, despite opting for a quiet life, would hardly become obsolete. In fact he would capture the imagination of two of the best minds of his generation, Herman Melville and Ralph Waldo Emerson. We must then inquire more deeply into why both men made special journeys to meet this twice-stricken and self-proclaimed "unlucky man."

This chapter is concerned with how Pollard could survive and subsist, both spiritually and materially, after his twin seafaring losses. Indeed, to both Melville and Emerson, Pollard stood for much more than New England grit, but instead something larger betokening the human cost of the nation's heedless industrial development and pursuit of capital. The personal element, however, was also paramount. Pollard's career had been ruined, at least in part because of these greater forces, yet the former captain showed remarkable emotional and psychological fortitude, given a crucible that would have driven others to madness. Perhaps this achievement emerged from his having a temperament and philosophy akin to that of Emerson, who, faced with the crushing losses of his own wife and son, could "in the solitude to which every man is always returning" find "a sanity and revelations which in his passage into new worlds he will carry with him." Perhaps Pollard could similarly quiet his own demons with the mix of hope and strength that allowed Emerson to "never mind the ridicule, never mind the defeat: up, again old heart!—it seems to say—there is victory yet for all justice."[2] Whether or not Pollard held these qualities to the same extent as Emerson, it is certain that the captain did not endure his days alone. In this sense he must have known that the young republic's individualist ethos was something of a myth. He must have understood this even on a stubbornly conservative island like Nantucket, with its Puritan and Quaker traditions, which resisted new social developments and held fast to its existing order. Survival, as Pollard well knew from his seafaring days, was never an isolated affair.

The *Iliad* begins not with the Homeric cataloging of ships, symbolizing national and military pride, but with Achilles pouting upon the discovery that his war prize, Briseis, has been stolen from him. The Greek hero is inconsolable, withdrawing into his tent and sulking precisely when his comrades need him most. His response is not just one of inner self-pity, but a blend of social humiliation and public shame. Indeed, such factors were integral to the ancient culture and motivated the decisions of mortals as well as conniving, self-interested gods. Pollard's fall from grace into the position of night watchman was also motivated by his own society's shame culture. But Achilles's withdrawal and his corresponding lack of contribution to society, Pollard knew, would have been intolerable by Nantucket standards. Pollard's refusal to disappear and sulk, then, may have had as much to do with his society as with his personal attributes. As Emerson and Melville almost certainly appreciated, Pollard's dignity was irrevocably linked to Nantucket's rough-hewn Protestant work ethic.

The social function of the night watchman on Nantucket traces back to a need for civic order—in areas from fire protection to crime prevention—during its earliest days of settlement in the 1660s. The historian Edward Byers observes that "public safety was the chief consideration that justified Nantucket's secular court regulation and punishment of personal behavior." The islanders' lack of tolerance for unruly behavior at night, in particular, arose from their desire to control relations with Indians, whom they feared, given their tendency to "get drunk, fight, or commit great disorders." But along with troublesome Indians, "lower class whites" committed crimes and engaged in "antisocial and often drunken behavior that disrupted the community peace and threatened the safety of its more 'respectable' citizens."[3] Before such offenders could be brought to justice, a night watchman was needed to arrest and detain them. Not only was the night watchman indispensable in initiating the judicial process—he was also the visible and embodied first line of defense against idleness, "the most heinous sin committed on Nantucket," as J. Hector St. John de Crèvecœur, the Tocqueville of the eighteenth century, observed on one visit.[4]

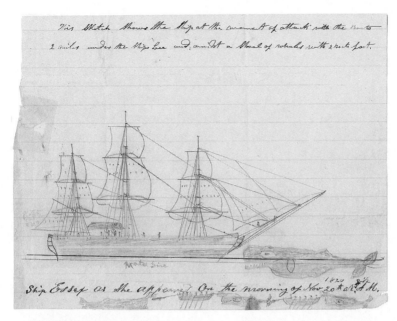

This Sketch shows the Ship at the moment of attack with the Boats
2 miles under the Ships Lee and, amidst a Shoal of whales with 2 mate fast.

Ship Essex as She appeared On the morning of Nov 20th at 8 AM. 1820

Nickerson's sketch of the *Essex*. Courtesy of the Nantucket Historical
Association, MS106–3.

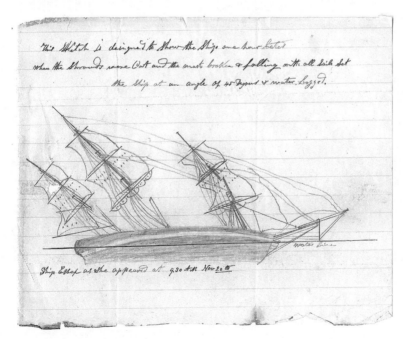

This Sketch is designed to show the Ship one hour later
when the Shrouds were Cut and the masts broken & falling with all Sails Set
the Ship at an angle of 45 degrees & water Logged.

Ship Essex as She appeared at 9.30 AM Nov 20th

Nickerson's sketch of the sinking *Essex*. Courtesy of the Nantucket
Historical Association, MS106–4.

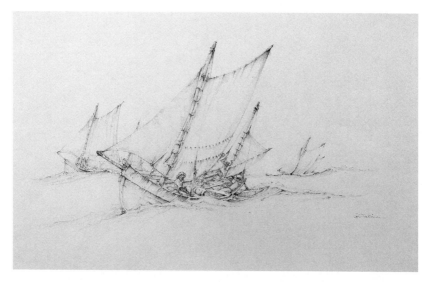

Departing Henderson Island, Gary Tonkin. Courtesy of the New Bedford Whaling Museum.

Coffin's Fatal Lot, Gary Tonkin. Courtesy of the New Bedford Whaling Museum.

Ramsdell the Executioner, Gary Tonkin. Courtesy of the
New Bedford Whaling Museum.

NARRATIVE

OF THE

MOST EXTRAORDINARY AND DISTRESSING

SHIPWRECK

OF THE

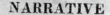

OF

.NANTUCKET ;

WHICH WAS ATTACKED AND FINALLY DESTROYED BY A LARGE

SPERMACETI-WHALE,

IN THE PACIFIC OCEAN;

WITH

AN ACCOUNT

OF THE

UNPARALLELED SUFFERINGS

OF THE CAPTAIN AND CREW

DURING A SPACE OF NINETY-THREE DAYS AT SEA, IN OPEN BOATS,

IN THE YEARS 1819 & 1820.

BY

OWEN CHASE,

OF NANTUCKET, FIRST MATE OF SAID VESSEL.

NEW-YORK:

PUBLISHED BY W. B. GILLEY, 92 BROADWAY.

J. SEYMOUR, Printer.

1821.

Chase's *Narrative.* Courtesy of the Nantucket
Historical Association, RBNAN–Chase Narrative.

List of *Essex* crew members. Courtesy of the Nantucket Historical Association, MS10–469a.

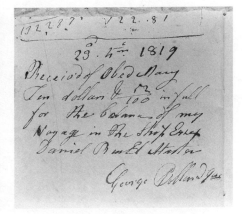

Chase's payment for *Essex* voyage. Courtesy of the Nantucket Historical Association, GPN4587

Pollard's payment for *Essex* voyage. Courtesy of the Nantucket Historical Association, GPN4586.

Thomas Nickerson. Courtesy
of the Nantucket Historical
Association, GPN4361.

Dr. Kelly Gleason Keogh investigates a ginger jar at the *Two Brothers*
shipwreck site at French Frigate Shoals. Courtesy of NOAA/Greg McFall.
Fig. 12. Plan for the *Two Brothers*. Courtesy of the New Bedford Whaling
Museum.

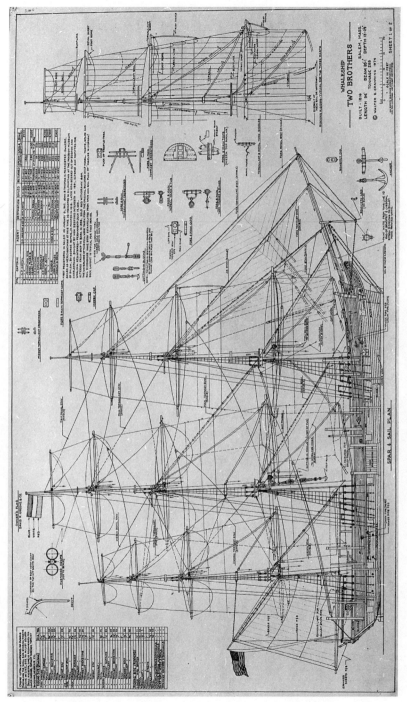

Plan for the *Two Brothers*. Courtesy of the New Bedford Whaling Museum.

Bird's-eye view of Nantucket. Courtesy of the Nantucket
Historical Association, sc735

LEFT Owen Chase.
Courtesy of the
Nantucket Historical
Association, GPN4448.

BELOW *A Nantucket
Sleigh Ride*, Grant
Gordon. Courtesy
of the New Bedford
Whaling Museum.

"His Head half out of water . . . he again struck the ship."

Attacking whale, *Cosmopolitan*, 1904. Courtesy of the
Nantucket Historical Association, P10230.

Pollard, wanting nothing to do with idleness himself, selected an occupation that allowed him to actively combat the island's foremost sin and thus earn islanders' basic respect. As night watchman, he could assume a socially beneficial role in the eyes of the community, firmly on the side of the industrious against their most feared opposite. For Pollard, perhaps, and other Nantucketers in need of relief, the island's welfare system had lately been changing. In 1822, just before the captain's return from the *Two Brothers* failure, relief services that had routinely provided the poor with food and shelter were repealed, to be replaced by a work farm premised on the idea that all recipients of public funds should earn their keep. This decision, issued by a committee assembled to solve the problem of the island's growing indigent population, might be seen as a force that would ultimately, if silently, help pressure Pollard into securing his useful occupation. The committee went so far as to denounce the support of the needy by their own families. They condemned such relief beyond the island's almshouse, which had exceeded its capacity to tend to the poor, because "support of paupers in their own families . . . silently adds to the accumulating number of poor, saps the founts of industry, and holds out to the indolent impunity from the natural punishments of their crimes, and to the intemperate a bounty for debauching and vice."[5] Such thinking issued not from base intolerance of Indians and lower class whites, but from the fundamental Nantucket abhorrence of any practice that undermined the Puritan, and in turn Quaker, virtues of industry and frugality.

Being a night watchman on Nantucket in 1823 thus was the occupation not of a "nobody" but of a vital guardian, a role demanding nothing less than the maintenance of a cherished ethos. The value and prestige attached to the whaling community was extraordinarily high in 1823, thanks to surging profits, with the industry's golden age to peak just a decade later. Along with that newfound affluence came a heightened awareness of ostentatious displays of wealth. Pollard, given his two failed voyages, would be vulnerable to no such accusations. But, as noted, he was very much at the mercy of Nantucket's shame culture, driven by gossip and innuendo serving as a means of safeguarding the island's highly visible and increasingly international reputation. In 1823, Nantucket, and not

New Bedford, was still the busiest port in the international whaling trade. Never before had so many outsiders set foot on the island, drawn from the South Seas to Australia and soon to depart with vivid impressions of this "elbow of sand" and its denizens, who "born on the beach should take to the sea for their livelihood!," as Melville describes the situation in *Moby-Dick*. We see, then, in the suspicion of dishonor to the island's status a sort of dichotomy between visibility and invisibility, world fame and isolation, prominence and obscurity in "these sea hermits." Ardently dedicated to their geographical and political separateness from trends sweeping cities such as New York and Boston, the formidable Nantucket seafarers, "issuing from their ant hill in the sea, overrun [*sic*] and conquered the watery world like so many Alexanders; parceling out among them the Atlantic, Pacific, and Indian oceans, as the three pirate powers did Poland." The "hermits" inhabiting a self-governed "ant hill" thus emerged as world-renowned mariners who seemed to own the sea, "other seamen having but a right of way through it."[6]

Like Nantucket itself, Pollard was simultaneously the most visible and invisible ship captain in antebellum America. Working to keep the peace and maintain order while others slept, he literally had removed himself from the light of day. As famous as James Cook, from the previous century, Pollard was widely recognized for the disasters he had endured and his case's heavy moral complexity in a nautical culture otherwise focused on bravery, ambition, and commercial gain. But Pollard had little concern with the social world beyond Nantucket, which functions like its own nation, making "its own war and peace" with "a strong national feeling," as Emerson observed. Pollard's main concern, despite his respectable civic role as night watchman, was what Emerson referred to as the island's ingrained tendency to be "very sensitive to everything that dishonours the island because it hurts the value of stock till the company are poorer."[7] For Nantucketers, reputation was indeed something to be protected in the interest of the company's "stock," at the time numbered in thousands of barrels of whale oil and spermaceti, secure in ships traveling at full sail toward the Nantucket bar from the globe's four corners.[8]

As we saw earlier, Nantucket's shame culture would also help explain Owen Chase's response to the *Essex* disaster. Chase evinced defensiveness whereas Pollard was humble, especially after the *Two Brothers* wreck, a disparity perhaps best accounted for by differing temperaments. Chase, however, also made aggressively offensive moves, pursuing career success and the corresponding financial reward with a zeal that, he must have thought, would eventually win the admiration of Nantucket's residents (even though he had relocated to New Bedford). Pollard, meanwhile, knew that his two losses hurt the company's "stock" and sought to do no further harm. His actions also reflected an awareness of how, according to Byers, "through the use of social ostracism and ridicule, the community informally enforced its system of values."[9] Where a "deviant" act on the level of cannibalism, not to mention lesser acts, could "cause a schism, and set every tongue a-going," some had predicted the ruin of families associated with Pollard. Yet his presence now symbolized, among other things, humble service as a check against the mounting material extravagances that threatened to alter Nantucket's collective identity forever. Prosperity was now a force to be reckoned with, given that "never since the foundation of the town had there happened anything which so much alarmed their primitive community," as Crèvecœur aptly notes.[10]

By 1823, Nantucket community values—supported by Pollard through his work as a night watchman—had transferred from the island's government into the hands of voluntary reform associations, with emphases ranging from temperance to antislavery to labor reform and advocacy for the poor. In his new, very low-paying job, Pollard's work melded at least somewhat with the voluntary public service roles provided through the emerging reform associations—and less with the private institutions associated with Quaker culture's focus on individualistic effort. The job in this sense, as well as others already mentioned, would have garnered him respect and acceptance. As for his Quaker ties, the faith itself had become more informally practiced on the island, and individuals' expressions of service toward the common good were viewed favorably.[11] The concept of nonpracticing Quakers might lead one to suspect that the faith's natural informality had permeated the community, which became something of a church without walls. If Nantucket's nonpracticing Quakers had a high priest of humble, enduring dignity in the face of a difficult past, it was Pollard.

Though no longer a practicing Quaker, Pollard was now helping uphold the island's long-standing code of moral certitude. Despite institutional shifts away from the earlier predominance of Quakerism, Nantucket in 1823 had hardly been transformed into a bastion of radical freethinking or laissez-faire mores, as would Rhode Island and Concord in the next decade. Instead, a common set of principles, especially with regard to industry, labor, and humility, prevailed. As for Pollard, by night he apprehended wrongdoers; by day a judge determined their fate. The paradoxes were rich for the former captain, who was tied to the great transgression of cannibalism and to his seafaring losses but was now helping enforce Nantucket's laws.

In a Nickerson quotation we saw earlier, the former cabin boy remarks that "Captain Pollard has since [his whaling days] lived on the island, greatly respected by all whose business [or] pleasure brought them in contact with him and died lamented by a large circle of friends." This sentiment runs counter to the antipathy Pollard elicited from Owen Coffin's mother. Joseph Warren Phinney, who was raised as part of the captain and his wife Mary's extended family, testifies that "Captain Pollard was the gum-shoe man of the town. The boys were supposed to be in the house by nine o'clock & he used to make a tour of the town, a long hickory pole with an iron hook at the end under his arm." However menacing his weapon, which he brandished like a modified harpoon, Pollard was harmless. Hardly a John Claggart, the sadistic military police officer and master-at-arms who Melville imagined decades later in *Billy Budd*, the former captain never led through intimidation. Instead, Pollard bore the manner of a trusted fatherly figure whom Phinney recalls as "a short fat man—jolly, loving the good things of life." Could this have been the twice-stricken soul who had howled in anguish while describing the *Essex* ordeal? Phinney's recollection paints more of a carefree, kindly, eccentric character torn from the pages of Dickens than the tortured, tragic figure one might expect. According to Phinney, Pollard's stoutness was the object of considerable jest, as "they used to say" that "his wife, who had been a tailoress, when he needed a new pair of breeches laid him down on the cloth and marked him out on it. When he wore out the knees he turned them round hind side fore'most." Phinney may have been needling Pollard in part to shield him from far more serious accusations, including of self-righteousness, had neighbors perceived he was assuming too serious a role for himself. For better or worse, the portrait also distracted from evidence showing Pollard's depth of character and acts of spiritual supplication. His respect for those *Essex* sailors who died on his watch was embodied in his own ritual recognition—equal parts commemoration, confessional, and tribute—atoning "once a year on the anniversary of the loss" of the ship. Until his death, every day on November 20, "he locked himself in his room and fasted."[12]

"THE MOST IMPRESSIVE MAN . . .
I EVER ENCOUNTERED"

Pollard inadvertently attracted attention by hiding from it. Not only did he enjoy a "good name and the esteem of the local citizens," but he also captured the attention of Melville and Emerson. Yet how could Melville have found in this short, fat, jolly old man a source of wisdom and inspiration that would find its way directly onto the pages of his epic poem, *Clarel*, the final major literary work of his career? On July 8, 1852, in one of the most significant encounters of Melville's life, the *Moby-Dick* author "saw Capt. Pollard on the island of Nantucket, and exchanged some words with him." Those words were exchanged in the context of Melville's spiritual and existential crisis, his struggle to come to grips with fate, free will, and the role of divine providence in what appeared to him a godless universe. Pollard's bearing, which reflected the manner in which he lived out his fate, seemed to touch Melville more than any particular words he uttered. In that bearing he found "the most impressive man, tho' wholly unassuming, even humble—that I ever encountered." Melville's reverence expressed here for Pollard can be seen to overturn his less-than-sympathetic reaction, written prior to meeting Pollard in person, summing up the captain's existence after his two wrecks. Under the heading "Sequel" Melville writes that based on secondhand information, "Pollard, it seems, now took the hint, & after reaching home from the second shipwreck, moved to abide ashore. He has ever since lived in Nantucket. Hall told me that he became a butcher there. I believe he is still living."[13] The reference to Pollard's life as a butcher is as inaccurate as it is cruel, and Melville went on to express alarm at the faulty seamanship that led the crew astray from a safe haven in Tahiti, an error, as previously discussed, attributable mainly to Chase's influence. Later annotations reveal an enlightened Melville correcting his identification of Pollard as a butcher with the carefully inscribed words "A Night Watchman," which he triple-underscored and inserted after the phrase "he is still living."[14]

Reflecting his exalted views of Pollard, Melville would later, in his *Clarel* notes, head a page "Eclipse," while setting at the bottom, like the two bases of a triangle, "Noah after the Flood" and "Cap. Pollard. of Nant."[15] This was Pollard in Melville's imagination, a man who had survived the apocalypse, which was also an eclipse in which God appeared to die. Melville's portrayal of Pollard's demeanor would be a stark contrast to Phinney's jovial patriarch. "Never he smiled," writes Melville of Pollard, who heroically rather than ridiculously patrols the streets: "Dire need constrained the man to pace / A night patrolman on the quay / Watching the bales till morning hour / Through fair and foul." No mention is made of his homemade hickory pole. Just as Phinney pictures Pollard devoutly fasting to honor the memories of the *Essex* dead, Melville notes that he "Oft on some secret thing would brood." The key to understanding Melville's fascination lies in Pollard's disposition, which he found "not sour / In spirit, but meek and reconciled; / Patient he was." The early critical failure of *Moby-Dick*, Melville's own shipwreck of sorts, had embittered him to the extent that he would tell Hawthorne en route to the Holy Land that he had decided to be annihilated. Crucially Pollard seemed to bring Melville back to his Calvinist roots: "In Calvin's creed he put his trust; / Praised heaven, and said that God was good, / And his calamity but just."[16]

Pollard, perhaps more humbled than ashamed by the tragedy he experienced, was all the same no timid, risk-averse, God-fearing Starbuck (who happened to be an active Quaker). Also, in contrast to the disconsolate Melville after *Moby-Dick*'s initial reception, Pollard appears to have found peace through an acceptance of his fate. Pollard's sense of spiritual poise in the face of career-ending and reputation-*up*ending chaos appealed to Melville for good reason. Not only had *Moby-Dick* failed to win early public approval, but his following works, *Pierre* and *The Confidence-Man,* functioned something like the *Two Brothers* venture in Pollard's career: both were second chances at redemption that failed in large part due to his own haste and impatience, stabs at the domestic novel and mixed-genre forms that would prove just as reckless as Pollard's chase for his companion vessel in the French Frigate Shoals.[17]

Melville's professional struggles, and his ensuing stare into the cosmic abyss, prompted him to seek insights in the Holy Land. This journey came in the late 1850s, some years after Melville's encounter with Pollard and just around the time when he had abruptly stopped writing novels. It is fitting that, of all his writings, *Clarel,* which tells of a search for spiritual stability in Jerusalem, would be where Melville immortalized Pollard, having briefly mentioned him in conjunction with the *Essex* disaster in *Moby-Dick.*[18] Yet just as he repeatedly alludes in his nautical fiction to the survival impulse—from Queequeg's confrontation of his own mortality and subsequent refusal to die, given his unfinished business ashore to Ishmael's visceral awareness of the sharks that await sailors excessively prone to reverie—Melville would derive from Pollard a new respect for the spiritual anchor of humility demanded of Calvinism. If Pollard could subsist, "He ate what came, though but a crust," with faith in "Calvin's creed," why couldn't Melville do so also?[19] "The Happy Failure," a short story from Melville's magazine fiction of the late 1850s, would testify to his hope that his decision to stop writing novels would engender wisdom rather than the bitterness that would eventually plague him throughout not only his Holy Land trip but also his decades of work as a customs agent.

Despite Melville's turnabout on Pollard, rumors of his working as a butcher persisted well into the twentieth century. The sensational depiction of the captain by a mid-twentieth-century magazine writer, A. B. C. Whipple, for example, casts Pollard's postwhaling life not as a "happy failure" but as that of a cracked madman undone by ridicule from an unforgiving Nantucket culture. In his 1952 *Life* article "Three-Month Ordeal in Open Boats," which he expanded into the book *Yankee Whalers in the South Seas* (1954), Whipple would shape the coming decades' perceptions of the former sea captain and his tragedy. Whipple, who like his nineteenth-century forebears modified the facts of the *Essex* wreck, continued his charade in his 1978 *Vintage Nantucket*, which flouts the historical record to distill and intensify his yarn. The most glaring of these alterations in the 1978 book involved Chase, whose third wife, Eunice Chadwick, had an illegitimate son, Charles Frederick, while Chase was at sea in 1838; Whipple, however, casts this love child as having been born in January 1821, just as the *Eagle* arrived in Nantucket with Chase and three other *Essex* survivors. The obvious intent here was dramatic effect. For the record Chase's first wife, Peggy, had died in 1824, a week after the birth of their third child. Chase's second wife, Nancy Slade Joy, the widow of *Essex* casualty Matthew Joy, died in 1833 while he was on board the *Charles Carroll*. Only one month after his return did he marry Eunice, who charged with the care of four children from her husband's previous wives conceived a child with another man just nine months after Chase had returned to sea on the *Charles Carroll*.[20] Whipple, then, added adultery and potential divorce, with all the pain and humiliation entailed, to the existing irresistible details of the *Essex* tale.

Just as Whipple redrew Chase to compound his tragic circumstances and thus enhance his readers' Schadenfreude, he also sought to transform Pollard into the island's resident lunatic. Pollard, of course, had not been devoured whole by the shame culture of Nantucket, even though this culture was quite real. Whipple had apparently seen none of the subtlety, none of the irony, none of the transformed relationship to God that Melville had so movingly seen. That figure of renewed obedience to God and respect for his fellow man would not emerge until the 1980s with *The Jonah Man*, Henry Carlisle's novelized life of Pollard.

Whipple's largely fabricated tableau of Pollard on patrol as "fire watcher" has him stationed "in his post in a tower high over Nantucket town, like a whaleman on his crosstrees." The garrulous father figure remembered by Phinney is nowhere to be found in Whipple's crude caricature. He muses of Pollard that "it is no wonder that his mind began to slip as old age came on," basing his claims of Pollard's madness on an off-color Nantucket joke reframed as a real conversation. Asked in the joke if the captain knew Owen Coffin, Pollard answers, "Know him? I et him."[21]

Whipple's 1952 *Life* article, betraying a Cold War fear of weak leadership, rendered the *Essex* as a possible allegory for America's worst nightmare of political-economic ruin, eventuating in the consumption of its own for survival. The author impugns Pollard's character by suggesting he knew about Pitcairn Island, at the southwestern edge of the Marquesas, and thus was guilty of egregious neglect in not insisting his crew sail for it rather than the South America coast. The fabrication thus pinned on Pollard what should have been understood as Chase's error in insisting the crew sail for the South American coast, a fear-based solution that prevented the sailors from charting toward islands they knew were overflowing with fruit, fish, fowl, and freshwater, precisely the sustenance they so badly needed. The unknown entity was the inhabitants, but a more skilled leader would have accepted this risk. Perhaps most unfair is the *Life* article's conclusion that Pollard had drifted irretrievably into madness, when this was precisely the fate that had befallen Chase.[22] Alongside its distortions, this widely circulated *Life* story failed to extend true knowledge of the Essex details beyond academicians and Nantucket antiquarians and to the broader American reading public.

Whipple even invents scenes to portray Melville as discovering in Pollard the source of Captain Ahab, a long-buried innuendo until its reappearance online following the discovery of the *Two Brothers* (discussed in the next chapter). Emerging from the swirling fog, Pollard comes as a revelation to Melville in Whipple's stagy scene: "'Who,' said the creator of Captain Ahab, 'is that man? I have never seen such a tragic face in all my life.'" To which his interlocutor replies, "'That's George Pollard. He was the captain of the *Essex*.'"[23] As we will see in the discussion of Carlisle's book, fictionalizing the *Essex* story can add to its imaginative richness. But to pass off in a mass-market magazine a fabricated version of the tale rewrites history and harms the memory of the real lives associated with the tragedy.

A TALE OF TWO CANNIBALS

Fasting was included in Pollard's annual ritual because cannibalism was the worst of the horrors attending the *Essex* ordeal. This step once again demonstrated the former captain's humility and deep remorse, as well as his active desire for spiritual and psychological recovery. Just as being a night watchman showed he did not fear the dark, his refusal to eat indicated he was willing to look directly into his agonizing past. He could then revisit the instances that might otherwise have driven him insane, from the arranging of the lottery, to the killing of the shipmates, to the stripping of flesh from bone for consumption. Worth mentioning is that the mixed results of exposure therapy for PTSD victims hold that revisiting such moments can worsen the experience for some.[24] But Pollard seems to have benefited from revisiting the trauma. If survival depended on community for both the process of selection and the meat to be eaten, Pollard effectively inverted both features in his ritual by isolating himself socially and refusing to eat. To fast for a day is to starve under controlled circumstances, to meet the far edge of the sort of desperation that would drive one to cannibalism. This ritual, likely a reflexive decision by Pollard, may well have aided in his self-recovery. Perhaps even more resoundingly, it could not have better illustrated the sanity and fortitude with which he lived his life on Nantucket after his whaling career.[25]

Whereas Pollard fasted and faced the past, first mate Chase, who had been largely responsible for the crew's three-month battle with starvation, never paused to formally recognize the calamity with which he had been involved. Indeed, his frenetic life at sea after the wreck consisted of earning record profits on multiple voyages strung together up until his retirement on Nantucket. He could not discuss the *Essex* event without breaking down. Upon his death food stores were discovered squirreled away in the far corners of his Nantucket home. Chase's psychological compensation for the trauma was glaringly obvious in his hoarding, no doubt meant to ensure such a desperate course would never have to be taken again.[26] This hoarding was easy enough to contrast with Pollard's annual denial of nutrition, and his corresponding willingness to confront unbearable realities.

A closer look at Chase's psychological decline points, among other things, to the impressive nobility of his counterpart Pollard's course. In 1868 Chase's cousin Phoebe B. Chase laid bare in a letter to the sailor's former sister-in-law Winnifred Battie what those who knew him had already concluded. "Owen is insane," she wrote of the seventy-two-year-old former seafarer, and "(will eventually be carried to the insane hospital)." He "sobbed and called me cousin Susan (taking me for sister Worth) held my hand and sobbed like a child, saying *O my head, my head.*" She winced at how "pitiful" it was "to see the strong man bowed, then his personal appearance so changed, didn't allow himself decent clothing, fear's [*sic*] he shall come to want."[27] The great whaleman with unmatched earnings had thus been reduced to clutching his throbbing head and irrationally fearing financial ruin to the point that he insisted on cloaking himself in a vagabond's garb. He would eventually be moved to a mental institution and considered untreatable.

We thus see in Chase's decline both his relationship to capital and, in his insanity, the classic marks of unresolved guilt. As this book has explored, Chase—and not Pollard—held the larger share of responsibility for the *Essex*'s downfall. While Pollard was at least somewhat responsible for the unsuccessful outcome of the *Two Brothers*, his conscience was comparatively clean. Even in the case of the *Essex*, he knew the crew needed to partake of human flesh to survive, and that had the sailors followed his counsel, they might have avoided the cannibalism fiasco to begin with. Thus Pollard, rather than Chase, matches the portrait of the healthy return to daily life John Leach and Jo Campling describe in their discussion of recovery and post-trauma in *Survival Psychology*. If the circumstances warrant it, and the contingency suggests no recourse but death, then cannibalism survivors are likely to face a decent prognosis, full recovery, and surprisingly integrated and well-adjusted lives in their communities.[28] This portrait describes Pollard exactly. Most Nantucketers knew that need was real, and understood cannibalism as a long-running liability for the whaling industry. For Chase's part, no record exists of him suffering any social ridicule for his cannibalism, but he seems to have imposed suffering on himself, seemingly for distancing himself from having caused the tragedy and maintaining that distance over his career. Then, once the flight inevitably came to rest in old age, his demons caught up with him.[29]

As our discussion has shown, Chase's 1821 account of the *Essex*'s last voyage was not "the plain and faithful narrative" Melville, and many others for that matter, took it to be. The former first mate had written misleadingly, and most of Nantucket had believed him. Pollard, although living out his life modestly, was for the most part supported by his home island, as evidenced by the sacredness associated with the *Two Brothers*—from the time it bore him back to Nantucket after his rescue off South America to his days as the island's night watchman. Pollard, who never sought to defend himself by publishing his own narrative version of events, carried the tragedy deep within him. The island's tendency to look out for its captain is displayed in an 1879 Nantucket *Inquirer and Mirror* story recalling the momentous "Sunday, August 5th, 1821, the day the ship *Two Brothers* was announced in sight from the watch tower, for she had Capt. Pollard as a passenger." Pollard had become a standard-bearer for "these afflicted men of the sea, suffering . . . as none had in any of our long career of whaling life."[30] The community had not, by and large, blamed Pollard for bringing his dual failures upon himself. In a sense the entire community took some responsibility for his second voyage by choosing the *Two Brothers* as the vessel, virtually sailing along with him onto the open sea. Indeed, Pollard was no Ahab flying his own flag but instead represented all afflicted seafarers, as well as representing his home island. He was deemed useful and even celebrated rather than being torn down as a failure.

The *Essex* crew may have had the dubious distinction of suffering more than any other in Nantucket's lengthy whaling history, but its association with cannibalism was nothing new in the world of seafaring. When the French frigate *Medusa* sank in 1816 off the west coast of Africa, the story spread across the globe of the craft's destruction, which left 150 people clinging to an intact portion of the hull. As many began to die of a combination of starvation and injury, others fought over who would be consumed to save the rest. No civil and just procedure such as a lottery was carried out during these desperate circumstances. Instead, order broke down and fighting soon escalated to murder, as the crewmen began clawing at each other's flesh. Nantucketers would have known of this infamous instance according to the testimony of the emaciated group of fifteen who were eventually rescued after surviving on the bodies of the thirty-five who had perished.[31]

Although none of the *Medusa* survivors were tried or convicted of murder, trials under similar circumstances were certainly held in later decades. In 1884, for example, the killing of shipmates to stave off death by starvation was pronounced an act of murder in a court ruling brought by the English crown against survivors of the wreck of the *Mignonette*, a thirty-two-foot English yacht. Whereas the defense of Captain Tom Dudley argued that under extreme circumstances laws of the land can be broken, the prosecution ultimately prevailed on the contention that "a man who, in order to escape death from hunger, kills another for the purpose of eating his flesh, is guilty of murder although at the time of the act he is in such circumstances that he believes, and has reasonable grounds for believing, that it affords him the only chance for saving his life."[32] The less-than-coherent verdict here flatly contradicts itself with a qualification that proves far more convincing than its rigid adherence to the "law of the land." Ironically Nantucket's shame culture cast a more fair and just verdict on Pollard than this court would have. Had that *Mignonette* ruling been made prior to the *Essex* disaster, we may not have seen such a humble yet remarkably stable Pollard in his retirement. Cannibalism at sea would become a subject of civil litigation only near the time of Pollard's death, thus allowing the former captain a far more comfortable existence in a culture far less inclined to file lawsuits and press charges in such cases.

Nantucket's inclination was to protect its seamen rather than prosecute them. The island thus leaned toward lifesaving and the defense of navigators in peril. Edouard Stackpole notes that as early as 1803 "Nantucket had petitioned Congress for the development of a harbor of refuge" to serve as a lifesaving station to aid the innumerable vessels that foundered in the shoals and capsized on the infamous sandbar off the island's shore.[33] The *Whalemen's Shipping List*, a journal that began as a commercial ledger for captains, owners, and loved ones of those at sea, was crowded with advertisements for marine insurance. When it ran articles, many of which involved Nantucket vessels and sailors, they were almost invariably defenses of navigators, reading like claims written to appease insurance adjusters by arguing that the whalemen bore no fault in the frequent cases in which not only vessels but also multiple barrels of precious and hard-won whale oil were lost at sea. Nautical liability was entirely the focus, for example, of a March 25, 1845, report in the *Shipping List* of "the loss of the ship *Holder Borden*." In language designed to release liability and return a handsome settlement to all investors, thus buffeting the industry's financiers, the piece describes how "the ship struck on a shoal and *stuck*," an emergency to which the crew promptly responded. Its members duly "hauled all the sails aback and used every exertion to get her off. . . . We tried every means that lay within our power to get her afloat," the report assures readers, but to no avail. These lines appeared directly next to a series of large advertisements headed "Mutual Marine Insurance" and offering coverage ranging from $15 to $500,000. Prompting the insurance company to prepare its payment, a May 6, 1845, report explicitly highlights that despite the loss of the *Hamilton* of Sag Harbor forty miles north of Rio Grande, Argentina, including "4,500 bbls [barrels] of oil lost," "there is insurance on the *Hamilton* in New York for twelve thousand dollars on vessel and eighteen thousand on cargo, which but partly covers the cost." Other reports point to faulty charts or nautical equipment to preempt any suspicion of faulty seamanship. The headline "Important to Navigators" warns that the *English Nautical Almanac* "has an important error . . . the equation of time is directed therein to be *added* while it should be *subtracted*." But the very name of the Booby Shoals off Sydney and what was then New South Wales would indicate that captains could also be made fools of in areas known to be treacherous. All the same, *Shipping List* reporters strenuously advocated for their men at sea, contending that the captain and crew of the *Thule* in June 1845 "struck on the shoal NOT laid down on the chart" but nonetheless in the proximity of Booby Shoals.[34]

Had he lived in the later culture, more apt to indict navigators like Captain Dudley rather than defend and insure them as the *Shipping List* had, Chase rather than Pollard would have had far more to fear. Even in the Nantucket shame culture, which threatened real social and economic marginalization for sins committed and taboo behaviors, Chase stood to lose much more than Pollard, especially considering that he returned to Nantucket flush with profits from his string of successful whaling voyages. Chase's paranoid fears of losing these assets, "fears he shall come to want," as his cousin wrote, were likely rooted in his sense of vulnerability to the community's condemnation, if not a formal court's sentencing.[35] Aware that "civil authorities frown on the unnecessary practicing of cannibalism," he must have sensed that any inkling of a possible alternative to this outcome for the *Essex* would have stirred reproof.[36] Thus the practice of consuming human flesh under threat of starvation, whatever the baseline cause, may have been associated with the eccentric and sociopathic profile of intentional cannibalism.

Pollard was a survivor in a radically different way than Chase. The captain may have considered suicide as the *Two Brothers* was sinking, but it was not out of remorse for dispatching and consuming his cousin on his previous voyage. The depth of his melancholy instead came from his sense that "the gods shipwrecked him again upon unknown rocks and breakers," as Melville wrote in *Moby-Dick*.[37] This, more than the prospect of cannibalism, threatened to undo Pollard. All *Essex* survivors thrived to some extent, while Chase, who had committed the critical error, suffered the most psychologically in the long run. Interestingly, as implied earlier, people who engage in cannibalism and survive tend to lead happy and healthy lives thereafter. "Becoming a productive member of a community," such as Nantucket in Pollard's case, "raising successful children, and enjoying prosperity are more common endnotes to the lives of involuntary cannibals than suicidal depression and drug use."[38] The key term here is *involuntary*. Pollard could easily and truthfully categorize himself that way, while Chase vigorously argued for that status against his own negligence. But he knew his insistence to sail for South America was indeed emphatically voluntary, an act of domineering will over that of his captain, whose will is universally recognized as preeminent according to all written and unwritten codes of the sea. No ship is a true democracy, but Chase was a captain before he held the official title—not only would his first pivotal decision prove to be the worst and most fatal before decades as a whaling commander; it also led to America's most visible and storied shipwreck of the century.

JONAH MAN

For the first fifty years of settlement of Nantucket, there was no formal religion. Then in 1708, after a series of Quaker missionaries had proselytized on the island, one in particular struck island resident Mary Coffin

Starbuck as profoundly inspirational. She used her considerable influence to found the Monthly Meeting of Friends in her home, which later spread and attracted a wide following. It took little time before Starbuck had effectively transformed the community from a nondenominational eclectic mix of believers seeking asylum from Puritan tyranny to one dominated by the Quaker principles of pacifism, personal liberty, temperance, and hard work, foundational values that would prove deeply consonant with what would soon become global deep-sea whaling. Following the island's humble origins in subsistence farming and shore whaling, both of which were taught to Nantucketers by the island's exceedingly cooperative Native Americans, came the 1712 discovery of sperm whales by Christopher Hussey. The cache of valuable oil, which offered better material for making candles and better, clean-burning fuel to light lamps, was far greater in sperm whales than in the previously hunted right whales. Nantucketers now had a burgeoning economy supported by its new Quaker ethic, which among other things distinguished them from mainland Puritans. Remaining neutral during the Revolutionary War, Nantucket defended this position by citing Quaker pacifism. But Nantucketers profited by lifting British blockades of food and building material shipments essential for their survival.[39] The following years would see Nantucket's small, Quaker-inspired community drive the U.S. entry into global trade.

Pacifism, as Melville sardonically points out in *Moby-Dick*, never prevented Nantucket Quakers such as the *Pequod* owners, Peleg and Bildad, from admiring the heathen Queequeg once they glimpsed his hunting skill. These were thus Quakers with a desire for vengeance for Melville, who astutely exposed a far deeper conviction in the profit motive than in pacifism. After the War of 1812, Nantucket had fallen on hard times mainly because the island's neutrality left its whaleships vulnerable to being stolen or destroyed by either side. At the war's end, however, in the years leading up to Pollard's voyages, the world's richest whale-hunting grounds were discovered in the deep Pacific waters south of Japan—whose isolationist government prevented all citizens, including shore-bound whalers and fishermen, from leaving the nation and summarily executed all those who did so upon their arrival on shore. With the golden age of whaling now reaching its zenith, wealth poured into tiny Nantucket, effectively transforming the modest shacks on Main Street into mansions.

Pollard's modest home stood out among those of his wealthy neighbors. At the corner of Center and Broad Streets, near a series of businesses run by enterprising Nantucket women, a district that became known as Petticoat Row, stands Pollard's home. Holding a prominent spot in town, it is now occupied by an art dealer, with only a small plaque indicating that the *Essex* captain who influenced Melville's *Moby-Dick* had lived there. Like Jonah in Nineveh preaching the gospel of moderation and humility during an era of lavish wealth, Pollard came to embody such a cautionary ethos. His conspicuous presence in the heart of town counterbalanced the surging affluence and vanity of the shipowners who had now made their fortunes. Pollard in essence reminded all that he had been swallowed by the whale, been vomited on shore, and emerged not an impetuous, reluctant follower of God's command but a willing servant to divine will. "A Jonah is he?" Melville would later ask rhetorically in *Clarel*. Responsive to the community's needs, prepared to shoulder the burden of his past trauma with dignity, Pollard like Jonah faced up to his neighbors. "Call him, and he would come," Melville writes, reinforcing the notion of Pollard as a living embodiment of Jonah.[40]

In Carlisle's novelized life of Pollard, the former captain holds his head high upon his return to Nantucket after the *Two Brothers* wreck: "Down new Dollar Lane and onto Main I drove, standing up, Nantucket-style, sennit hat back on my head, nodding greetings to passersby, draymen, wagoners, shopkeepers." The portrait renders an unashamed Pollard, "letting one and all know that if the sea had played a few tricks on me it had not gotten to my pride, that I was home to stay and with no apologies to anyone." Jonah, according to Father Mapple in *Moby-Dick*, bears his message of humility before God without a sense of having done wrong himself, considering that he has more than done his penance by facing mortality in the belly of the whale. Like Jonah, Pollard would lead not the life of a guilty man but one redeemed from his shortcomings. Carlisle astutely depicts Pollard wrestling with his ambiguous status, wondering if "I [will] live the rest of my days as an outcast on this Island, deprived of peace, ordinary dealings, friendship, love, faith."[41] But as the evidence from his long life attests, this was hardly the real Pollard's fate—nor was it the fate of Carlisle's fictional version.

In Carlisle's text, assuming the role of night watchman, demeaning though it may appear for a former ship captain, was hardly that, nor was it an act of financial desperation to stave off becoming the town beggar. "Rather, it was my pride asserting itself in earnest," as Carlisle's Pollard writes in his journal. Indeed, he would not promote himself, nor campaign on behalf of his reputation, mainly because, unlike Chase, he had nothing to hide. Pollard was confirming that he "had no need to worm respect from a community that dared not stand in judgment of me." His resolve, in *The Jonah Man*, to "walk their streets at night with an appearance of humbleness such as has never been seen on this Island" paradoxically casts him as having more power and influence in the context of the mansions, expanding commercial district, and overall wealth permeating Main Street.[42] More than any other era in Nantucket's long history, the early 1820s proved the ideal setting for this Jonah man to roam its streets and make himself not only tolerated but appreciated and even loved by the community. As his obituary in the Nantucket *Inquirer and Mirror* would recount, "He was still a young man when he retired from the sea and closed the strange, eventful part of his life." This memorial bore no judgment or slight to Pollard's dignity in this highly self-conscious community. As Emerson had noted, anything to damage Nantucket's reputation threatened to damage the island's rising stake in global trade. But Pollard had literally worked himself back into the community to earn its love: "For more than forty years he has resided permanently among us; and now leaves the record of a good and worthy man as his legacy to us who remain."[43]

In 1835, more than a decade after Pollard's service on Nantucket's night patrol began, Obed Macy, the island's earliest historian, duly recorded what had become apparent to all residents. By contrast, Macy makes no mention of Chase in his telling of the *Essex* story, and 72 Orange Street, where Chase lived, is today in a state of striking disrepair. On an otherwise opulent street, in a famously genteel town, the home is stripped of shingles and the yard is jammed with rusting junk seemingly accumulated over decades. As if this superficial appearance weren't unsettling enough, whispers of drug dealing in and near the old Chase home abound, along with innuendo regarding psychosis in the family. As of this writing, few have come to the defense of the first mate's memory. No commemorative plaque can be found at 72 Orange Street, with the island's shame culture apparently having issued its verdict on who was responsible for the loss of the *Essex*.

Pollard's decision to stop sailing was more than an act of self-exile by which he might gain wisdom through resignation. He sailed again on a merchant ship but knew the pursuit of whales was in his Nantucket blood. If he were to do any work bearing meaning and significance, it would be on Nantucket, the island of his ancestors, and involve the most estimable of all functions of ship captains—ensuring the safety of his crew, now figured as the people of Nantucket. He would be their protector and night watchman, their captain to sail them through their darkest hours.

Chapter 6

〜〜〜〜〜〜〜〜〜〜〜〜〜〜〜〜〜〜〜〜〜〜〜〜

THE REAL AHAB

Despite all the evidence showing George Pollard Jr.'s peaceful postwhaling existence on Nantucket as a contrast to Owen Chase's zealous return to sea after the *Essex* tragedy, the February 2011 blogosphere proclaimed Pollard the "real" Captain Ahab and his ship the authentic counterpart to the *Pequod* upon reports that the *Two Brothers* had been discovered.[1] This Internet mash-up took itself and its claims to historical accuracy quite seriously, an outgrowth of what the *Guardian* has called "open journalism," in which average citizens use new media to communicate relevant data to flesh out stories written by staff writers.[2] Often, however, these online voices are wrong and can perpetuate false conclusions based more on conjecture than substantiated fact.

The online rush to link Pollard with Ahab reflected a desire to use empirical evidence in the form of a sunken ship to finally pin down a cagey author like Melville.[3] These "aca-fans," as media scholar Henry Jenkins has characterized them, seemingly yearned to identify Ahab's historical antecedent, but they fell short in part because of a lack of contemporary publicity about Chase, Pollard's real foil and a significant cause for his demise as a sea captain.[4] Chase not only prompted the crew to take an impracticable route to safety—he also later singularly pursued the hunt for Old Tom in hopes of psychologically destroying the whale that would haunt him into old age—a whale he and his mates had been unable to destroy amid the South Pacific on November 20, 1820.

Just as the mythic whale took on a monstrous presence in contemporary culture, it seems to have swelled in Chase's psyche. Like that of Chase, Ahab's drive—he does not stop his pursuit of the whale despite

Starbuck alerting him to new leaks discovered in the casks—stems not simply from the loss of a ship but specifically from a personal confrontation with a whale. Unlike Pollard, Chase was on the ship at the moment of the whale's collision and made tactical maneuvers to avert the blow. That the whale bested him, and that the eventual consequences would be so gruesome, weighed upon his conscience while simultaneously driving him furiously back to sea. So just as Ahab is comparatively accountable for the sinking of the *Pequod*, Chase at least shared responsibility with the whale for the sinking of the *Essex*.

CHASE'S WHALE

If Chase had been captain of the *Essex*, and if its sunken remains were discovered as were those of the *Two Brothers*, online commentators would have immediately seen the correspondence and adopted him instead of Pollard as the real Ahab. An alternative scenario played out, however, whereby online news media from bloggers to the BBC seemed to "remix" Ahab into Pollard, not regardless of their dissimilarities but paradoxically because of them.[5] Digital culture is rife with participation in the writing of that composite biography of the "real Ahab," affirming Henry Jenkins's postulation that "nothing motivates readers like the prospect of becoming the author or performer of your own new text."[6] Web commentators here invented an Ahab that did not exist. Pollard's online presence thus transformed Ahab into a sympathetic figure by muting the villainous characterizations and "remixing in" his humanity as reflected in his repeated failures.

Among other reasons, Pollard is unlike Ahab in that he acquiesces twice to the will of the majority, first to take the long voyage home and then to cast lots. The first decision, of course, precipitated the second. This chapter, however, concerns itself with revisiting Chase's moment with the whale, and how it would forever shape his future, the lasting memory of the *Essex* disaster, and shipwreck narratives thereafter. As previous chapters have shown, Pollard's disposition was never Ahabian in the slightest. He never coerced or cajoled his crew into following his lead; his leadership was instead modest, understated, and hardworking, an approach aimed at rallying his crew by example. Never did he attempt to seduce, deceive, or otherwise persuade the crew to his will as Ahab does in the "Surmises" chapter of *Moby-Dick*. It is perhaps true that Pollard's democratic tendencies were inadequate for managing his first mate's errant impulses. Pollard, then, might be more accurately compared to Starbuck in *Moby-Dick*, given his failure to successfully challenge Chase's deadly directive to sail for South America. Reminiscent of the *Essex* captain, Starbuck quails at his only opportunity to save the *Pequod* crew from being sacrificed at the hands of Ahab's suicidal mission.

In once again comparing Chase to Ahab, one notes that Melville, fascinatingly, has imposed the sin of inaction on Starbuck in "The Musket" chapter, dramatizing his inner monologue as he steals into the captain's cabin with his loaded weapon and an opportunity to save his own life along with everyone else's in one shot. But he does not shoot. Likewise, Chase's failure to act accounts for the first of his two errors that would lead to tragedy. Namely Chase, and not Pollard, was on the ship as the whale approached and might have saved it from sinking with a kill. In Nickerson's account, Chase's indecision is explicit. In his own account, it is avoided.

Nickerson was the first to see the whale approach and, according to his own account, "called out to the mate [Chase] to inform him of it." Then "on seeing the whale" Chase "instantly gave me an order to put the helm hard up, and steer down towards the boats." This evasion maneuver is unassailable, a tactic that indeed shows good seamanship under the circumstances, given that there was no time to throw a harpoon at the creature to divert its trajectory. But after this incident Chase had *ample* time to arm himself and prepare to throw the harpoon at the startled whale, which was "then setting under the ship's bottom." Chase had accordingly made the appropriate preparations to subdue the animal, which suddenly "came up on the starboard side and directly under the starboard quarter." Now ideally positioned to dispatch the whale and save the crew from another blow, Chase stood at the rail, his harpoon raised above his shoulder and his eye fixed on the approaching gray mass: "This last position gave the mate a fine opportunity to have killed him with a throw of his lance." But in weighing the risks of damage to the boat during the creature's death frenzy, he balked. As Nickerson reports, "His first impulse" was to hurl his weapon, "but on a second look observing his tail directly beneath the rudder his better judgment prevailed lest a flourish of the tail should unhang the rudder and render the ship unmanageable." Herein lies Chase's first crucial mistake. Nickerson puts the dilemma into a perspective with which no one would likely be more intimate than Chase himself: "But could he have foreseen all that so soon followed he would probably have chosen the lesser evil and have saved the ship by killing the whale even at the expense of losing the rudder."[7]

This was clearly Chase's whale to kill, not Pollard's. Out of sight of the main ship, Pollard was on a chase boat hunting other whales when the collision occurred. This situation itself carried some controversy. At the time some whaleship captains and owners condemned the practice of leaving the main ship in order to lead whale chases. In the case of the Essex, this meant Chase was effectively left behind to serve as captain, although lacking the qualifications or title. So Pollard might have been charged with putting the entire enterprise at unneeded risk by venturing out. But the other side of the story was that Pollard relished working alongside sailors rather than lording his power over them by remaining detached and invisible in his cabin. Thus only under extreme circumstances of illness or injury would Pollard eschew traveling out with his fellow mates in a chase boat to hunt whales. This explains why the first mate found himself charged with such monumental decisions as the whale neared.

The myriad claims adjusters whose ads crowded the *Whalemen's Shipping List* would certainly have been interested in such a detail. Pollard's absence may indeed have raised skepticism regarding the crew's fitness to respond to an enraged whale. But somewhat ironically, Chase's *Narrative* effectively exonerates Pollard on this count by placing hyperbolic emphasis on the whale's cunning and savagery, on a creature supposedly undefeatable by even the most able seaman, whether mate or captain. This assessment also placed the legal onus on a force of nature well beyond mortal control. In reality, though, as Nickerson's then unpublished account shows, the first mate was clearly in a position to save the crew but failed to deliver. Chase's focus on the rudder when faced with an attacking whale was unconscionable. Yet even as Nickerson's testimony is damning to Chase, the former cabin boy evinces no perceivable ill will toward the first mate, instead suggesting Chase would have thrown the lance had he known the full consequences of holding on to it. All the same, Nickerson's apparent compassion for Chase does not mitigate the scale of the first mate's error thus exposed.

The other eyewitness account of the incident was penned by second mate Thomas Chappel in an 1824 Religious Tract Society pamphlet; Chappel had accompanied Pollard in the chase boats to hunt whales. Chappel, for his part, nowhere mentions that Chase had been left in command of the ship, an omission that leaves readers sensing a rather helpless and faceless collective identity in "the crew." With no reference to human agency, Chappel instead focuses on the whale as it darts, then returns to strike the craft. Only when it is clear that the boat will sink does he recall how "the crew exerted themselves to the utmost" to cut away the masts so that "the ship righted, but she was a mere wreck & entirely unmanageable; the quantity of oil on board alone kept her from foundering."[8] Given that Chappel was then away from the boat, this account was likely derived from the remaining crew members' oral reports. Had Nickerson reported to Chappel on Chase's response to the incident, which he apparently did not, the second mate almost certainly would have entered it in his account. Meanwhile Chappel's elision of Chase's command speaks to the expectation that the first mate was no match for such an emergency.

On June 12, 1821, the *Boston Daily Advertiser* reported that "Yesterday, ships *Hysco*, and *Eagle*, arrived from the Pacific Ocean with sperm oil. In the latter came Owen Chase, mate, Benjamin Lawrence, Thomas Nickerson, and Charles Ramsdell, seamen, late of the *Essex*, of this port." The news story noted, "Capt. Pollard was left ill at Valparaiso, not having recovered from his severe sufferings."[9] Pollard's absence from this convoy would suggest erroneously to many that the captain was the weaker sailor and had suffered more on his voyage in the open boats. In truth, the location of the respective open boats reveals Pollard to have been a more competent navigator than Chase. According to Edouard Stackpole's history of the event, Pollard's boat was "within a few miles off the island of St. Mary's near the coast of Chile" when it was sighted by rescuers.[10] Chase and his two companions, by comparison, were still far off at sea when spotted by the brig *Indian*, up to fifty miles away from the nearest land, Masafuera Island. Chase's competence, especially under intense pressure, clearly lagged behind Pollard's just as the effects of acute starvation set in for the first mate's emaciated crew.

Writing in 1835, the fair-minded Obed Macy also paints an unflattering portrait of Chase's encounter with the whale. In his account he focuses directly on human agency, and in particular on Chase's misapprehension of the situation's risks, making explicit that the whale that sank the *Essex* was the first mate's responsibility. While "the captain and second mate were left with their boats pursuing the whales," Macy writes, Chase "discovered a large sperm whale near the ship, but, not suspecting the approach of any danger," and thus fatally underestimating the urgency of the situation, it gave him and the crew "no alarm, until they saw the whale coming with full speed toward them." Thus taken by surprise, "they were astonished by a tremendous crash," shocked not by the impact itself so much as by the fact that it had been caused by the whale, visible to all, that moments earlier had been swimming toward the ship.[11] Macy does not clearly evoke Chase with harpoon raised and paralyzed with indecision as Nickerson does, but he certainly reveals that the whale had been sighted in advance of the collision, implying that Chase had the opportunity to take evasive or defensive action but declined to do so.

In Henry Carlisle's *Jonah Man*, discussed at some length in chapter 5, the author bases his portrayal of Chase's hesitancy on meticulous research into the various accounts, particularly Nickerson's. At one point in Carlisle's rendition, Chase yells to the youngest member of the *Essex*, "Put her hard up!"[12] This line is a dramatization of Nickerson's written account that reads, "On seeing the whale he instantly gave me an order to put the helm hard up, and steer down towards the boats." Clearly reflecting Nickerson's account of Chase's decision-making lapse, Chase is portrayed as eyeing "the whale a hundred yards from the ship, his head toward her." Nickerson's own sense of urgency—he calls out, "Sperm whale off the weather bow!"—sharply contrasts with Chase's restraint, his delay only allowing the whale more time to build its momentum toward the ship.

"As the mate watched—hesitating whether to lower his partially repaired boat in pursuit of the creature—the whale spouted." Instead of depicting him standing frozen at the rail with harpoon in hand, as in Nickerson's account, Carlisle protects Chase by having him rightfully question the prudence of launching his leaky and haphazardly patched chase boat. Nevertheless, Carlisle captures Chase's failure to respond by highlighting the causal connection between his hesitation and the escalating danger in their midst. In that moment of delay, the whale "then sank from sight and seconds later broke the water a ship's length away, headed directly for the vessel at a rate of about three knots, the ship then making about the same speed."[13]

After this first strike, and forewarned of the liability for such a collision, one might have expected Chase to take better measures to avoid the second. Here Carlisle has Chase pathetically calling "Hard up!" yet again, this time after spotting the whale *beginning* its advance toward the ship a mile off. Benjamin Lawrence now calls out, "'Here he comes! He's making for us again!'" The narrator continues, "Chase turned to see the whale, about a mile distant almost directly ahead, bearing down on the ship at great speed and with what seemed to the mate, in his words, 'tenfold fury and vengeance in his aspect.'"[14] With a mile of distance to maneuver the ship out of the whale's path, Chase again displays questionable navigational prowess, as portrayed in the novel. It would seem reasonable that a first mate could order the ship to alter course, come about, or even reverse ground entirely in the time it would take a whale traveling at six knots (6.9 miles per hour) from a mile away.[15] The whale would have taken exactly eight minutes and forty-two seconds swimming at that speed to reach the boat, hardly a split second but rather ample time for Chase to have averted the disaster, even according to Carlisle's charitable reconfiguration of events.

Since Carlisle adopts Nickerson's testimony that Chase clearly had ample time to react, it is worth examining Chase's skill in judging distances and trajectories at sea. Considering there was time to avoid one or both of the collisions by altering the ship's course, Chase was clearly not seasoned enough in handling a large vessel like the *Essex*, let alone the small chase boat he commanded en route to Chile. Further inquiry is thus warranted for Stackpole's illuminating suggestion that the separate courses of Pollard's and Chase's boats reveal insights into their respective navigational skills. Specifically Chase's decision to tack north on January 26, 1821, was suspect. After tacking southeast, for exactly one month in an open boat, from Henderson Island into a stubborn trade wind, Chase altered course, opting for a more direct line toward shore at the cost of considerably slower progress. To his good fortune, this decision brought him to an area of high sea traffic to and from Chilean ports, a turn that would eventuate in his boat's rescue. By comparison Pollard began his north-by-northeast tack later, on February 11, and thus made more expeditious progress toward the coast.[16] It was to his great misfortune that he had headed due south of the major ship route and thus missed the opportunity to be rescued at sea the way Chase had. As for Chase, were it not for the ship that rescued him so far out at sea, his time to shore might have been too slow to survive. Chase was also the most anxious of the three open-boat leaders, as expressed in his *Narrative* (the third being Obed Hendricks), about staying together with the other two boats, reflecting his recognition that he was the weakest navigator of the three. Indeed, the struggle to keep the three boats from separating hampered the crew's progress. Chase's sense of his navigational shortcomings proved to be justified when, on January 12, 1821, his was the first boat to lose contact with the other two, and he and his mates suffered the rest of the voyage in complete isolation until February 18. Of course all three boats, including Chase's, faced extremely difficult weather, wind, and high seas. Yet although Chase made his best effort to remain with the other boats, his competence at sea was not up to the task.

Thus, filling out the portrait of Chase's questionable leadership are his refusal to throw the harpoon and his failure to remain with the other two boats, along with his earlier-discussed dispute with Pollard over the direction in which to sail after the wreck. From these actions came a tragedy of starvation, cannibalism, and months at sea in open boats. For Chase the lifetime effect of these actions was the forging of an iron will aimed at mastering the sea and wreaking vengeance on every whale he would ever encounter. Guilt tinged with humiliation no doubt fueled his furious quest for retribution and compensatory triumph, resulting in his record-breaking whaling hauls. These hauls allowed him to reverse the sins of his past in the most measurable way available. Like Heathcliff of Emily Brontë's *Wuthering Heights*, a novel penned during the mid-1840s, Chase would remake himself into a captain-and-businessman riveted to his profit-driven agenda, all according to and condoned by the rules of free-market capitalism, which offered a socially acceptable channel for his vengeance. So was *this* Ahab?

"STRONGLY ERRING"

In his biographical study of Chase, Thomas Heffernan posits a direct relationship in Melville's epic poem, *Clarel*, between the captain as Pollard and his mate as Chase. But on a closer look Melville seems to have forged his characters differently and in such a way that sheds new light on Chase's kinship to Ahab. Although Captain Nehemiah's downfall echoes Pollard's in the *Essex* disaster, the captain in *Clarel* is more Ahab than Pollard. Indeed, instead of intending *Clarel* as a vehicle to retell the *Essex* story, Melville meant the poem to be an imaginative blending, an act of creative alchemy.[17] With respect to details, a "hidden rock" and not a whale sinks the boat in *Clarel*, a clear enough allusion to the wreck of the *Two Brothers*. But the fear of uncharted waters and desire to travel for a previously visited port clearly suggest Chase, who shared Nehemiah's aversion to "those waters then obscure; a maze." Thus: "The isles were dreaded—every chain" by Melville's fictional captain, suggesting Chase's fear of the Marquesas. Melville emphasizes the weight of the following miscalculation by Chase: "Better to brave the immense of sea, / And venture for the Spanish Main, / Beating and rowing against the tides" . . . "Than float to valleys 'neath the lee, / Nor far removed, and palmy shades." The grave effects that would follow Chase's flawed reasoning here, including a gross underestimation of the sea and its vicissitudes to which he exposed the crew, register in Melville's final judgment of Chase's decision: "So deemed he, strongly erring there."[18]

Melville's Captain Nehemiah is willful here, hardly the victim of fate whom "the gods shipwrecked," as Pollard is represented in "The Affidavit" chapter in *Moby-Dick*.[19] Instead, Nehemiah carries out a near replica of Chase's ill-considered decision to master the ocean (this time the Atlantic), seeking to outdo tide and relentless trade winds. Chase's seamanship correlates with an Ahabian refusal to act by the consensus to which Pollard had been so deeply committed—but that ultimately, as discussed, proved to be a weakness. The strong-willed Chase even seizes on Pollard's agreeable demeanor by making the captain appear to have supported his decision to sail for the mainland, when in fact he had only acquiesced to the crew's consensus: "It was also the captain's opinion, that this was the season of hurricanes which prevail in the vicinity of the Sandwich Islands; and that consequently it would be unsafe to steer for them."[20] Melville himself does not miss this tactic, and places the blame where it belongs, squarely on Nehemiah.

Chase's and Pollard's respective next voyages following the *Essex* tragedy also suggest strong ties between Chase and Ahab. Pollard took his next command not out of brazen, isolated ambition but upon the urging of two *Essex* shipmates, Ramsdell and Nickerson, along with effectively the entire island of Nantucket, which bore a huge influence on such matters. Pollard sailed out of Nantucket on his voyage, whereas Chase sailed from the rival upstart whaling hub of New Bedford. It was both an ideal place for Chase to escape the glare of Nantucket's insular social world and a port that had suddenly surged in the global race for whale oil.

Of course Melville is no different from his peers in "remixing" and adapting the facts for a work like *Clarel*. As David S. Reynolds contends, Melville is doing more than simply working with the raw materials of popular nautical narrative, which would help propel American literature to new heights in the nineteenth century.[21] He is also very much reworking Pollard's shipwrecks in order to emphasize aspects of Chase's faulty seamanship and culpability. To this end Melville reverses the order of events that doomed Pollard's career so that his first wreck is caused by "a hidden rock" splitting the hull of his ship, and his second is brought about by a whale attack. The dilemma of where to sail for land—the clear reference to Chase's misjudgment—comes not after the confrontation with the whale but instead after the ship runs aground on a shallow reef. Pollard of course had struck the shallow rocks of the French Frigate Shoals near Hawaii to end his second whaling expedition, and came directly home after his rescue. Melville thus reimagines Pollard's career-ending shipwreck so that "a whale / Of purpose aiming, stove the bow," after which "Owners and neighbors all impute / An inauspiciousness" for heightened dramatic effect. Nehemiah can only be called "a Jonah" if a whale had the final word on his career by precipitating his last tragic incident at sea.[22]

Although the professional trials of Chase and Pollard are blended into the arc of Captain Nehemiah's career, Melville aligns the most reprehensible aspects of the *Clarel* character with the headstrong first mate. Nehemiah accounts for his survival by acknowledging not only his own personal strength of mind and body, key attributes of Chase's self-portrait in his *Narrative*, but also his sheer force of will. "I *willed* it," Nehemiah proclaims with pride, exuding a self-aggrandizing quality Pollard never espoused. Furthermore, in his notes on the *Essex* written long before the composition of *Clarel*, Melville describes Pollard, as noted earlier, as a "wholly unassuming, even humble" man acutely aware of the ability of circumstances beyond his control to shape his destiny. Chase, for his part, held the distinguishing characteristic of defiant individualism, fueled by the belief that he could single-handedly destroy the white whale that had haunted him since the *Essex* disaster.[23] Chase believed, further, in his autonomous power to drive away his demons both through the rhetorical force of his *Narrative* and by navigating ships without either *Essex* survivors or even fellow Nantucket mariners but instead based out of New Bedford and filled by strangers and foreigners from across the globe.

By contrast, Pollard never lost faith in the collective will of his Nantucket community, most of which rallied around him at every stage in his career. Despite spreading dark rumors about Pollard, the islanders' actions spoke louder than their words. Nantucketers, after Pollard's second voyage, folded him back into the clan, helping promote his success rather than casting him out. His success, they believed, was their success. Nor did the island initially reject Chase, who initiated his own exile with the goal to overwrite his part in the *Essex* tragedy by dominating the seas. This general assessment problematizes Heffernan's correlation between Pollard's supposed willfulness and that of Bartleby, the scrivener (of all Melville characters!), made on the thin evidence that Melville penned his story of the intractable office clerk sixteen months after meeting the *Essex* captain.[24] The connection is far-fetched, among other reasons, when one considers Melville's subtitle, "A Story of Wall Street." Pollard's life, further, is distinguished not by what he would prefer *not* to do but, rather more remarkably, what he could in fact do through his new role as night watchman and social servant for Nantucket's greater good. This quiet, unassuming existence rooted in the community could not be further removed from Chase's Ahabian mania to triumph at sea. "'Strong need'st thou be,' the rescuers said" upon Nehemiah's return to shore after his first wreck. But the notion of strength is ironic, especially as it relates to an ill-conceived decision not to sail for the nearest land. In that case Chase was guilty of "strongly erring" by acting on the most dangerous of all options open to the crew.

THE COST OF NOT KILLING

The November 1834 *Sailor's Magazine and Naval Journal* contains a natural history article entitled simply "The Whale." Published by the American Seamen's Friend Society and offering practical advice to professional seafarers, the journal held very little advertising, and indeed no marine insurance solicitations appear within its pages. Its distance from the insurance industry comes naturally by way of its stated purpose to reach the "two millions of seamen, scattered up and down in the world, mingled among all nations; and to this day the greatest proportion of them are famishing for the bread of life, while no man breaks it to them."[25] This goal of bringing religious fellowship to an otherwise alienating commercial industry was thus combined with an equal emphasis on professionally useful data. The periodical is meant for actual sailors, whereas the *Whalemen's Shipping List* is clearly for mainland readers, given its original purpose of providing sailors' loved ones with a list of ships, captains, and cargo, along with departures and arrivals. The *Shipping List* also informed whaling investors of the outcome of voyages. Owners would have been especially interested in hearing about the fate of their ships if they hadn't learned the news by other means. In the case of a wreck, owners could count on a narrative account craftily designed to persuade insurance adjustors associated with the myriad insurance advertisements on the pages. As discussed in the previous chapter, narrative accounts of sunken vessels in the *Shipping List* rarely if ever exposed negligent seamanship of the sort Chase was ostensibly guilty of. These were accidents, readers were told, driven by insurmountable forces of nature.

In the *Sailor's Magazine*, with its indifference to insurance settlements and unusual blend of practical advice and spiritual sustenance, pieces entitled "Nautical Enterprise" and "A Tax on Sailors" share space with temperance- and piety-related articles such as "Total Abstinence" and "Texts of Scripture in Relation to Temperance." As for the "Whale" title from 1834, the magazine's stories on whale behavior tended to be more accurate, given the absence of ulterior interests. If a story about the whale's rage appeared, it was designed to defend whalemen from claims adjusters seeking negligence assessments and thus an excuse for not paying compensation for lost ships. Negligence was not the primary driver for Chase's defense in his *Narrative*, which was more immediately concerned with "impression management" and his future prospects as a captain. Impression management explains why he omitted mention of his failure to throw the harpoon, which likely would have galled his professional peers. Only the teenage Nickerson would emerge as the truth teller on the harpoon incident, precisely because he had no professional interest at stake in reporting Chase's display of weakness.

But Nickerson's truth itself, as we saw, showed empathy for Chase regarding his presumed worry over the potential damage a frenzied whale would do to the ship's precious rudder—even as the more likely explanation of events was that Chase had simply been caught off guard and failed to act. According to the magazine's studiously accurate description, had Chase thrown the harpoon at the whale at the correct moment, he almost certainly would have averted the feared damage to the rudder and the rest of the ship.

In what was then common knowledge among whalemen, as the *Sailor Magazine* reports, "the whale is extremely timid; when struck by a harpoon, instead of making, with his whole force, at his enemy, he sinks immediately from ten to fifteen fathoms in the water," a depth that would have easily cleared the *Essex*'s hull and averted disaster. The whale, the story reports, is capable of "sometimes dragging the whole weight of the harpoon with him," which, for Chase, would have meant having whale and weapon clear the vessel, thus saving it from a damaging collision. This downward flight behavior is the creature's natural response to an attack from above the surface of the water. The animal would be operating not on the horizontal plane experienced by his captors, but on a vertical one. After this immediate retreat downward—sometimes misinterpreted as the creature's malicious method of drowning whalemen caught on the line, and appearing in *Moby-Dick* during the final three-day chase and in Captain Boomer's clash with the whale—the creature will typically swim away and sometimes survive. "The whale, when struck, makes off with the harpoon in his flesh, at the rate of eight or ten miles per hour," a fact Chase should have known as the first mate of a thirty-person whaling vessel like the *Essex*. To sum up, a darted whale "descends to avoid the pursuit, or to flee the danger that awaits him," an initial reaction followed by flight behavior that would have left the *Essex* unscathed.[26]

Despite this evidence, the myth of Chase's blamelessness as it relates to the harpooning incident—perhaps the most crucial alteration shaping perceptions of the event—still persists in some circles. Even today at the Nantucket Whaling Museum, presentations to mainly tourist audiences make no mention of Chase failing to throw his harpoon at the pivotal moment. Chase's omission of this detail in his *Narrative* kept it away from the official memory of the incident, especially in the 1834 *North American Review* article that relied exclusively on his testimony. Chase, along with his ghostwriter, could not have more effectively managed his image for popular consumption, with the strategic text emerging precisely as the whaling industry moved from being a local commercial interest to a global trade phenomenon.

Chase's *Narrative* not only informed the seminal *North American Review* article, but also inspired a reading textbook for schoolchildren in which Chase insinuates Pollard's guilt by falsely claiming the captain refused to discuss the tragedy when asked, thus implying guilt and something to hide.[27] Chase's *Narrative* encouraged this embellishment. In fact Pollard was always surprisingly forthright when anyone asked him about the incident—and more and more people asked, given the incipient boom in whaling, from 1818 to 1822, when Nantucket's fleet expanded from fifty-seven vessels employing 1,222 sailors to eighty-four ships for 2,000 mariners. Especially given this growth, Chase's 1821 publication of his *Narrative* helped spread news that was already on the lips of many gossiping sailors. The event became an international sensation, spurred in part by the explosion of the trade. On Nantucket alone, the population of "free people of color" such as Portuguese from the Azores and Kanakas from the Sandwich Islands rose from 274 in 1820 to 580 in 1840, indicating the widening international reach of the whaling industry.[28] As the industry spread, so too did the *Essex* tale, particularly as minted by Chase.

As Chase had suspected would happen, news agencies reported avidly on the *Essex* disaster almost as soon as it was discovered. The November 1820 shipwreck followed by the February 1821 rescue were first covered in a tiny paragraph in the *Gazeta ministerial de Chile* (April 28, 1821). Reports then appeared in the *New Bedford Mercury* one week later and Australia's *Sydney Gazette* the next month (June 9, 1821). Despite the Chilean and Australian papers being close geographically to the event, their accounts were hardly accurate. The Nantucket *Inquirer and Mirror* was next with the story, an accurate account drawn from Pollard's rescuer, Captain Aaron Paddock, of New York's whaleship *Diana*. Paddock had recorded his testimony and sent it immediately to Nantucket. The letter arrived before Pollard and his mates did, and word of the catastrophe spread south to the *Maryland Gazette and Political Intelligencer*, which published its piecemeal story drawn from "An Extract from a Letter to the Editors" and a second segment "from our Boston correspondent, Mr. Topliff."[29] Because these stories were not informed by Nickerson's account, none bears any mention of Chase's decision not to kill the oncoming whale, instead portraying the crew as utterly helpless and victimized by the enraged creature.

Chase's *Narrative*, as we saw, skirts responsibility by assigning agency to the whale and placing the first mate and crew in the hands of a merciful and benevolent God. Chase certainly emphasizes his own piety in his *Narrative*, regularly alluding to divine providence and his faith. This would have the effect of encouraging twentieth-century critics and readers to align Chase with Starbuck, as Heffernan does. "Above all," he writes in his 1980 study, "Owen Chase combines the probity, religious devotion, courage, and industry that radiate from Starbuck, the virtues that simultaneously awe and sadden" Melville. But as discussed earlier, even Melville did not take Chase at his word, calling into question, through underlined text and a question mark in the margin, his assertion that "there was not a hope now remaining to us but that which was derived from a sense of the mercies of our Creator."[30] How could God be considered remotely merciful, given the horrendous misfortune, ill-timed sequence of events, and errors in judgment that led these men toward slow death by starvation? Melville was justifiably incredulous.

There is little evidence to suggest that Chase was nearly as pious as his *Narrative* made him out to be. In fact few sailors were, given the reported estimate by the American Seamen's Friend Society that a mere 3 percent of mariners were pious. The Society's Register Office recorded that "1,426 seamen entered their names during the year 1830, of whom 45 appeared to be pious; and 130 vessels were recorded as being navigated without the use of spirituous liquors."[31] Indeed, the society openly allowed that by evidence of sailors' reading material alone, they "in many cases supply themselves with licentious books, the evil influence of which is incalculable."[32] Chase of course was not above killing a whale, nor did he feel morally obliged to protect the animal. Although Chase could have hardly been counted among the devout—he was no Starbuck constrained by Quaker pacifism and blanching at the operative moment to dispatch Ahab and save the *Pequod*'s crew—his decision not to throw the harpoon can at least be assessed as a moral conundrum shaped by the thoroughly religious context, and its curious relations to commercial enterprise, of his Nantucket upbringing.

Paradoxically the Quaker creed that surrounded the youthful Chase regarded killing as a categorically unpardonable sin in the eyes of almighty God. Although Nantucket church records do not indicate Chase was formally part of the Quaker religion, some evidence strongly suggests he was associated with the tradition. His sister-in-law Winnifred, the wife of Joseph M. Chase, appears consistently in the surviving Nantucket record of Quaker meetings. Joseph Chase's family descendants maintained that the Chases were Quakers, leaving little doubt that Owen had participated in this family tradition.[33] Furthermore, Chase persistently places his piety on prominent display in his *Narrative* by extolling an eternally benevolent and protective God, as well as God's function at the epicenter of a business saturated with the blood of nature's largest living creature. He and the crew suffered monumentally, however, thus calling into question the authenticity of the strained Quaker benediction with which he ends his *Narrative*. There he credits his return home "to a beneficent Creator, who had guided me through darkness, trouble, and death, once more to the bosom of my country and friends."[34]

The Quaker pacifism of his Nantucket upbringing should have encouraged Chase to throw the harpoon and destroy the whale at the decisive moment rather than preventing him from doing so. This is because, far from cementing his commitment to pacifism, as if he were the historical antecedent to Melville's Starbuck, Chase's failure of decisiveness inaugurated a lifetime of violence. Considering the hundreds of whales Chase would claim in the decades to follow, not killing the whale that sank the *Essex* bore the marks of a transformative moment—for which he apparently could never forgive himself—inspiring a seeming vow to reach the pinnacle of commercial whaling success, or die in the process. The consequences of not killing for Chase were high; he is like Starbuck in his moment of cowardice, like Ahab in his compensation thereafter.

Most Quakers, as we have seen, could reconcile their religious and moral pacifism with an equal zeal for the pursuit of capital. Their frugality, business sense, and work ethic were generally not driven by wanton greed or extravagance, notions antithetical to the religion. Instead, their commercial drive seems to have come from more than a century of enduring forbidding conditions, in the form of frigid winters and sometimes meager food supplies, on an island that did not lend itself to farming or even, until 1820 or so, profits from the sea. Thus we see how Quakerism and a business mind-set could coexist without the charge of hypocrisy. As Melville observes in *Moby-Dick*, Quakers could "come to the sage and sensible conclusion that a man's religion is one thing, and this practical world quite another. This world pays dividends."[35]

Chase's own biography reads like that of a Quaker who knew those dividends could more than cover any previous material losses. In a sense

Chase might also have believed that his professional drive could help him achieve spiritual atonement for his sins. Chase's career reads something like that of Melville's Bildad: "Rising from a little cabin-boy in short clothes of the drabbest drab, to a harpooner in a broad shad-bellied waistcoat; from that becoming boat-header, chief-mate, and captain, and finally ship-owner." Chase himself followed such an "adventurous career," with one key exception that he would not reinvest his earnings in the whaling industry but instead seek to grow his assets more rapidly in real estate, bonds, and the booming railroad industry.[36] By 1854 he had bought sizable shares in the Indiana Central Railroad, Nantucket's own Pacific National Bank (named for the whaling industry's main source of revenue), and New Bedford's Wamsutta textile mills. Unique to Chase, and very unlike the archetypical Quaker shipowner Melville captures in Bildad, who in older age peacefully accrues capital by investment in the sea trade, was his late decline. His buying food in double quantities and hiding it in the attic and rafters, as even his most sympathetic biographer, Heffernan, must confess, were not idle rumors. These were probably signs of Chase's insanity, Heffernan acknowledges, because "certainly if fantasies of starvation are going to come back after almost fifty years, there are few people whom they should so reasonably trouble" as the *Essex* first mate, with harpoon aloft and clenched tightly, recoiling from the shock of the whale's blow.[37]

By age twenty Chase had been in whaling for nearly eight years. Although his father, Judah, was a farmer and not a mariner, Chase had grown up with four older brothers who ascended to the rank of captain by their late twenties or early thirties.[38] All began their apprenticeships at sea at the earliest possible age, and would go on to enjoy great success in their sailing careers. Chase naturally followed the lead of his four older brothers, and was surely driven to compete with them. The stakes were high, however, and the risk of failure was very real. According to Crèvecœur, the training, which usually began at age twelve, entailed going "gradually through every station of rowers, steersman, and harpooner; thus they learn to attack, to pursue, to overtake, to cut, to dress their huge game." The rigors of training were designed to sort the youth into two categories, one consisting of those with glorious futures, the second likely facing obscurity.

Crèvecœur continues, "After having performed several such voyages, and perfected themselves to the business, they are fit either for the counting house or the chase."[39] Of those fit for the chase, a select few who could prove themselves as exceptional seamen and leaders would be groomed to become whaleship masters. Like other Nantucket boys, Chase dreaded the prospect of not achieving the standard his brothers set; relegation to the counting house would have been a professional death sentence entailing unbearable humiliation.

Given the culture of early and rapid vocational development in a highly dangerous industry, it is not surprising that many unseasoned hands found themselves in positions of authority. Indeed, the rush to man whaleships and draw a labor force from a relatively sparse island population—complementing ethnic sailors such as Portuguese and South Sea Islanders along with African Americans—regularly placed Nantucket youth in situations entirely beyond their competence. Melville's *Redburn* and *Billy Budd* are lyrical testaments to youth thrown into such physically and morally overwhelming circumstances at sea. These situations, in which inexperienced whalemen routinely were forced to execute pivotal decisions, helped drive the creation of protocols aimed specifically at keeping "the most experienced man at the position of greatest responsibility."[40] In this quest, drastic, seemingly self-defeating measures were taken to remove the inexperienced from the point of attack on chase boats. Namely, after attaching to a whale, the boatheader would defer his position at the bow to the more senior boatsteerer, who would plant his lance in the creature and cinch the capture. The obvious problem here was that two men standing and changing places in a rough sea risked capsizing the boat. But the tradition remained fixed nonetheless, mainly because of lost whales at the hands of incompetent boatheaders. A nurse never delivers a newborn if a competent doctor is present.

Owen Chase was only twenty-four on November 20, 1820, when he faced the proverbial decision of his life. Although he was clearly out of his element in terms of rank, position on deck, and operation, he had very likely been left behind to tend the ship on other occasions while Pollard led the chase. If this were the typical arrangement throughout the voyage, it would have severely limited Chase's immediate experience wrangling whales, and certainly not from the side of the main vessel. This can reasonably be construed as a defense of the first mate—and the role of manning the ship during the hunt was likely, for the most part, uneventful—but Chase all the same should have been capable of spiking a whale at close range, especially one visibly approaching for some ten minutes.

After Chase's moment of indecision, then, his headstrong resistance to Pollard's suggestion to sail east is especially notable, both in evincing a fear of the very cannibalism the crew would eventually encounter and in representing defiance not commonly seen at sea, except under mutinous circumstances. On the latter count Captain Edward S. Davoll's recorded commands represent the culture of authority and leadership at sea, which was necessarily blunt and unilateral to protect against the inherent seafaring risks: "If you are not for me, say so, for if you are not for me you are certainly against me."[41] Although Pollard would never utter such a sentiment, given his democratic style, Chase was certainly against him when it came to setting their open boat course. Interestingly Chase turned against Pollard only once the *Essex* had disappeared beneath the water's surface, reflecting a seemingly knee-jerk attempt to regain the control he had moments ago relinquished. By overturning Pollard's decision and directing the crew's course, Chase was now unjustifiably occupying the role of captain without bearing the rank.

As with Chase, Ahab does not respond to conflict with resignation; he continues to sail into harm's way despite all reasonable arguments against it. Ahab does not heed Starbuck's warning, and keeps fighting until he loses his prosthetic limb in three clashes with the whale. By the end he is left a bubble in the sea. Chase himself is also ultimately broken apart, reduced to dementia, debilitating headaches, and his hoarding compulsion. Obsession is at the core of both figures. Chase died a shell of a man, a mere shadow of the strapping seaman of his most famous portrait, which arrests the viewer with piercing eyes and square jaw, evoking strength, poise, and stability.

For Chase, and to a lesser extent Nickerson and Chappel, the telling of the *Essex* experience functions as a revenge narrative. Losing the ship and more than half of its crew members, Chase was determined not to also lose his career, just as Ahab was determined to avenge his lost leg and sanity to the whale. Chase did not want to pursue his career only as a means of survival but also to lash back at the cruel and unjust moral universe that allowed the tragedy to occur in the first place. If Chase, in his worldview, transforms the whale into a force of evil stripping the brave whalemen of what should be rightfully theirs, including their dignity, humanity, and sanity by effectively subjecting them to cannibalism, the creature then becomes freighted with universal, rather than simply anthropomorphized, agency. Chase kept pursuing the whale, a creature of his own invention, ambition, and ultimate undoing.

The *Essex* narratives habitually lay blame on the whale itself for the ship's destruction. Blaming a force of nature, of course, relieves captains and mates of liability for the shipwreck. It is precisely on this note of the seamen's utter vulnerability that we begin the coda on the agency of the whale itself—whether malevolent beast or instrument of God's will—and its characterization throughout the various narratives of the sinking of the whaleship *Essex*.

Coda

~~~~~~

A WHALE'S MOTIVES

In the *Natural History of the Sperm Whale* (1839), a text Melville consulted closely in writing *Moby-Dick*, the surgeon and natural historian Thomas Beale affirmed what the expanding whaling industry, with its escalating human casualties from confrontations with the species, had been loath to admit. The sperm whale, he concluded, is "remarkably timid, and is readily alarmed by the approach of a whale boat." Thus "it is difficult to conceive any object in nature calculated to cause alarm to this leviathan."[1] Such sources of alarm do include swordfish, which commonly attack sperm whales. The whale responds not hostilely but by vigorously pumping its dorsal fin to attain top speed, often darting upward to breach into the open air.[2] Although not predators, swordfish can nonetheless injure whales, and such breaching helps explain the whale's response to the whalemen discussed earlier. On the rare occasions when killer whales hunt sperm whales, the latter typically cluster in a herd, responding socially in concert rather than individually with violent retaliation.[3] An approaching whaleboat, likewise, was less likely to provoke an attack than to elicit clustering and eventual flight from potential confrontation. Although the sperm whale's head appears built for combat—its spermaceti case is located at the very fore of its brow, providing for ideal head protection in high-impact collisions, not unlike a boxing glove designed to maximize the blow delivered, while minimizing damage to the fighter's fist—the animal's nature is distinctly peaceful, as seen in its response to conflict by diving deeper and outracing its predators.

Whaling historian Eric Jay Dolin explains that the sperm whale's forehead, and spermaceti case, is a vestige from its prehistoric ancestors, whose males commonly rammed each other in competition for females.[4] Needless to say, such ramming no longer takes place. The spermaceti case, meanwhile, also helps the whale dive to astonishing depths, a feat that awed Melville, where it hunts for food, mainly octopus on the ocean floor. Given its ability to displace water pressure at extreme depths for up to several hours, the waxy, gelatinous case serves the primary function of protecting the whale's brain from the debilitating condition known as the bends.[5] Female whales have the same anatomical feature, suggesting its subordinate rather than primary use prehistorically as a weapon for male competition. This situation may be contrasted with that of most ram species, which have horns for engaging in the head-butting mating ritual, whereas ewes lack them. The sperm whale's brow is further used for fleeing the rare assault from a killer whale.

The evolutionary biologist Adam Summers, along with other natural historians, has nonetheless extended into the realm of science a fringe perspective that vilifies the whale, consonant with Owen Chase's 1821 *Narrative* of the *Essex* shipwreck. Despite evidence to the contrary, Summers extrapolates from the spermaceti case an essentially belligerent nature for the whale, with the forehead its preferred weapon. Summers argues that the storied sinking of antebellum whaleships—the most visible of which were the *Essex* and the *Ann Alexander*, in 1851—occurred because the bulky hovering vessels were easy targets for the aggressive creature. He paints the whale as a pugilist, and whaleships as "punch drunk opponents just begging to be blind-sided—dream targets for an angry sperm whale."[6]

Melville himself seems to refute such a claim in *Moby-Dick*. In "The Battering-Ram" chapter Ishmael regards the "dead blind wall" of the brow less as an offensive weapon than a shield against threats in nature as well as "the severest pointed harpoon," which when stuck with "the sharpest lance darted by the strongest human arm impotently rebounds from it."[7] And even as the whale might be provoked to use its "battering ram" for defense, it is more likely to use its teeth, yet again only in self-defense, as Melville himself knew well and thus depicted in the *Samuel Enderby* chapter of *Moby-Dick* (chapter 100). Using its teeth—a last line of defense after herding and flight, and as seen "in biting that line"—Moby

Dick shreds Boomer's arm from shoulder to wrist and dispatches Ahab in the novel's final debacle.[8] Even then, Ahab's drowning upon being jerked underwater points more to his own careless mismanagement of the line, combined with ill timing, than it does to a willful tactic deployed by the whale. Melville immortalizes the whale's use of its teeth in describing how, "suddenly sweeping his sickle-shaped lower jaw beneath him, Moby Dick had reaped away Ahab's leg, as a mower a blade of grass in the field." Here the whale has simply responded with justifiable aggression to Ahab, who, seizing "his line-knife from his broken prow, had dashed at the whale, as an Arkansas duelist his foe, blindly seeking with a six inch blade to reach the fathom-deep life of the whale."[9]

Notwithstanding such encounters, in only a tiny fraction of collisions did whales successfully sink ships using their heads as battering rams. More often the ships emerged unharmed from such crashes, whereas the whales were left lacerated, mangled, and dismembered. If "flight is the usual reaction of sperm whales to danger," then why would so many assume them truculent by nature?[10] Even Ishmael—who, under the influence of Ahab's quarterdeck speech, argues for Moby Dick's status as a "murderous monster" with an "uncommon magnitude and malignity"—cannot ignore the species' blissfully serene and peaceful nature, as poetically recorded in the herding and socialization passage in "The Grand Armada." Even as Ishmael admits to hating the whale, at least temporarily, given that his "shouts had gone up with the rest" in the crew's ritual vow to destroy Moby Dick, the whale's hunters are still typically acknowledged as the cause of the beast's most fearsome behavior.[11] In an example of the whale being cast as acting defensively, he, "after doing great mischief *to his assailants*, had completely escaped them [emphasis mine]." Ishmael takes this to represent "the perils of the Sperm Whale fishery at large," which had been "marked by various and not unfrequent instances of great ferocity, cunning and malice *in the monster attacked* [emphasis mine]."[12] Despite the portrayal of the whale's villainy, Melville's prose carefully casts its viciousness only in conjunction with its assailants; attack thus heightens the power of its wild reactions. "More than all," Ishmael notes, "his treacherous retreats struck more of dismay than perhaps aught else." In Ishmael's perhaps most explicit acknowledgment that the murderous whale is not lying in wait for whalers, he muses that the "unconscious power" of the whale's "very panics are more to be dreaded than his most fearless and malicious assaults."[13] Such emphasis on alarm, panic, and flight, therefore, rather than predilection for conflict, begins to paint the whale not only as a victim but as a master of transoceanic migration for survival—on this, Ishmael speculates that whales will elude their captors by gravitating to the distant and icy poles. Such hues become more pronounced in later chapters, such as the meditation on extinction in chapter 105, "Does the Whale Diminish?"

Given the rapid increase in whale hunting throughout the first half of the nineteenth century, it stands to reason that instances of whale retaliation were also sharply on the rise. In most accounts the whale typically plays the role of savage brute, if only because brutes with lances and harpoons had savagely attacked it in the first place. Given the industry's desire to maintain its aggressive capitalist pursuit, its practitioners were predisposed to vilify the creature rather than appreciate its poised tranquility. Chase's *Narrative* follows this tendency not only to glorify the courage demanded of the profession but also, as noted, to release himself from responsibility for the sinking of the *Essex*. Laying blame on an enraged whale, wholly unaccountable and impossible to interrogate, is a convenient slip, a crafty exit from the spotlight regarding his own mismanagement of the crisis. Thus we turn to the precise circumstances that led to the sperm whale's fatal collision with the *Essex*.

FIGHT OR FLIGHT

The history of whaleships' encounters with cetaceans is strewn with fatalities both human and animal, and these fatalities rose only with the industry's pre–Civil War boom. Along with the uptick in human fatalities, unsurprisingly, the creature's reputation worsened. The whale had anyway been cast as the natural enemy of righteous seafarers seeking profits through whale oil. Chase likewise routinely aligns his work with God's will, thus casting the whale as the embodiment of satanic evil. In the context of literary Romanticism, similar scenes of dramatic moral conflict would play out in Mary Shelley's *Frankenstein* (her work, along with that of other Romantics, was heavily influenced by Milton's *Paradise Lost*[14]). Likewise, the contemporary Hudson River School of landscape painters commonly evoked moral conflict in scenes of apocalyptic clashes between sunlit Edenic verdure and gloomy rock formations and ominous rolling clouds. Chase was thus working within a Romantic context flush with hyperbolic moral allegory, wherein natural figures such as the whale would be recognizable through biblical, literary, and mythical representation. This was decades before an indifferent natural world would emerge from the pen of naturalists such as Stephen Crane (1871–1900), especially in "The Open Boat."

In reality, however, those human deaths were often the consequence of whales' simply fleeing for their lives. For Chase and others who have experienced a trauma, though, psychologists and legal experts alike describe a reflexive need to impute intentionality by various agents involved. According to a recent scholarly work on the subject, "the concept of intentionality brings order to the perception of behavior in that it allows the perceiver to detect structure—intentions and actions—in humans' complex stream of movement." Introducing an animal's stream of movement only complicates matters. Imputing intentionality, furthermore, "supports coordinated social interaction by helping people"—especially captains of sunken whaleships like Chase—"explain their own and others' behavior," such as that of nonhuman participants, "in terms of . . . underlying mental causes." Most important, "intentionality plays a normative role in the social evaluation of behavior," especially in the case of deviant behavior that inflicts harm "through its impact on assessments of responsibility and blame."[15] This was precisely the psychosocial mechanism, coupled with moralistic dualities central to prewar Romanticism, through which the whale was vilified and the whaleman valorized in the early nineteenth century.

As whaling extended past the Civil War years, a different picture began to emerge, with natural historians no longer able to ignore that "a great number of cases are on record in which vessels have been in collision with whales, usually to the greater damage of the latter." By then anecdotes of malicious whales bursting hulls were vastly outnumbered by instances of ships blasting into the creatures. The resultant carnage occurred, on one occasion, "when two days out from New York, bound for the West Indies, a whale was struck with such terrific force as to cut the animal into two parts." Sadly "the captain had altered his course to avoid the collision," precisely as Chase might have done when he spotted the whale approaching the *Essex*, "but was too late."[16] In the case of the *Essex*, the ship had crossed the path of what was likely a fleeing whale from the group of four that Pollard had been pursuing. The whaleship was not traveling at nearly the speed necessary to kill the creature outright, yet the greater velocity and sturdier bow of a postwar ship may have dealt it a fatal blow.

Today we understand whale collisions as an active crisis for marine conservation. As of April 2012, collisions with whales had reached such troubling levels that a new iOS app, Whale Alert, was introduced to help North Atlantic mariners avoid striking endangered right whales. The product comes as a response to the sharp rise in unreported accidents, adding to the confirmed incidents. New data on the northern right whale show that "mortality and serious injury due to commercial fishing and shipping [collisions] are significant factors limiting their recovery," thus explaining why their population mysteriously stagnated around a mere three hundred for decades. The findings show that "ship strikes are more immediately lethal" than entanglement and account for precisely 44.6 percent of all documented deaths from 1970 to 1999.[17] These are the oceanic equivalent of roadkill, animals dying in droves not owing to hunting but to high-volume transportation through their natural habitats. A similar cause was cited a century ago, when in a sampling of six different collisions with whaleships, all were all found to be due to incidental contact. "In all cases," involving the *Alexander M. Lawrence No. 4*, *Adelia E. Carleton*, *Admiral Sampson*, *Grecian*, *Wladimir Reitz*, and *Puma*, "it seems that the collision was quite by accident."[18]

Whereas a whale is much more likely to be struck and killed by a vessel than it is to attack one head-on, the creatures that do strike are usually hounded, harassed, and antagonized into doing so, such as the whale that sank the *Ann Alexander*. (The pugilist in that case was clearly not the whale but Captain John DeBlois, whose own truculent disposition will be discussed later.) Moreover, in 1842, during a decade when allegations of the creature's violent nature had reached a fever pitch, two dead whales with broken jaws discovered off Plymouth, Massachusetts, were immediately assumed to have sustained their injuries while fighting. But even the cultural mood could not prevent whalemen and scientists from rejecting, upon further investigation, the initial assumption that they had "fatally injured each other" since "the usual peaceable nature of this species is rather against such a supposition."[19] They could only conclude that collisions with whaleships had caused the fatal injuries.

Crew members' implication in a whale's fight for survival often proved harrowing. For example, whales were not uncommonly caught on anchors, stirring panic on deck equal to that of the submerged animal, which would usually die in the process. The Nantucket *Inquirer and Mirror* reported just such an incident in 1855 involving the schooner *Valentine Doane*: "So violent were the whale's struggles to free itself that it broke the anchor, but received such injuries from its frenzy that it shortly died and was later found floating on the surface." As a testament to the whale's power to destroy the strongest nautical equipment—the steely root grounding any seafaring vessel—"the broken anchor was on exhibition for some while at Harwich," the *Valentine Doane*'s home port.[20] The concern here—as demonstrated in the celebration of imperial power through big-game hunting, a concept that gained considerable traction during the early nineteenth century—was not the suffering of the animal but "romanticized admiration for the dangers faced by whalemen, as heroic crusaders in an industry crucial to national and global prosperity," as ecocritic Philip Armstrong explains.[21] Such exalting of the human over the natural world takes on connotations not only of nationalism and geopolitical domination but also of the heroism of commercial enterprise, a point Chase emphasizes in his *Narrative*.

Amid innumerable instances of whales fleeing while caught in lines or tethered to anchors, one in particular reflects the appalling violation of the animal. In the 1720s, in a harbor near Cape Cod, an anchor roughly the size and shape of a whale's phallus apparently became lodged in a female whale's uterus. Thus tethered "by the orifice of the *Uterus*, and finding herself caught, [she] tore away with such violence, that she towed the ship out of the harbor as fast as if she had been under sail with a good gale of wind to the astonishment of the people on shore for there was nobody on board." Once out on open water, the whale dived deep and the cable gave way. Whereas the sloop was recovered, "this whale was found dead some days after on shore with the anchor sticking in her belly."[22] Thus we have a figurative rape and murder of the species, made especially grotesque by the anchor's industrial provenance. This is a long way from the anchor suggesting a warrior's broken lance—a token of bravery demanded in facing such a formidable foe.

As such incidents illustrate, whaleships and their equipment effectively represent traps rather than targets for cetaceans. Compounding their vulnerability is sperm whales' peculiar blind spot, given the placement of their eyes on either side of their head, which impairs their ability to avoid a ship or other foreign objects, such as lines and nets. The whale is thus sometimes a risk in being liable to inadvertently ram ships while fleeing from attacking whaleboats—and to collide with whaleboats while fleeing ships. Its blind spot extends from the snout's midpoint straight ahead, precisely the point of contact before its giant brow; the fields of vision on each side of its head do not converge at this center point, making the animal oblivious to objects immediately ahead as it swims. A frantic whale in full flight from flying harpoons, then, is not likely to be fastidious about avoiding natural obstacles, let alone those alien to its natural habitat like a whaleship. Meanwhile, an extraordinary lateral range of vision enables the whale to scan almost the entirety of its perimeter. More precisely, the whale's "blind sector has been estimated as extending through about 10 degrees in front." Thus, "in order to take advantage of these blind spots, early whalemen approached either directly from the front or rear, keeping spout and hump in a single line of sight."[23] Whales have been known to swim alongside a ship or among human swimmers, sometimes even rising up out of the water. But in the process of eluding hunters, the whale would not be at its leisure to survey the territory. Accelerating just below the surface near a whaleship cruising in a high wind at full sail, the whale typically was blind to the submerged hull, often totally unaware of it until stunned by contact.

In light of this context on the whale, the *Essex* was unique in that it was the first whaleship on record to have sunk after colliding with a whale. This was the case even though countless tales of whales destroying chase boats had been in circulation for nearly a century. Significantly, virtually every whaling narrative after 1820 not only showed an awareness of the incident but retold the story with the sort of Romantic tropes and fervor then prevalent in literature, art, and drama. Chase had finally provided the whaling industry with a defining narrative and villain—the whale—playing on the increasingly outlandish, yet wildly popular, travel and adventure genre then driving the literary market. The evil whale, through Chase's *Narrative,* thus became a product for and by commercial whaling—not Jonah's whale, cast in the Bible as an agent of God, but a vicious force of nature unambiguously opposed to the pursuit of profit. Here, then, was the profit that could lead to national economic dominance and thus imperial geopolitical prominence. This narrative, which Chase advanced tentatively for fear he would encounter skepticism over his claims about the whale's intentionality, ran starkly counter to any notion that the collision had actually occurred as an accident due to the whale's natural instinct to flee. Not only *Moby-Dick* but scores of other popular narratives rushed into print with tales of vindictive nonhuman agents, monsters in every sense of the word, from Cornelius Mathews's *Behemoth* to Shelley's *Frankenstein.*

Only a handful of skeptics rebelled against the handy notion of a calculating whale as the enemy of the world's most lucrative trade, alleging that these yarns represented the very sort of sea story satirized by Jonathan Swift. More recently Philip Armstrong has argued that *Moby-Dick*'s commercial failure came about because readers resisted, rather than embraced, the notion of animal agency out of a desire to defend capitalist agency and thus supremacy over the natural world.[24] But readers and reviewers indeed praised the inclusion of a malevolent whale in Melville's magnum opus. What they disapproved of was the whale's inability to fit into a clear moral allegory, uncomplicated and told with narrative linearity. Melville instead offers multiple sources of agency— whale, lines, Ahab—in a nonlinear way that favors complex ambiguity over crisp good-evil dualism, thus forcing the reader to face constant inversions of the hunting narrative. Who is chasing whom?, Melville seems to ask at so many junctures, such as when Ahab suddenly finds himself the helpless rodent, shrieking and waterlogged, to Moby Dick's playful and cruel aquatic feline.[25]

The dualism, however, is amply present in Chase's *Narrative*, which relies on multiple baseless assumptions about the animal's intentions to build its one-dimensional, sinister portrait. One key assumption is that because the whale "came directly from the shoal which we had just before entered, and in which we had struck three of his companions," he was therefore "fired with revenge for their sufferings."[26] Even if the whale had come from Pollard's boats, the animal is unlikely to have been able to seek out and find the *Essex* so quickly, as if it possessed some extraordinary power (yet one essential to its mystification by Chase) to identify and then hunt down the whalemen's mother ship. More probable is that the whale was fleeing the attack, swimming at full speed toward the whale-ship, and collided with it accidentally, with the strike owing in part to the whale's speed, in part to its blind spot. I would further suggest that the whale collided with the *Essex* not because it randomly crossed its path but because fleeing whales tend to swim windward (or upwind), the direct trajectory from Pollard's boats toward the ship. This theory actually comports with Chase's description. "He struck her to windward," Chase reports, "directly under the cat head."[27]

THE *ESSEX* WHALE

On November 20, 1820, three boats departed from the *Essex* in pursuit of whales, commanded respectively by Pollard, Chase, and second mate Matthew Joy. Chase's boat was damaged in the fracas and returned to the *Essex*. "The captain and second mate were left with their boats pursuing the whales," as Macy reports in his 1835 *History of Nantucket*.[28] Chase had been bested in the hunt, interestingly, because of his proximity to a whale, which had thrashed about after Chase had sunk the harpoon into its flesh. Yet Chase's own description does not ascribe malicious intent to the whale in this instance: "Presently one rose and spouted a short distance ahead of my boat; I made all speed towards it, came up with, and struck it; feeling the harpoon in him," instinctively contorting in pain, "he threw himself, in an agony, over towards the boat (which at the time was up alongside him)." This mention of the whale's position "alongside" the boat is crucial because it indicates the creature had not purposefully lunged a great distance but instead had incidentally whipped the boat with its tail. Chase clearly should have left more space—at least enough to allow for the animal's dangerous frenzy—between his boat and the whale before launching the harpoon. Yet even as Chase should have anticipated the whale's likely response and the risk to the boat, he nonetheless blamed the creature for willfully "giving a severe blow with his tail [that] struck the boat near the edge of the water, amidships, and stove a hole in her."[29]

The next event proves further that this whale was in full flight mode, terrified and bent on escaping the area. With his boat damaged, Chase cut the line "to disengage the boat from the whale, which by this time was running off with great velocity." Chase himself had recognized the grave danger a stricken whale represented and thus "succeeded in getting clear of him" to evade the animal's path to escape. This whale is not Ahab's "calculating, deliberative, rational and malign agent"; nor is it, as Robert Zoellner claims, operating randomly, without direction, focus, or purpose.[30] Yes, the whale is acting in alarm, but it is certainly doing so with more intent, specifically to escape, than Zoellner's depiction of a nonconscious creature that "does not *choose* . . . does not *decide* . . . does not *follow* any apparent plan of action."[31] In its way, the panicked creature is aware of executing a series of deft maneuvers to achieve liberation from its captors. Chase, while acknowledging the whale's behavior as a direct response to pain, still feels outdone by a beast he thought he had captured. For any fisherman, cutting the line on a significant catch is a galling admission of defeat. To emerge from that surrender with a damaged boat—for which Chase blames the creature that "struck" and "stove a hole in her"—would add insult to injury.

After he tried to patch the whaleboat's hole, Chase mobilized the *Essex* as if it were a chase boat and "put the ship off toward" Pollard and the second mate, a function for which it was never designed, given its bulk, lack of maneuverability, and limited peripheral visibility. Unlike light craft designed for pursuit, ships were more effective in spotting whales at a great distance from masthead lookouts and for processing and storing whale oil, making them something like floating factories. Thus moving a ship toward whales under attack would have been dangerous and speaks to Chase's haste in this situation. When Chase returned to the ship to find the whale—presumably the one he had harpooned—ramming it, he chose not to rejoin the hunt by boarding the other boat attached to the ship but instead to frantically patch his damaged boat with canvas at the same time that he pursued the whale. The more prudent course would have been to keep the ship moored, rather than sailing into harm's way, and eventually launch a new boat. Additionally Chase would have been better served by leaving the patching job for the long, monotonous periods attendant on such voyages. But his wounded pride and bruised ego seem to have fixed him on vengeance directed at the whale, whether achieved from the ship's deck or from his leaky canvas-patched boat.

While Chase was fumbling with the canvas patch, one of the fleeing whales had swum upwind toward the ship, in exactly the opposite direction from the one in which the whaleboats had just been rowed, downwind, toward the shoal in search of whales. The animal now appeared to Chase some "twenty rods off our weather-bow . . . with his head in a direction for the ship." The whale was clearly moving in a way that suggested flight, whatever its trajectory, characterized by equal parts speed and endurance, rather than racing to deliver a blow. Then "in less than two or three seconds he came up again, about the length of the ship off." Only as the whale closed in did Chase register alarm and thus claim that the creature approached with "great celerity." This was perhaps only because a whale in the distance appears to be moving much more slowly than one "but a ship's length off."

Chase's whale was likely following the tendency according to which "sperm whales, when running, flee to windward." The whale's instinct to swim windward is so strong, as frequently noted by natural scientists, "that the whales, if the air is calm, usually turn to the direction from which the wind blew last, and never deviate by a compass point from their flight in this direction."[32] This whale's flight from the shoal, then, which was also against the current, would have been the strong-swimming creature's seemingly best tactic to lose its pursuers. It was with head turned windward, tail pumping, and momentum blistering that the whale had the misfortune to run directly into the *Essex*'s hull.

Louie Psihoyos, a filmmaker and *National Geographic* photographer who recently earned an Academy Award for the documentary *The Cove*, about the destruction of the world's dolphin population, explains that a whale which had been attacked out of sight of the mother ship would not likely seek out the ship and assault it.[33] This corroborates my claim that the whale was not attacking, so much as fleeing according to its natural pattern of windward escape when, hindered by its blind spot, it struck the vessel. Only after this impact did the stunned whale turn back on the boat with its teeth and, in attempting to bite the hull, inadvertently ram its long, well-padded snout through it. So startling and unexpected was the first contact that the whale probably returned for a second blow as an act of self-defense against the boat, which it perceived to be a predator. Recent dramatic renderings of the incident, such as in Jay Parini's *Passages of H. M.: A Novel of Herman Melville* (2010), do not measure up to what whale behaviorists and natural scientists describe. Parini's fiction draws out precisely the vilification of the whale established in Chase's *Narrative*, enhancing the animal's savagery and the whalemen's victimization, while muting Chase's qualifications. Note the strategic use of the passive verb amid this melodramatic portrayal. The *Essex* "had been hit broadside by a ferocious, self-destructive, monomaniacal whale," he writes, while failing to mention, as do other accounts, that the whale died in the process. Thus superimposing Ahab's kamikaze vengeance on the whale, he renders an animal delirious in its rage, delivering a crazed beating, hungry for death and destruction. A whale, however, is not a shark, which Parini's beast curiously begins to resemble here: "It punctured a deep, fatal hole in the ship's hull. Bizarrely, the whale refused to desist, attacking again and again." Now "the frantic crew" all become victims—including Chase himself, who had just returned to patch his whaleboat—with none of them bearing any causal connection to the whale's behavior. This ruined crew, purportedly holding no responsibility for the whale's attack, is reduced to "murder and cannibalism" for survival.[34] Even though this description comes in undisguised novel form, it is nonetheless striking for being both the most recent retelling of the

Essex story and the most widely circulated novel on the subject explicitly intended for a wide audience.

Parini's portrait indicates that the malevolent *Essex* whale is alive and well in today's culture and producing a steady stream of profit. Witness, for example, the low-budget film *Moby-Dick 2010*, which reimagines the whale as a satanic, three-hundred-foot sea monster that gleefully swallows entire whale-watching ships, gorging without discrimination on peaceful "save the whales" ecotourists as well as his hunters. Yet the conservation movement has gained traction, one not to be confused with today's passive, dilettantish, and sentimental whale watchers.

Psihoyos, who collected visual evidence of dolphin massacres to marshal support for their protection, deploys a no-holds-barred activism in the tradition of Hunter S. Thompson and warrants more attention here. In *Racing Extinction*, which debuted in January 2015 at the Sundance Film Festival, Psihoyos addresses the situation of the North American right whale, following in the bold footsteps of Graham Burnett's *The Sounding of the Whale* (2012). Burnett describes how "a history of whale science can shed considerable light on the changing understanding of nature in the 20th century." Essential to that history is Burnett's chapter "The Prince of Whales," on A. Remington Kellogg, who lobbied to alter the public's view of the whale as a malicious creature. Along with creating the Council for the Conservation of Whales, now the International Whaling Commission, Kellogg published an influential article in the January 1940 issue of *National Geographic* on whales and their intelligence, battling editors who instead wanted him to emphasize their viciousness and even suggested he title the piece "Whales: Lions of the Sea." He stood his ground. "Left and right he fought off editors' desires to sensationalize cetacean 'monstrosity' and at one point wrote to a colleague, 'The publisher has the idea that all the pictures should be exciting, such as a whale running its head through a steamer,'" a not unfamiliar image for *Essex* aficionados, "'and then winking its eye at the astonished crew,'" malice aforethought intact, as in Chase's *Narrative*. As for depicting whales as lions, Kellogg retorted, "'Whales are very distantly, if at all, related to the cat tribe. . . . Except when mortally wounded, they are inoffensive and noted for their timidity.'"[35] Chase's rendition of the event, according to

Kellogg's paradigm-shifting understanding of whale behavior, is a product not only of his desire to preserve his own reputation as a whaleman and future as a captain but also of nineteenth-century public perceptions of whales as the vicious beasts so often portrayed in the popular press. Inherently timid animals, of course, do not make formidable foes in romantic hunting narratives, whether at sea or on land. Kellogg's science thus undermined the basis of the romantic sea narrative by robbing it of its villain, and perhaps its most charismatic character—a situation well understood by Melville, who dedicates so much of *Moby-Dick* to detailing the legend, lore, and manner of the white whale.

The image of Moby Dick as ubiquitous, brooding, battle-scarred, and above all solitary is a romantic conceit designed to serve as Ahab's foil. Likewise similar portraits of the *Essex* whale grossly misrepresent this inherently social animal. According to Chase, the whale came from a shoal where the sailors had just "struck three of his companions."[36] The image of the whale as exhibiting sharklike behavior, stalking the seas alone, waiting to wreak havoc on humans, is the most crucial ingredient of this foundational nineteenth-century fish story. It is not surprising that the beast's malice aforethought amounts to greater liability, increases the stakes of the crime committed, and thus makes the whale an unpardonable sinner. If the whale were a criminal in court, it would be charged not with involuntary manslaughter but indeed with premeditated murder, a felony according to both earthly and higher law.

Chase himself knew his attempts to prove malicious intent by the whale went against the grain of two basic understandings already well established by 1820: "The mode of fighting which they always adopt is either with repeated strokes of their tales, or snapping of their jaws together; and that a case, precisely similar to this one, has never been heard of amongst the oldest and most experienced whalers." Only after Chase's inaugural account of such an attack was published, and here he acknowledges his is the first, did tales of whales similarly ramming ships proliferate. Not only does Chase admit the whale had never before been known to attack by deliberately colliding with a whaleship, but instead was understood to retaliate with its jaws and tail—he also confesses that it could only be by "destiny of design" that "a sudden and most deadly attack had been made upon us, by an animal too, never before suspected of premeditated violence, and proverbial for its insensibility and inoffensiveness." He concludes, "Every fact seemed to warrant me in concluding that it was anything but chance which directed his operations." He pins agency on the whale, deeming it driven by resentment, fury, and calculating mischief, despite it being a "hitherto unheard of circumstance, and constitutes, perhaps, the most extraordinary one in the annals of fishery" for a whale to execute such a plotted attack.[37]

The plot, according to Chase, was conceived out of revenge for the assault on the whale's "three companions." But for a whale to seek out a ship that far away—far enough out of sight and earshot that Pollard and his mates were unaware the *Essex* had been fatally damaged—and for the whale to have presumably identified the mother ship is, as the Psihoyos discussion shows, utterly implausible. As mentioned before, after the first blow, the stunned whale likely shifted into fighting mode, sought to engage its jaws, and in the process punctured the ship's bottom just below the bow. The two blows, therefore, constitute an accidental collision followed by a defensive retaliation, the latter a reflexive instinctual response. A fleeing animal under attack should not be confused with one hunting down its attackers' base of operations and destroying it, however stirring and irresistible the latter scenario appears.

Chase's occasional critics included Francis Allen Olmsted, who in his 1840 retelling of the *Essex* ordeal appended an excerpt from a highly skeptical commentator that appeared in the *North American Review*. "No other instance is known," this virtual imitation of a fiction writer's release of liability notes, "in which the mischief is supposed to have been malignantly designed by the assailant, and the most experienced whalers believe that even in this case, the attack was not intentional." The comment then raises the obstinate character of "Mr. Chase," who "could not be persuaded to think so." As an eyewitness, according to this commentator, Chase cannot be trusted: "He says all he saw, produced on his mind the impression of decided and calculating mischief on the part of the maddened leviathan."[38] In an 1851 issue of the *Whalemen's Shipping List*, a similar, scathingly sarcastic view was aired. Although "the case of the *Essex*" showcases the "great power of the whale," the author points out that

Chase had lied. "Cases, it is true, of the destruction of ships by the attack of whales have not been of frequent occurrence," he concludes. That the *Essex*, like the *Ann Alexander*, on which his piece was focused, has "been sent to the bottom of the sea by the attack of a whale is just as sure as anything can be in this world," he quips, "and we pray that we may never be called upon to chronicle the similar destruction of a canal boat by the ferocious attack of a horse." This skeptic's comments coalesce nicely with Melville's spectrum between "Monstrous Pictures of Whales" and "Less Erroneous Pictures of Whales," as chapters 55 and 56 of *Moby-Dick* are known. Ishmael observes, "There are some indigestible facts that lead us to think that the writer has taken in more than his whale could."[39]

If the attacking whale is as plausible as a predatory horse, then the question of the whale's second strike at the *Essex* nonetheless bears further consideration, given its peculiar circumstances. The second strike, it must be accepted, was no accident but, as Thomas Heffernan points out, was "the whale's trying to bite the ship."[40] Dr. David Ramsay's log of the *Surry*, the ship that rescued the stranded *Essex* sailors on Ducie Island, describes how after the initial collision, the whale "lay along side the ship and tried to bite some part of it, but could get no hold, she then took a sweep round . . . and came dead on to the ship which was going about 6 knots . . . drove her head into the bow and then left the ship."[41] However hostile the whale may have been on this second strike, it was only, as we have seen, responding to the first accidental collision. Hal Whitehead supports the theory of the whale's self-defensive instinct in his correspondence with Nathaniel Philbrick, which dispels Henry Carlisle's fictional portrayal, whereby the sound of Chase's hammering attracted the whale. He reasons that since the animal hears sounds primarily through the water, the chaos of Pollard's attack would have created a cacophony of aquatic vibration overwhelming any hint of Chase's boat repair. Further, even if the whale had detected the distant muffled sounds of his patching work, the creature is highly unlikely to have sought out and attacked the source of those noises, instead associating them with danger and fleeing. Carlisle's whale, in this sense, is simply an elaboration, bearing signs of 1980s-era scientific discoveries in echolocation, of Chase's vindictive beast. Whitehead also discredits the idea that the bull whale would be protecting the females under attack, a scenario reprising normative human gender roles played out in the melodramatic key of the chivalrous defense of damsels in distress. Instead, contact between the sexes within the species is "brief and impermanent." He concludes that the whale struck the *Essex* accidentally and that "this contact greatly disturbed the animal, resulting in the second event, which does read like an 'attack.'"[42]

The first strike, however, is the one that has almost uniformly gone down in history as a predatory attack. Intentionality is taken for granted in comments such as, "The bull sperm whale that made the unprovoked attack upon the *Essex* also rammed with its head."[43] Henry T. Cheever's *Whale and His Captors* (1850) sensationalizes the second strike, noting that the whale "started with great speed directly across the vessel's course to the windward." The windward direction, as we saw, is the whale's instinctive direction of flight, opening up the alternative interpretation that the second collision was also accidental. Interestingly, Cheever's account is not so strident as others in attributing malicious intent to the animal, referring to it as the "*seemingly* malicious whale [emphasis mine]."[44] The hundred-plus years between Cheever's account and those of Parini and Carlisle generally tend to play down these matters of instinct to darken the whale's intent in our time. Carlisle is right about Pollard, but not about whale science, an area that also evades Eric Jay Dolin's otherwise powerful history.[45] Dolin's recent comprehensive history of whaling indulges in pure fabrication to enhance his narrative effect. To preface his embellished rendition of the *Essex* tale, he provides what is a fully accurate illustration of the 1807 *Union* disaster, reversing the usual scenario in which the animal strikes the ship: "It was cruising at a good clip off Patagonia when it plowed into a large sperm whale, a collision that left a gaping hole in the hull. Capt. Edward Gardner, realizing that the pumps were no match for the torrent of sea water rushing into the hold, called for the men to abandon ship." To their good fortune, or "Divine Providence to bear us and protect us from harm," the crew of sixteen was well enough supplied with provisions and navigational instruments to survive eight days at sea covering a total of six hundred miles until landing on Flores Island, where they were finally rescued. But then Dolin proceeds to use the whale that sank the *Essex* to overstate the opposite case, going so far as to suggest that the whale not only rammed the port side of the bow intentionally but drove the ship backward by propelling itself through the water. Interestingly, Chase tells of the second strike with relative understatement, with no mention of a ship-stopping blast followed by a tail-pumping boot of the massive vessel previously carrying three knots, presumably with the whale's head buried in the hull, the cetacean equivalent of a torpedo.[46] Of the whale's behavior during the second collision, Chase merely writes, "We took the second shock," and then watched as the whale "went off to leeward, and we saw no more of him."[47]

All these liberties taken with the incident speak to how fertile the original details were for sensationalization. The more human the whale can seem—especially imbued with raging emotion harnessed into a tactical scheme—the more dramatic the spectacle of its attack. The details related to the whale attack are pivotal beyond the intrigue they generate, with the details certainly capturing Melville's imagination, given his personal experience with various whale assaults. Though none of the whale attacks in *Moby-Dick* perforate ship hulls in the manner of the *Essex*, they achieve a much more diverse repertoire of moves than Chase's whale. Melville turns the creature into something of a martial artist with pinpoint precision: the whale smites Macey from a boatload of men "bodily into the air," sending him falling "into the sea at a distance of about fifty yards" in the *Jeroboam*'s story; punts a chase boat skyward, cartwheeling end over end like a football; deftly uses its line to collar Ahab into the depths; employs its considerable jaws to snap off the arm of Captain Boomer, of the *Samuel Enderby*; and in perhaps its most spectacular feat, remarkable for its perfectly timed poetic justice and sheer lyrical violence, soars above the *Town Ho*'s rails to pluck the vile and vicious Radney from the deck just as the sadistic captain is about to unleash his wrath on the recalcitrant Steelkilt.[48] Melville alternately turns the whale into a ballerina, an outsized kitten toying with the chase boats, and an agent of a righteous Calvinist God that can at other moments appear aligned with Satan, closer to Chase's creature. Beyond mere theatrics, the whale's feats dramatize a morality play in these works as well as in the lesser-known nineteenth-century tale of a whale destroying the *Ann Alexander*.

Although he was not the first to assign malice aforethought to the whale, Chase had rendered the most visible and celebrated account in nautical history of a ship being sunk by a whale. Then, on November 4, 1851, John DeBlois, captain of the *Ann Alexander*, characterized the whale that had destroyed his vessel on August 20 of that year in similar terms in the *Whalemen's Shipping List*. Like Chase, DeBlois maligned the whale in order to conceal his professional deficiencies and ultimately deflect responsibility for the wreck. DeBlois's key indiscretion prompting the debacle was his naïve playing into the hands of another ship's commander, who would fleece him of a pod of whales. After a congenial gam, Captain Jared Jernegan of New Bedford had convinced DeBlois to partner with him by holding similar "tacks during the night so that we could keep together," under the promise that they would consolidate their oil cargo in the morning. Upon awakening, DeBlois noticed Jernegan "was 12 miles off on my lee quarter" seeking the main share of whales for himself, with all hands under strict orders "not to put up sail unless they saw me coming towards him." Thus humiliated before his crew, DeBlois furiously raced toward Jernegan. After hours of pursuit, he finally reached him at midday. "I was pretty mad over his trickery," he admitted, "and sung out on coming within hailing distance, 'Have you left any whales?'" Like Melville's Stubb, who fools the French whalemen into giving up their precious and highly valued ambergris, Jernegan gloated in his triumph, "taking a dead whale aside." Then pitying his dupe, he replied, "'Oh yes, one has started west northwest.'"

Armed with this information and refusing to play the fool, DeBlois struck out for the animal to rescue his wounded pride. "I didn't want anything besides the whale," he confessed, motivating his men with the reward of an early return to port, a kind of equivalent of Ahab's doubloon, should they raise this creature from the deep. DeBlois cried out, "Get that whale and your voyage will be five months shorter!" The men promptly responded by closing in on the creature and landing a harpoon in its back. The whale, however, shattered the boat, then doubled back and made a failed run at the other chase boat. This "fighting whale" then approached, and "turning on his side, looked at us, apparently filled with rage at having missed his prey," the captain recalled. Undaunted, DeBlois returned to the ship to continue the chase, each time losing the whale the moment he and his crew approached it. Upon ordering the men to lower a new boat, the captain was stung by the crew's refusal. "I don't care a d-n! Go ahead!" he brayed. But the crew would be neither forced nor cajoled. Just then, the whale swam off, seemingly for good, diving down into the deep. Tallying his losses with resignation, DeBlois withdrew from the rail, but just then the whale "hurled himself against the bow four feet from the keel and just abreast of the foreswifter," jolting the men, who had been lulled into believing they had lost the whale and thus taken to the perfunctory task of bracing up the mizzen and main topsails. Water rushed into the hold, the ship keeled over, and the crew dived into the remaining boats, where they bobbed about on the rolling sea for forty-eight hours until rescued.

In covering for his own indiscretions, DeBlois made certain to avert two errors commonly associated with the *Essex* disaster. First, he refused the crew's request to sail south from their location in the heart of the South Pacific two to three thousand miles west of the Peruvian coast, and instead insisted that they head for the equator, where they could rely on rainwater to quench their thirst. (Chase, of course, had demanded with support from the crew that Pollard sail southeast for the west coast of South America.) His other directive was to keep the boats together on the same trajectory, and to let the faster of the two move ahead, so that if the first boat were to encounter a ship, "the rescuers [could] bear down to the other boat. In this way we were increasing our small chance of being saved." These implicit references to the *Essex* become explicit two paragraphs later, when he describes how his entire crew could not help comparing their situation to "the fearful suffering of the crew of the *Essex* directly."[49] Chase's *Narrative* indeed drove the mounting fear that, after two days without sustenance, cannibalism would be their only recourse. Not only did the *Essex* disaster shape DeBlois's account of the sinking, with the captain spinning his decisions as prudent correctives to Pollard's oversights, it menaced the hearts and minds of the crew as they awaited rescue.

The *Ann Alexander* would famously inspire a toast to the attacking whale from Melville, who proclaimed the ship's fate a "Crash!" from "Moby Dick himself." "What a commentator is this *Ann Alexander* whale," he mused. "I wonder if my evil art has raised this monster."[50] Five years later Davis W. Clark's retelling of the *Ann Alexander* wreck in a compendium titled *The Most Striking Narratives on Record* describes the whale "seemingly animated with the prospect of speedy revenge" as it attempts to destroy two whaleboats. The captain resolves to chase the whale with the ship, a foolhardy decision indeed, given the loss of the two boats. At dusk the whale drops with the setting sun and seemingly disappears, leading the men to believe it has fled. "Subsequent events proved, however," in Clark's words, "that the whale had formed a deadly resolution to destroy the ship which had given him so much annoyance."[51] Plotting, scheming, and lying in wait, this creature, like the *Essex* whale, thus energizes the tale with its premeditated malice, blasting a hole in the ship two inches from the keel.

By the turn of the twentieth century, a new narrative of the event by Willis Abbot placed even greater emphasis on the whale's "mere lust for combat," effectively transforming the whalemen into so many lambs to be "sacrificed to the whale's rage."[52] In fact the *Ann Alexander* whale, like the animal that sank the *Essex*, was not the one with the lust for combat. DeBlois, more accurately, was that creature. According to his own admission, his "blood was up and [he] was fully determined to have that whale, cost what it might," a token of his fury and willingness to sacrifice the crew's safety for the catch, which would help the captain maintain his self-described prowess and reputation for "killing every whale he had ever fastened to." As we saw, though, his impetuosity alarmed the crew members, who protested, "O captain, you ran too much risk of our lives!" But all hands, the captain feebly retorted, "were as anxious as I to catch that whale, and I hadn't the least idea that anything like this would happen." His self-justifying rhetoric bears the unmistakable influence of years of second-guessing and skepticism of Pollard's command. Whereas DeBlois allows, "I was burdened with the responsibility of having these precious lives on my hands," he disowns any wrongdoing. By appealing to the group's collective consent, he contends that "to be blamed for what we were all eager to try"—even as his testimony clearly indicates the crew's resistance to his commands at several key points—"was a little too much."[53]

But Captain DeBlois was notoriously dogged in his pursuit of whales, exhibiting a "stubbornness, and ambition to succeed and excel." The whale that retaliated against him had endured uncommon harassment and abuse from a tenacious assailant, who was "completely fearless of life, limb and equipment," regarding each whale as if it were a "personal antagonist, to be killed, no matter what the cost," a gamble for which he and his crew paid dearly with the loss of their ship.[54] Fiercely competitive and inflexible, DeBlois wrote his narrative with an equally steely resolve to capture the elusive white whale of fame. His narrative is obviously in dialogue with that of the *Essex*, not only for its overt reference to the *Ann Alexander* crew suffering forty-eight hours of starvation at sea, but also for affirming, through repeated extracts of dialogue, that his men did actually believe he should be the one to advise them at key moments in the crisis. This narrative approach is bluntly self-serving. Unlike Pollard, this technique seems to say, DeBlois had the faith of his crew.

Another similarity between Chase's *Narrative* and the DeBlois disaster involves the use of the whale's teeth. Just as the *Essex* whale attacked the hull with its teeth after being struck by the ship, evidence of the *Ann Alexander* whale's strike can be found in tooth marks in the copper near the ship's keel, noted by the men when they returned to the capsized ship, a detail indicating that the whale had attacked with its teeth rather than its spermaceti case. A sperm whale has teeth only on its lower jaw, which itself is set back from its toothless upper jaw. Given this anatomical configuration, one can assume that the whale had lunged at the *Ann Alexander*'s keel, with the forehead necessarily leading the charge, since it juts out so much further than the low, recessed jaw. Thus the whale's unusually long snout slammed into the target, perforating the copper and wood several feet before the teeth, the true assault weapon, could make their impression.

Given the aforementioned instances in which sperm whales bit through lines, shattered whaleboats, and dismembered whalemen like Captain Ahab and Captain Boomer in *Moby-Dick*, there is good reason to believe sperm whales used their teeth offensively as well as in self-defense. The use of the teeth rather than the brow for such purposes is, as noted, well documented by marine biologists. "The sperm whale's usually reported method of attack on a small boat is to turn over on its back or side and approach belly up, with the jaw agape," explains David Caldwell. Clearly "the jaw is powerful, and whaleboats have been bitten cleanly in two by sperm whales."[55] Cases of the head being used in ramming are supported by scantier, and far fishier, anecdotal evidence, most of which points toward an unsuccessful attempt by the whale at biting, due to angle and momentum toward the target (usually a ship's hull rather than a chase boat). Nineteenth-century scientists like Thomas Beale were fully aware of the habit among seamen to create legends about whales with aliases such as Timor Jack and New Zealand Tom for their supposed outlaw behavior, transforming such animals into "the hero of many strange stories . . . much exaggerated accounts of real occurrences."[56]

One of Melville's favorite sources for *Moby-Dick*, Frederick Bennett's *Narrative of a Whaling Voyage around the Globe* (1840), perhaps best sums up the era's understanding of the whale. Bennett's explanation of the whale's tendency to make "willful, deliberate, and even judicious attempts against human pursuers," like in Chase's *Narrative*, reviles the creature for its wickedness. Chase acknowledges that the creature was "never before suspected of premeditated violence," but then, like Bennett, presents the *Essex* whale as his personal discovery, suggesting that the creature might not actually be so docile and peaceable, and pointing, like the day's phrenologists, to the shape of the whale's skull to explain its inherent truculence. Only in Bennett's and Melville's later descriptions does Chase's new aggressive whale become understood in more sophisticated terms, incorporating its will to survive as the main driver behind the dangers it posed to whalemen. "Actuated by a feeling of revenge," Bennett explains, crucially noting the whale's defensive position as the cause for its wild, unpredictable rushes, "by anxiety to escape its pursuers, or goaded by desperation by the weapons rankling in its body"—and only under such mortal threat—does the animal "act with deliberate design to do mischief."[57]

The impulse to impose agency "on a dumb brute . . . that simply smote thee from blindest instinct" and to be "enraged with a dumb thing," as Starbuck rightly asserts to Ahab on the quarterdeck, is alarmingly perverse and "seems blasphemous" according to his Quaker ethos.[58] Ahab's urge, as with Chase and DeBlois, was as old as the sea itself—drenched in thousands of years of myth sprung from what cognitive scientists call a "hyperactive agency detection device." Mariners have forever seen harbingers of death in nature, malevolent whales lurking beneath the ripples on the ocean, just as humans have forever attached exaggerated significance to their sensory worlds, whether in search of the divine or of the satanic. "We see faces in clouds, hear denunciations in thunder," as the writer Barbara Ehrenreich explains, "and sense transcendent beings all around us because we evolved on a planet densely occupied by other 'agents'—animals that could destroy us with the slash of a claw, arbitrarily and in seconds."[59]

However ancient and timeless this agency detection device, the whale's agency became both more sensationalized and more complicated as mid-century approached. New understandings of human culpability emerged, as Ahab's scruples would come under Melville's scrutiny. As we have seen, however, Chase's own intentions behind his depiction of the *Essex* whale would remain virtually unquestioned for centuries, and his maligned creature would haunt nautical lore over the same years. Like Shelley's *Frankenstein*, that "fighting whale" is Chase's own hideous offspring, born docile yet made wicked through human depravity. Born free and embodying vigor and physical beauty, like Melville's Billy Budd, the whale would find itself ensnared in a narrative trap devised by the fallen Chases and Claggarts, bent on concocting tales of evil where only innocence seemed to lie, all for the desire—boiling to bloodlust—to protect and promote their professional careers.

Owen Chase, aided by his skillful ghostwriter, cornered the book publishing market with his *Narrative*, forever shaping the tenor, plot, and sequence of the *Essex* whale chase in the popular imagination. When word spread of the wreck some two centuries ago, periodicals—from newspapers to popular story paper weeklies to highbrow magazines to the penny press—were there to publish their versions of the story. The book publishing industry would also seize on the tale's popularity, prominently marketing adaptations of it, along with other similar stories, in everything from natural history texts to whalemen's accounts to boys' adventure stories. Long after Melville reshaped the *Essex* tale for *Moby-Dick*, the weekly press, by way of the predatory Leon Lewis, pursued the elderly Thomas Nickerson's written record of his voyage aboard the *Two Brothers* as well as the *Essex*.

The real Pollard behind these tales—the humble night watchman referenced by Emerson and Melville—lay buried under all the media manipulation, the fanfare, and the angling for America's most coveted sea story. Given the media's power to enforce cultural understandings of captaincy, responsibility, and self-sacrifice, it would seem virtually impossible for a captain to survive his ship's loss, especially with fatalities among the crew, and still enjoy public respect. Yet despite attempts to malign him as a cracked and haunted seaman, Pollard enjoyed precisely this respect. As Nantucket's night watchman, his goodwill demonstrated on each of his voyages continued throughout his life on shore. Chase, for his part, lived out the experience so many ironically had presumed Pollard to have suffered, enduring the guilt of his errors and headstrong miscalculations that sealed the fate of the *Essex*. Chase's heroism could never be measured in the barrels of oil he brought to shore from decades of relentless whaling after the *Essex* tragedy. The quiet dignity, instead, of the conscientious yet star-crossed Captain Pollard should finally resonate with us in the twenty-first century, just as it resonated in the nineteenth century with Melville and Emerson—the two most significant voices of their generation to recognize the singularity of Pollard's forbearance, given his two wrecks. Guided by Emerson and Melville's compassionate apprehension of the twice-failed captain, this book has sought to redeem Pollard's memory from a teeming and furious sweep of print and now digital mythmaking. This "real captain Ahab" was no Ahab.

Thus Pollard deserves to be resurrected as a significant figure in cultural history shaping nautical lore—and not only isolated to America's major antebellum whaling ports. His redemption speaks to broader human themes of ambition and carrying scars with dignity, while humbly serving one's loyal community. Indeed, roughly two months after the *Essex* tragedy stunned Nantucket—the tiny island with a mighty hold on world commerce whose seamen's geographical reach rivaled those of the era's empires—Pollard again shipped out, with two *Essex* veterans and his community's support.

This book has attempted to place this tale of two captains in its proper perspective, not only to show the wide incongruence in various narratives of the same event, but to show precisely how each narrator's predicament and motives directed these divergent retellings. Pollard, interestingly, never engaged the storytelling industry spawned by the sinking of the *Essex*, an event that would shape the development of print and later digital culture. While he never put pen to paper to record his experience, defend his name, or set the record straight, he was, however, remarkably candid and transparent about reporting his experience to inquiring strangers. This was the Pollard Melville so admired—the captain free of pretense or affectation who refused to mask his scars and pain, instead bearing them with almost Whitmanian American dignity. This was the captain who also deeply impressed the most accomplished and celebrated ship commander of the era, Charles Wilkes.

Wilkes, famous for winning U.S. congressional support to lead the nation's last naval circumnavigation of the globe from 1838 to 1842, aimed at exploring uncharted waters from the Antarctic to the Bering Strait, met Pollard in August 1822 in a gam with the *Two Brothers*. Pollard was off the coast of Ecuador when he encountered the precocious twenty-four-year-old midshipman aboard the U.S. Navy schooner *Waterwitch*. Hauntingly, Wilkes, eager to hear Pollard's story, had asked the captain why he would venture out to sea so soon after enduring such a devastating loss. Wilkes recalled that despite sailing "for the same area of the ocean where he had encountered so much," where "it was to be expected that some effect of his former cruise would have been visible in his manner or conversation," Pollard instead "was cheerful and very modest in his account, and very desirous to afford us all the aid we might want," especially food, which one might have imagined such a captain to hold tightly, given his past experience. Little did Wilkes or Pollard's supportive Nantucket islanders know then, but the *Two Brothers*, too, would sink. Wilkes, meanwhile, left the encounter duly impressed that he "had by accident become acquainted with a hero, who did not even consider that he had overcome obstacles which would have crushed 99 out of a hundred." Given Pollard's "vividness about his descriptions of the scenes" and such poise and composure, his listener could barely "believe that the actor could have been the narrator so modest and unassuming was his account," and crucially, "most truthful."[60]

Narrator and participant during the *Two Brothers* journey, and even after its failure, were roles Pollard played at a distance indeed, as attested by his ability to discuss the event with a perfect stranger. Even among Nantucketers who had been close to those lost on the *Essex*, establishing such separation between their roles as "participants" and as narrators proved too difficult, and they struggled to tell the tale with composure. Although some islanders profaned the event with tasteless jokes, others found its mere mention sacrilege, with word circulating on the street that "the *Essex*" should not be uttered on Nantucket. Pollard appeared to be sufficiently in touch with the experience to avoid burying it; he could, and always did, answer anyone who asked of it, even after the loss of the *Two Brothers*. Chase, however, literally told a different tale, one that would suggest that in seeking to cope psychologically, he established a vast distance between himself and the event, between his roles as narrator and participant. Chase suffered more, yet enjoyed greater monetary success, in the wake of the tragedy. His decision to capitalize on the narrative, to eschew Pollard's unfiltered use of his own voice and instead assemble a tale calculated for profit, is articulated in his *Narrative*'s note to readers. The polished ghostwritten yarn designed to build up his image and defend his reputation may have become the period's best-selling account of the event, but it seems to have kept Chase further from coming to terms with his own fatal actions on the voyage. Only the former cabin boy Thomas Nickerson would similarly succumb, later in life, to the temptation to profit from the tale—even though this effort would never come to fruition—with his careful omissions and sensationalistic twists designed simultaneously to dignify his image and to sell the story. Although Chase earned vast wealth in the whaling industry, in his retirement he descended into madness, surely induced in part by his failure to face his actions on board the *Essex*.

Most likely a fleeing whale—hardly a vengeful one—collided with the *Essex*; Chase, not Pollard, was guilty of the faulty seamanship that precipitated the tragedy; and Owen Coffin drew the short straw that prompted his execution, which Charles Ramsdell carried out as dictated by a second lottery. The captain most certainly did not shoot Owen Coffin; nor did he shoot the cabin boy, Nickerson.[61] These are neither incidental nor trivial facts, but truths suppressed from the memory of the event that would have otherwise profoundly altered it to the benefit of both Pollard's and the whale's more deserving reputations. Chase's *Essex* story was a sort of *Jaws* of the nineteenth century, maligning whales and accelerating mass hunting on par with what Peter Benchley's character assassination would do to the great white shark, a role he later recanted to become the creature's greatest advocate.[62] As for Pollard, he was a survivor in the most dignified sense of the word, a man who may have momentarily preferred to remain on the sinking deck of the *Two Brothers* and let the sea roll over him as it has rolled for near eternity, but who returned to service, humanity, and the Nantucket Island that loved him.

NOTES

Prologue

1. Thomas Farel Heffernan, *Stove by a Whale: Owen Chase and the "Essex"* (Middletown, CT: Wesleyan University Press, 1981); Nathaniel Philbrick, *In the Heart of the Sea: The Tragedy of the Whaleship "Essex"* (New York: Penguin, 2000); Edward Leslie and Sterling Seagrave, *Desperate Journeys, Abandoned Souls: True Stories of Castaways and Other Survivors* (New York: Houghton Mifflin, 1988); Obed Macy, *The History of Nantucket* (Boston: Hilliard, Ray, and Co., 1835); Owen Chase, *Narrative of the Most Extraordinary and Distressing Shipwreck of the Whaleship "Essex"* (New York: W. B. Gilley, 1821).

2. "The *Essex* Whale-Ship," *New Hampshire Observer*, March 18, 1822, 2.

3. Thomas Nickerson, Owen Chase, and Others, *The Loss of the Ship "Essex," Sunk by a Whale: First Person Accounts*, ed. Nathaniel Philbrick and Thomas Philbrick (New York: Penguin, 2000), 73; hereafter *Loss*.

4. The constructed nature of nautical narratives is discussed in Greg Denning, *Performances* (Melbourne: Melbourne University Press, 1996), and Jason Berger, *Antebellum at Sea: Maritime Fantasies in Nineteenth-Century America* (Minneapolis: University of Minnesota Press, 2012). For more on how mariners transformed their experience at sea into literature, see C. L. R. James, *Mariners, Renegades, and Castaways: The Story of Herman Melville and the World We Live In* (New York: Schocken Books, 1985), Wilson Heflin, *Herman Melville's Whaling Years*, ed. Mary K. Bercaw Edwards and Thomas Farel Heffernan (Nashville: University of Vanderbilt Press, 2004), Thomas Philbrick, *James Fenimore Cooper and the Development of Sea Fiction* (Cambridge: Harvard University Press, 1961), Margaret Cohen, *The Novel and the Sea* (Princeton, NJ: Princeton University Press, 2010), and Haskell Springer, *America and the Sea: A Literary History* (Athens: University of Georgia Press, 1995).

5. Nickerson, Chase, and Others, x.

6. For more on how mariners conceived of their narratives at sea and were "mindful of the demands of contemporary publication," see Hester Blum, *The View from the Masthead: The Maritime Imagination and Antebellum American Sea Narratives* (Chapel Hill: University of North Carolina Press, 2008), 115.

7. Retired sailors, many of whom were "desperate for money," "peddled their yarns about adventure on the high seas," receiving some editorial assistance, often from "impecunious hawkers" like Lewis who "catered to the public's appetite for adventure and entertainment." Myra C. Glenn, *Jack Tar's Story: The Autobiographies and Memoirs of Sailors in Antebellum America* (New York: Cambridge University Press, 2010), 2.

8. Ralph Waldo Emerson, *The Journals and Miscellaneous Notebooks of Ralph Waldo Emerson*, ed. William H. Gilman, Ralph H. Orth, et al., 16 vols. (Cambridge: Harvard University Press, 1960–1982), 4: 265.

9. Foundational studies of maritime themes and texts in the broader culture are Samuel Otter, *Melville's Anatomies* (Berkeley: University of California Press, 1999), and Wai Chee Dimock, *Empire for Liberty: Melville and the Poetics of Individualism* (Princeton, NJ: Princeton University Press, 1989).

Chapter 1 Who Shot Owen Coffin?

1. Thomas Nickerson, Owen Chase, and Others, *The Loss of the Ship "Essex," Sunk by a Whale*, ed. Nathaniel Philbrick and Thomas Philbrick (New York: Penguin, 2000), hereafter *Loss*.

2. Nathaniel Philbrick, *In the Heart of the Sea: The Tragedy of the Whaleship "Essex"* (New York: Penguin, 2000), 179.

3. Homer, *The Odyssey*, ed. Thomas R. Walsh and Rodney Merrill (Ann Arbor: University of Michigan Press, 2002).

4. Philbrick, *In the Heart of the Sea*, 92–103.

5. Ibid., 36, 102, 175. Coffin was six months from his nineteenth birthday when he died.

6. Sophocles, *Antigone, Oedipus the King, Electra*, ed. Edith Hall et al. (Oxford: Oxford University Press, 1998).

7. *Loss*, 71–72.

8. For a historical novel that reconstructs scenes with embellished dialogue and actions based on documentary evidence, see Anne E. Beidler, *Eating Owen: The Imagined True Story of Four Coffins from Nantucket*, An Old Nantucket Mystery (Seattle: Coffeetown Press, 2009).

9. A. W. Brian Simpson, *Cannibalism and the Common Law: A Victorian Yachting Tragedy* (London: Hambledon Press, 1994), 317. Philbrick, *In the Heart of the Sea*, 276.

10. *Loss*, 77.

11. Melville "finds in the *Essex* story more than the basic plot elements of his novel," as Hester Blum astutely observes, particularly "the sailor's impulse to catalogue and contain in the face of oceanic loss," a gesture we see repeatedly in *Moby-Dick*, from Queequeg's preparation of his own coffin to Tashtego's poignant, yet tragically vain,

attempt to save the *Pequod*'s flag while the ship sinks: see Hester Blum, "Melville and Oceanic Studies," *The New Cambridge Companion to Herman Melville*, ed. Robert S. Levine (New York: Cambridge University Press, 2014), 29.

12. Philbrick, *In the Heart of the Sea*, 151.

13. *Loss*, 71.

14. Ibid., 181.

15. Cyrus Townsend Brady, "The Yarn of the *Essex* Whaler," *Cosmopolitan*, November 1904, 72.

16. For more on the transmission of oral storytelling to print culture in Melville, see Mary K. Bercaw Edwards, *Cannibal Old Me: Spoken Sources in Melville's Works* (Kent, OH: Kent State University Press, 2009), and Kevin J. Hayes, who notes that "the legends of Mocha Dick [a sperm whale infamous for repeated clashes with whalers off the shore of southern Chile near the island of Mocha] and the sinking of the *Essex* provided partial inspiration, yet Melville would synthesize many legends before he finished his new book," some of them overheard at the countless gams in which he participated at sea, *Melville's Folk Roots* (Kent, OH: Kent State University Press, 1999), 78. Such encounters enabled him to "borrow multiple elements he had heard from other whalemen," Hayes, 79.

17. For more on the social psychology of scapegoating, see Neil J. Smelser, "Psychological Trauma and Cultural Trauma," in *Cultural Trauma and Collective Identity*, ed. Ron Eyerman et al. (Berkeley: University of California Press, 2004): 31–59

18. *Loss*, 181.

19. Herman Melville, *Moby-Dick*, ed. Harrison Hayford, Hershel Parker, and G. Thomas Tanselle (Evanston and Chicago: Northwestern University Press and Newberry Library, 1988), 26.

20. Melville, 316.

21. Ibid., 206.

22. *Loss*, 208.

23. Ibid., 209.

24. Thomas Heffernan, *Stove by a Whale: Owen Chase and the "Essex"* (Middletown, CT: Wesleyan University Press, 1981), 209.

25. Although Pollard himself was not a practicing Quaker, he likely would have been familiar with and even followed the principles of the faith, since he had been exposed to it through his devout grandparents. The family's Quakerism can be traced to Pollard's great-grandmother, Mehitable Pollard, a Quaker minister. Philbrick, *In the Heart of the Sea*, 175.

26. *Loss*, 181. Note that Coffin's mother was actually Pollard's aunt, not his sister, as Nickerson erroneously writes.

27. Ibid., 170–71.

28. Ibid., 69.

29. Edgar Allan Poe, *Poetry and Tales*, ed. Patrick F. Quinn (New York: Library of America, 1984), 1096.

30. Poe, 1099. For more on black sailors and the fear of violent revolution in Poe, see Kevin J. Hayes, *A History of Virginia Literature* (New York: Cambridge University Press, 2015), 187.

31. Charles Olson, *Call Me Ishmael* (Baltimore: Johns Hopkins University Press, 1997, 5.

32. Ibid., 5.

33. Philbrick notes that "certainly the statistic raises suspicion—of the first four sailors to be eaten, all were black. Short of murdering the black crew members, the Nantucketers could have refused to share meat with them," *In the Heart of the Sea*, 173. Such refusal to share may have actually happened more militantly than one might suspect, especially given Chase's description of how "when one of the white men awoke me, and informed me that one of the blacks had taken some bread . . . I immediately took my pistol in my hand, and charged him if he had taken any, to give it up without the least hesitation, or I should instantly shoot him!" *Loss*, 62.

34. No Author, *Six Species of Men; With Cuts Representing the Types of Caucasian, Mongol, Malay, Indian, Esquimaux and Negro with Their General Physical and Mental Qualities, Laws of Organization, Relations to Civilization, &c.* (New York: Van Evrie, Horton, and Company, 1866). As the title illustrates, such racial typologies were still espoused even after the Civil War. In the 1820s the ideology was even more regressive and divisive. For more on the vocational opportunity whaling represented to prewar blacks given legal slavery in the South and their exclusion from the professions in the North, see Philbrick, *In the Heart of the Sea*, 25–27.

35. Quoted in Philbrick, *In the Heart of the Sea*, 257; Reay Tannahill, *Flesh and Blood: A History of the Cannibal Complex* (New York: Stern and Day, 1975); Edouard A. Stackpole, *The Sea Hunters: The Great Age of Whaling* (Philadelphia: Lippincott: 1953).

36. Olson, *Call Me Ishmael*.

37. Ibid., 21.

38. For an excellent study of "the social and symbolic practices through which eating and food cultures inform the production of racial difference" as it relates to cannibalism in antebellum literature, see Kyla Wazana Tompkins, *Racial Indigestion: Eating Bodies in the Nineteenth Century* (New York: New York University Press, 2012), 1, 94–96, 112.

39. Henry Carlisle, *The Jonah Man* (New York: Knopf, 1984), 166.

Chapter 2 Damage Control

1. Henry Carlisle, *The Jonah Man* (New York: Knopf, 1984), 166.

2. Thomas Nickerson, Owen Chase, and Others, *The Loss of the Whaleship "Essex,"*

Sunk by a Whale, ed. Nathaniel Philbrick (New York: Penguin, 2000), 199; hereafter *Loss*.

3. *Loss*, 8.

4. Herman Melville, *Clarel: A Poem and Pilgrimage in the Holy Land*, ed. Hershel Parker (Evanston, IL: Northwestern University Press, 2008), 117.

5. *Loss*, 79, italics mine.

6. Thomas Heffernan, *Stove by a Whale: Owen Chase and the* Essex (Middletown, CT: Wesleyan University Press, 1981), 156.

7. As cited in Nathaniel Philbrick, *Away Off Shore: Nantucket Island and Its People, 1602–1890* (Nantucket, MA: Mill Hill Press, 1993).

8. See Cree LeFavour, "'Jane Eyre Fever': Deciphering the Astonishing Popular Success of Charlotte Brontë in Antebellum America," *Book History* 7 (2004): 113–41.

9. Edgar Allan Poe, *Poetry and Tales*, ed. Patrick F. Quinn (New York: Library of America, 1984), 1008.

10. Walt Whitman, *The Complete Poems* (New York: Penguin, 1986), 300.

11. Poe, 1069.

12. *Loss*, 14.

13. For an excellent discussion of the relative veracity of "logbook truths," naval memoirs, and the literary marketplace, particularly James Fenimore Cooper's "ambivalence about his choice to use American materials" in light of his refusal "to 'prostitute' himself to the market for British sea tales," see Hester Blum, *The View from the Masthead: The Maritime Imagination and Antebellum Sea Narratives* (Chapel Hill: University of North Carolina Press), 71–108.

14. Ibid.

15. Charles Sellers, *The Market Revolution: Jacksonian America, 1815–1846* (Oxford: Oxford University Press, 1991).

16. *Loss*, 14.

17. Lance E. Davis et al., *In Pursuit of Leviathan: Technology, Institutions, Productivity, and Profits in American Whaling, 1816–1906* (Chicago: University of Chicago Press, 1997), 390.

18. Davis et al., 389; Charles Nordhoff, *Whaling and Fishing* (New York: Dodd, Mead & Co., 1895), 2.

19. Although very real differences in this case separate the authorial circumstances of mariners and indentured servants, the maritime narratives themselves habitually play on the trope of slavery. For a powerful discussion of the analogy between sailor and slave, see Samuel Otter, *Melville's Anatomies* (Berkeley: University of California Press, 1999). Particularly useful is Otter's observation of "the collapsing of distance between sailor and slave" in Melville's *White Jacket*, a development that "threatens the narrator himself . . . and provokes a fantastic attempt at self-preservation." This pattern easily extends to *Billy Budd* as well as Chase's *Narrative*, 77.

20. Sebastian Junger, *The Perfect Storm: A True Story of Men against the Sea* (New York: W. W. Norton and Company, 2009), 74.

21. Leo Braudy, "Knowing the Performer from the Performance: Fame, Celebrity, and Literary Studies," *Publication of the Modern Language Association* 126, no. 4 (October 2011): 1071.

22. Heffernan, 158. And see Heffernan, 159, for an excellent survey of the data regarding the various courses the publication of the *Narrative* may have taken.

23. For details on Mathew Carey and his distribution network, see Ronald J. Zboray, *A Fictive People: Antebellum Economic Development and the American Reading Public* (New York: Oxford University Press, 1993), 37–54.

24. Braudy, 1072.

25. Ibid., 1074.

26. *Loss*, 15.

27. Ibid.

28. Poe, 1070–71.

29. For more on the publishing history of Poe's *Narrative of Arthur Gordon Pym*, see Kevin J. Hayes, *Poe and the Printed Word* (New York: Cambridge University Press, 2000), 64–73.

30. *Loss*, 16.

31. Elmo Paul Hohman, "Wages, Risk, and Profits in the Whaling Industry," *Quarterly Journal of Economics* 40 (August 1926): 230; see also Davis's discussion of "The Whaleman's Lay," 154–68.

32. Orestes Brownson, *The Laboring Classes: An Article from the "Boston Quarterly Review"* (Boston: Benjamin H. Greene, 1840), 13.

33. Davis, 186.

34. Blum, 213.

35. Davis, 387.

36. Ibid., 424.

37. Ibid.

38. National Maritime Digital Library, retrieved April 19, 2012, nmdl.org/aowv/whvoyage.cfm?VesselNumber=676 and nmdl.org/aowv/whvoyage.cfm?VesselNumber=1077.

39. Herman Melville, *Redburn: His First Voyage*, ed. Harrison Hayford, Hershel Parker, and G. Thomas Tanselle (Evanston and Chicago: Northwestern University Press and Newberry Library, 1969), 157; Martyn Smith, "Between Book and Reality: The Guidebook in *Redburn* and *Clarel*," *Leviathan: A Journal of Melville Studies* 13, no. 3 (2011): 30–40.

40. Melville, *Redburn*, 193.

41. *Loss*, 19.

42. Herman Melville, *Moby-Dick*, ed. Harrison Hayford, Hershel Parker, and

G. Thomas Tanselle (Evanston and Chicago: Northwestern University Press and Newberry Library, 1988), 116.

43. *Loss*, xii.

44. Ibid., 34.

45. Ibid., 40.

46. Ibid., 42.

47. Ibid., 56.

48. Ibid., 62.

49. Ibid., 167.

50. Heffernan, 11, 156.

51. Heffernan, 85; Captain Joseph Mitchell II, quoted in Heffernan, 86.

52. *Loss*, 21.

53. Ibid., 86.

Chapter 3 Nickerson and Lewis

Portions of this chapter were previously published as "The Nineteenth-Century Weekly Press and the Tumultuous Career of Journalist Leon Lewis," *Journalism History* 39, no. 3 (Fall 2013): 156–67.

1. Bonner sought a broad audience. In addition to serial fiction with weekly installments, the *Ledger*'s content included breaking news, political analysis, regular columns by popular writers such as Fanny Fern, biography, popular history, and guest commentary from statesmen such as U.S. congressman and secretary of state Edward Everett. The nineteenth century's most influential newspaper editor, Horace Greeley, chose Bonner's *Ledger* as the platform for his autobiography, published in weekly installments less than one year prior to his death. New York's most celebrated clergyman of the mid-nineteenth century, Henry Ward Beecher, who was the brother of Harriet Beecher Stowe, appeared prominently in the *Ledger*, enjoying a lucrative contract for his serial novel *Norwood; or, Village Life in New England* (1868). Matthew Hale Smith, *Sunshine and Shadow in New York* (Hartford, CT: J. B. Burr and Company, 1868), 604–21; David Dowling, *Literary Partnerships and the Marketplace: Writers and Mentors in Nineteenth-Century America* (Baton Rouge: LSU Press, 2012), 89–115.

2. Thomas Nickerson, *The Loss of the Ship "Essex" Sunk by a Whale and the Ordeal of the Crew in Open Boats*, ed. Helen Winslow Chase and Edouard A. Stackpole (Nantucket, MA: Nantucket Historical Association), 1984, 8; hereafter Nickerson Stackpole.

3. "As the facts concerning the passage of the open boats proceeds [*sic*] there are enough differences with the Chase story to intrigue the reader, as there are, naturally enough, similarities to Chase's accounts," Stackpole in Nickerson, 9.

4. For more on the broader cultural context of the nineteenth-century weekly

press, see Barbara Hochman, *"Uncle Tom's Cabin" and the Reading Revolution: Race, Literacy, Childhood, and Fiction, 1851–1911* (Amherst: University of Massachusetts Press, 2011); Frank Luther Mott, *A History of American Magazines*, vol. 2, *1850–1865* (Cambridge, MA: Harvard University Press, 1936); Isabelle Lehuu, *Carnival on the Page: Popular Print Media in Antebellum America* (Charlotte: University of North Carolina Press, 2000); Patricia Okker, *Social Stories: The Magazine Novel in Nineteenth Century America* (Charlottesville: University of Virginia Press, 2003); John C. Hartsock, *A History of American Literary Journalism: The Emergence of a Modern Narrative Form* (Amherst: University of Massachusetts Press, 2000).

5. Nickerson Stackpole, 10.

6. Mary Noel, *Villains Galore: The Heyday of the Popular Story Weekly* (New York: Macmillan, 1954), 76.

7. Stanwood Cobb, *The Magnificent Partnership* (New York: Vantage, 1954), 28–29.

8. Nickerson Stackpole, 8.

9. Leon Lewis, *Andrée at the Pole: With Details of His Fate* (New York: G. W. Dillingham, 1898), 10.

10. *New York Weekly*, March 17, 1864, 4.

11. *New York Weekly*, October 6, 1864, 3.

12. Noel, 71.

13. "Hon. Edward Everett and the *New York Ledger*," *Daily Cleveland Herald*, December 13, 1858, col. C.

14. *Loss*, 180.

15. *Loss*, 181.

16. Ibid.

17. *Loss*, 182–83.

18. Nickerson Stackpole, 9.

19. Jan Cohn, *Romance and the Erotics of Property: Mass Market Fiction for Women* (Durham, NC: Duke University Press, 1988), 70–71.

20. Leon Lewis to Robert Bonner, September 26, 1878, "Bonner Papers," NYPL.

21. Harriet Lewis to Robert Bonner, May 1, 1878, "Bonner Papers," NYPL.

22. Leon Lewis to Robert Bonner, n.d., n.m., 1898, "Bonner Papers, NYPL.

23. Patricia Cline Cohen et al., *The Flash Press: Sporting Male Weeklies in 1840s New York* (Chicago: University of Chicago Press, 2008), 1.

24. *Hartford Weekly Times*, April 23, 1853.

25. This also attests to Lewis's predilection for consorting in the world of the flash press, as seen in the lurid content of his 1879 *Penn Yan Mystery*. The *Whip*, the *Flash*, the *Rake*, and the *Libertine* all exposed scandals as a means of extorting and blackmailing and vowed to "keep a watchful eye on all brothels and their frail inmates": quoted in Cline Cohen et. al., 176. For more on the rampant corruption and organized crime in flash paper culture, See Leon Jackson, "Exposing Periodicals: Moral

Failure, Knowledge Networks, and Serial Culture in Antebellum America," keynote address, Knowledge Networks Conference, University of Nottingham, UK, May 27, 2011.

26. Quoted in Noel, 193.

27. Albert Johannsen, *The House of Beadle and Adams and Its Dime and Nickel Novels* (Norman: Oklahoma University Press, 1950), 2: 183–86.

28. Quoted in *Yesterday's Papers*, "'Leon Lewis' (1833–1920)," http://john-adcock .blogspot.ca/2011/08/leon-lewis-1833-1920.html.

29. Toni Johnson-Woods, "The Virtual Reading Communities of the *London Journal*, the *New York Ledger*, and the *Australian Journal*," in *Nineteenth-Century Media and the Construction of Identities*, ed. Laurel Brake, Bill Bell, et al. (New York: Palgrave Macmillan, 2000), 359.

30. "Being the Story of the Coming of a Deluge," *New York Times*, October 6, 1907.

31. Ibid.

32. Noel, 193.

Chapter 4 Lightning Strikes Twice

1. Jason T. Raupp and Kelly Gleason, "Submerged Whaling Heritage in Papahanaumokuakea Marine National Monument," *AIMA Bulletin* 34 (2010): 66–74.

2. Thomas Nickerson, "Loss of the Ship *Two Brothers* of Nantucket," Nantucket Historical Association Collection 106, Folder 3.5.

3. Stewart Gordon, *A History of the World in Sixteen Shipwrecks* (Hanover, NH: University Press of New England, 2015), 211–22.

4. "Traces of Cocaine Found on Hair Sample from *Costa Concordia* Captain," *Herald Sun*, February 20, 2012. "Cocaine Found on the Hair of Cruise Captain Francesco Schettino, Whose Ship Aground in Italy," *New York Daily News*, February 18, 2012.

5. Nathaniel Philbrick, *In the Heart of the Sea: The Tragedy of the Whaleship "Essex"* (New York: Penguin, 2000), 211.

6. Thomas Nickerson, Owen Chase, and Others, *The Loss of the Ship "Essex," Sunk by a Whale*, ed. Nathaniel Philbrick and Thomas Philbrick (New York: Penguin, 2000), 180–81, hereafter *Loss*.

7. Obed Macy, *The History of Nantucket* (Boston: Hilliard, Gray, and Co., 1835), 249.

8. Thomas Nickerson, "Loss of the Ship *Two Brothers* of Nantucket," Nantucket Historical Association Research Library, MS 106—Thomas Nickerson Collection, 1819–1876, Folder 3.5, 1a; hereafter Nickerson, *Two Brothers*.

9. Ben Simons, "Thomas Nickerson's Account of the Wreck of the *Two Brothers*," *Historic Nantucket: A Publication of the Nantucket Historical Association* 60, no. 3 (Fall 2010), 12.

10. *Loss*, 199.

11. Nickerson, *Two Brothers,* 1d.

12. Quoted in Evan Thomas, *John Paul Jones: Sailor, Hero, Father of the American Navy* (New York: Simon & Schuster, 2004), 9.

13. Nickerson, *Two Brothers,* 1e.

14. Ibid., 1f.

15. Eben Gardner (MS copy by William Randall), "Sea Account," Nantucket Historical Association Research Library, MS 15—Ships' Papers Collection, Folder 192.5, 1–2.

16. Nickerson, *Two Brothers,* 1f.

17. Gardner, 3.

18. *Loss,* 181.

19. Nickerson, *Two Brothers,* 1i.

20. Gardner, 1–2.

21. Heffernan only accounts for the fact that the captain of the *Martha* was John H. Pease, a relative of Captain Valentine Pease of the *Acushnet,* on which Melville journeyed in 1841: 150–51. Heffernan also transcribes the Gardner account strictly according to the original holograph, disregarding an earlier typed manuscript copy made in 1967, which takes liberties with the grammar, syntax, and diction of the original (150–51). Heffernan interestingly yields to Gardner rather than Nickerson as the authority on the event, reprinting the first mate's account in its entirety.

22. Herman Melville, *Moby-Dick,* ed. Harrison Hayford, Hershel Parker, and G. Thomas Tanselle (Evanston and Chicago: Northwestern University Press and Newberry Library, 1988), 90.

23. Ibid., 110. Captain James Cook was a British explorer famous for three voyages covering vast expanses of uncharted waters. He undertook the first of these missions to map unknown lands and oceans in 1766 and died in Hawaii on his third and final voyage in 1799. In 1803 Adam Johann von Krusenstern led a Russian two-ship expedition around the world, whose main objective was to establish the fur trade with Russian America, which is now Alaska, as well as to develop trade relations with China, Japan, and nations in South America. He returned safely in 1806 bearing maps and detailed records of his journey. The most popular source on the topic available to Melville, one that went through multiple editions from the 1840s to the 1860s, was Anonymous, *Voyages Round the World: From the Death of Captain Cook to the Present Time* (New York: Harper Brothers, 1844).

24. Mary Shelley, *Frankenstein* (New York: Cambridge University Press, 2000), 214.

25. Nickerson, *Two Brothers* 3–2a. Both prose narrative and poem are coupled in the NHA archive as parts of the same document, in keeping with what I argue were Nickerson's intentions for publication.

26. Ibid.

27. *Loss,* 193.

28. Ibid.

29. Review of *Leisure Hours at Sea*, by William Leggett, *North American Review* 5, no. 342 (1825): 454–55.

30. *Loss*, 181.

31. Nickerson, *Two Brothers* 3–2a.

32. Ibid.

33. Nickerson, *Two Brothers* 3–2b.

34. Ibid., 3–2d.

35. Ibid., 3–2e.

36. *Loss*, 17–18.

37. Nickerson, *Two Brothers* 3–2f.

38. Melville, *Moby-Dick*, 6.

39. Nickerson, *Two Brothers* 3–2f.

40. Melville, *Moby-Dick*, 163.

41. Nickerson, *Two Brothers* 3–2g.

42. Ibid., 3–2h.

43. Ibid., 3–2j.

44. Ibid., 3–2k.

45. Ibid., 3–2l.

Chapter 5 Night Watchman

1. Thomas Nickerson, Owen Chase, and Others, *The Loss of the Ship "Essex," Sunk by a Whale*, ed. Nathaniel Philbrick and Thomas Philbrick (New York: Penguin, 2000), 78, hereafter *Loss*.

2. Ralph Waldo Emerson, *The Collected Works of Ralph Waldo Emerson: Essays, Second Series*, vol. 3, ed. Alfred R. Ferguson, Joseph Slater, and Douglas Emory Wilson (Cambridge: Harvard University Press, 1983), 49.

3. Edward Byers, *The Nation of Nantucket: Society and Politics in an Early American Commercial Center, 1660–1820* (Boston: Northeastern University Press, 1987), 117. Excellent histories of Nantucket include Nathaniel Philbrick, *Away Off Shore: Nantucket Island and Its People, 1602–1890* (Nantucket, MA: Mill Hill Press, 1993); Edouard Stackpole and Melvin B. Summerfield, *Nantucket Doorways* (Lanham, MD: Madison Books, 1992); Edouard A. Stackpole, *Nantucket in the American Revolution* (Nantucket, MA: Nantucket Historical Association, 1976); Edouard A. Stackpole, *The Sea Hunters: New England Whalemen during Two Centuries, 1635–1835* (Philadelphia: Lippincott, 1953); Alexander Starbuck, *Nantucket Genealogies* (Baltimore: Clearfield, 2009); Robert J. Leach and Peter Gow, *Quaker Nantucket: The Religious Community behind the Whaling Empire* (Nantucket, MA: Mill Hill Press, 1997); Lisa Norling, *Captain Ahab Had a Wife: New England Women and the Whalefishery, 1720–1870* (Chapel

Hill: University of North Carolina Press, 2000); and Nathaniel Philbrick, "'Every Wave Is a Fortune': Nantucket Island and the Making of an American Icon," *New England Quarterly* (1993): 443–47.

4. J. Hector St. John de Crèvecœur, *Letters from an American Farmer* (Carlisle, MA: Applewood Books, 2007), 204.

5. Quoted in Byers, 300.

6. Melville, *Moby-Dick*, 64.

7. Ralph Waldo Emerson, *The Journals and Miscellaneous Notebooks of Ralph Waldo Emerson*, vol. 10, ed. William H. Gilman, Ralph H. Orth, et. al. (Cambridge: Harvard University Press, 1973), 63.

8. For more on the managerial function of Nantucket's success in the whaling industry, see Robert C. Ellickson, "A Hypothesis of Wealth-Maximizing Norms: Evidence from the Whaling Industry," *Journal of Law, Economics, & Organization* 5, no. 1 (Spring 1989): 83–97.

9. Byers, 175.

10. Crèvecœur, 203.

11. Many citizens may have stopped calling themselves Quakers, or ceased attending regular meetings, which were and still are held in plain buildings bearing no religious iconography and no pulpit from which an intermediary authority might hold forth over a rapt congregation. But Quaker culture still operated according to its blend of close-knit community and profound respect for personal individuality. To witness Quakers at worship is to see a group more intimately connected through the close physical space they share than through any organized ritual bonding them. No perfunctory words burden these meetings, and statements are uttered entirely on the volition of those present, in any order and on any subject deemed worthy.

12. *Loss*, 222.

13. Ibid., 78–79.

14. Harrison Hayford and Lynn Horth, "Melville's Memoranda in Chase's Narrative of the *Essex*," in Melville, *Moby-Dick*, 991.

15. Quoted in Olson, 109.

16. Quoted in Heffernan, 169.

17. After *Moby-Dick* was dismissed by critics, Melville pursued the mixed-genre form modeled after the French novel, according to Sheila Post-Lauria, *Correspondent Colorings: Melville in the Marketplace* (Amherst: University of Massachusetts Press, 1996).

18. For more on *Clarel* see Hershel Parker, *Melville: The Making of a Poet* (Evanston, IL: Northwestern University Press, 2008); and William Potter, *"Clarel" and the Intersympathy of Creeds* (Kent, OH: Kent State University Press, 2004).

19. Quoted in Heffernan, 169.

20. Heffernan, 122–26.

21. Quoted in Heffernan, 180.

22. Ibid, 181.

23. A. B. C. Whipple, "Three-Month Ordeal in Open Boats," *Life*, November 10, 1952, 144–56.

24. Richard A. Friedman, "Psychiatry's Identity Crisis," *New York Times*, July 17, 2015.

25. Nathaniel Philbrick, *In the Heart of the Sea: The Tragedy of the Whaleship "Essex"* (New York: Penguin, 2000), 212.

26. Ibid., 228.

27. *Loss*, 223.

28. John Leach and Jo Campling, *Survival Psychology* (New York: Macmillan, 1994), 177.

29. For more on new findings suggesting growth rather than disorder after trauma, and detailing the corrective and restorative emotional responses that can result from violent experiences, see Stephen Joseph, *What Doesn't Kill Us: The New Psychology of Posttraumatic Growth* (New York: Basic Books, 2011); and Lawrence G. Calhoun and Richard G. Tedeschi, *Posttraumatic Growth in Clinical Practice* (New York: Routledge, 2013).

30. *Loss*, 221–22.

31. Jonathan Miles, *The Wreck of the "Medusa": The Most Famous Sea Disaster of the Nineteenth Century* (New York: Grove, 2007).

32. Quoted in Daniel Diehl and Mark P. Donnelly, *Eat Thy Neighbor: A History of Cannibalism* (Gloucestershire, UK: Sutton Publishing, 2008), 45.

33. Edouard A. Stackpole, *Life Saving Nantucket* (Nantucket Island, MA: Nantucket Life Saving Museum, 1972), 13.

34. "Whalemen's Shipping List," Nantucket Historical Association, Research Library and Archives.

35. *Loss*, 223.

36. Shiguro Takada, *Contingency Cannibalism: Superhardcore Survivalism's Dirty Little Secret* (Boulder, CO: Paladin Press, 1999), 17.

37. Melville, *Moby-Dick*, 206.

38. Takada, 17.

39. Roland Leslie Warren, *Mary Coffin Starbuck and the Early History of Nantucket* (Pingry Press, 1987); Philbrick, *In the Heart of the Sea*, 8–9; Byers.

40. Quoted in Heffernan, 169.

41. Henry Carlisle, *The Jonah Man* (New York: Knopf, 1984), 221.

42. Ibid., 228.

43. Quoted in Carlisle, 259.

Chapter 6 The Real Ahab

1. Even in the face of overwhelming evidence, bloggers doubled down on their justifications for Pollard as Melville's model for Ahab. Online commentator Daniel Kuehn, for example, represented the legions who insisted that "captain Ahab was real," although "the real captain Ahab was more pathetic than the one in Melville's book," Daniel Kuehn, "Moby Dick Discovery," *Facts and Other Stubborn Things*, February 19, 2011, factsandotherstubbornthings.blogspot; "'Moby Dick' Captain's Ship Found," BBC Mobile News U.S. & Canada, February 12, 2011; "The Real Captain Ahab's Ship: Found," *Flavorwire*, February 12, 2011.

2. Justin Ellis, "Alan Rusbridger on the *Guardian*'s Open Journalism, Paywalls and Why They're Preplanning More of the Newspaper," Nieman Journalism Lab, May 29, 2012. On the merits and defects of citizen journalism, see Melissa Wall, *Citizen Journalism: Valuable, Useless, or Dangerous?* (International Debate Education Association and iDebate Press, 2012).

3. Archaeologists had been collecting artifacts of the *Two Brothers* wreckage site since 2008. The first scientific article appeared two years later, by Jason T. Raupp and Kelly Gleason, "Submerged Whaling Heritage in Papahanaumokuakea Marine National Monument," *AIMA Bulletin* 34 (2010): 66–74. A 2011 press release inspired major newspapers and magazines to cover the story, with the more reputable ones relying on lead archaeologist Kelly Gleason and the Nantucket Historical Association for their sources. *National Geographic News*, for example, stopped short of proclaiming Pollard "the real Captain Ahab," and instead cited the wreck and captain's more precise influences on Melville: Ker Than, "Rare 1823 Wreck Found—Capt. Linked to *Moby-Dick*, Cannibalism," *National Geographic*, February 11, 2011.

4. As a subset of fan communities and fandom, the aca-fan is discussed in Henry Jenkins et al., *Spreadable Media: Creating Value and Meaning in a Networked Culture* (New York: New York University Press, 2013).

5. Stefan Sonvilla-Weiss, ed., *Mashup Cultures* (New York: Springer, 2010), 18.

6. Ibid., 20.

7. Thomas Nickerson, Owen Chase, and Others, *The Loss of the Ship "Essex," Sunk by a Whale*, ed. Nathaniel Philbrick and Thomas Philbrick (New York: Penguin, 2000), 140; hereafter *Loss*.

8. Owen Chase et al., *Narratives of the Wreck of the Whaleship "Essex,"* ed. Robert Gibbings (Mineola, NY: Dover, 1989), 77.

9. Quoted in Thomas Nickerson, *The Loss of the Ship "Essex," Sunk by a Whale*, eds. Helen Winslow Chase and Edouard A. Stackpole (Nantucket, MA: Nantucket Historical Association, 1984), 81, hereafter Nickerson Stackpole.

10. Edouard A. Stackpole, *The Sea Hunters: New England Whalemen during Two Centuries, 1635–1835* (Philadelphia: Lippincott, 1953), 81.

11. Obed Macy, *The History of Nantucket* (Boston: Hilliard, Gray, and Co., 1835), 242.

12. Henry Carlisle, *The Jonah Man* (New York: Knopf, 1984), 106.

13. Ibid., 106.

14. Ibid., 107.

15. Chase judged "the speed of the whale [to be] about six" knots, *Loss*, 26.

16. Nathaniel Philbrick, *In the Heart of the Sea: The Tragedy of the Whaleship "Essex"* (New York: Penguin, 2000), 178.

17. Geoffrey Sanborn, *The Sign of the Cannibal: Melville and the Making of a Post-colonial Reader* (Durham, NC: Duke University Press, 1995), 205–6.

18. Quoted in Thomas Heffernan, *Stove by a Whale: Owen Chase and the "Essex"* (Middletown, CT: Wesleyan University Press, 1981), 168.

19. Herman Melville, *Moby-Dick*, ed. Harrison Hayford, Hershel Parker, and G. Thomas Tanselle (Evanston and Chicago: Northwestern University Press and Newberry Library, 1988), 206.

20. Notably the Sandwich Islands (Hawaii) should not be confused with the Marquesas Islands, a desired destination for Pollard and one not plagued by hurricanes.

21. David S. Reynolds, *Beneath the American Renaissance: The Subversive Imagination in the Age of Emerson and Melville* (New York: Knopf, 1988).

22. *Loss*, 167.

23. Ibid., 78.

24. Heffernan, 171.

25. "Preface," *The Sailor's Magazine and Naval Journal* 7 (August 1835): iii.

26. "The Whale," *The Sailor's Magazine and Naval Journal* 7, no. 75 (November 1834): 72.

27. The current Wikipedia page on the *Essex* relies primarily on Chase's *Narrative*, testifying to the enduring dominance of his testimony over Nickerson's.

28. Edward Byers, *Nantucket Nation: Society and Politics in an Early American Commercial Center, 1660–1820* (Boston: Northeastern University Press), 296–98.

29. *Maryland Gazette and Political Intelligencer*, June 21, 1821, 25D.

30. Heffernan, 166.

31. *Third Annual Report of the American Seamen's Friend Society* (Boston: J. Seymour, 1831), 6.

32. "Give the Sailor Good Books," *Sheet Anchor*, September 20, 1845, 140.

33. Heffernan, 8.

34. *Loss*, 72.

35. Melville, *Moby-Dick*, 74.

36. Ibid.

37. Heffernan, 144.

38. Ibid., 7–8.

39. J. Hector St. John de Crèvecœur, *Letters from an American Farmer* (New York: E. P. Dutton, 1957), 109–10.

40. Clifford Ashley, *The Yankee Whaler* (Boston: Houghton, 1926), 6.

41. Edward S. Davoll, "The Captain's Specific Orders on the Commencement of a Whale Voyage to His Officers and Crew," *Old Dartmouth Historical Sketches* 81 (June 5, 1981), 11.

Coda

Portions of this chapter were previously published as "Media, Myth, and the 'Fighting Whale' in Maritime Narratives," *Genre: Forms of Discourse and Culture* 47 no. 3 (Fall 2014): 255–83.

1. Thomas Beale, *The Natural History of the Sperm Whale* (London: John van Voorst, 1839), 46.

2. Ibid., 48.

3. The only major natural enemy of the sperm whale is the killer whale, according to marine biologist Hal Whitehead in *Sperm Whales: Social Evolution in the Ocean* (Chicago: University of Chicago Press, 2003). He notes, however, that "although they rarely kill sperms, the threat of killer whale predation, especially on the young, may have been an important factor in sperm whale evolution" (77). Their primary means of defense is by clustering in a formation, yet not always with heads out, as one might suppose, to use their prominent shield-like brows for protection. Just as frequently they adopt the "'Marguerite formation,' with their tails outward, their heads together, and their bodies radiating outward like the spokes of a wheel" (194). In conflicts the sperm whale is more inclined toward group defense than solitary attack.

4. Eric Jay Dolin, *Leviathan: The History of Whaling in America* (New York: Norton, 2007), 78.

5. A similar function has been found in a pocket of fat located near a whale's eyes. Just as spermaceti displaces pressure on the brain, "the only means available to aid the eye in the deep-diving mammal that is not available to its terrestrial counterparts is ... intraocular fat," which also aids in thermal control by providing insulation from cold temperatures that would threaten the neural function of the eyes and brain, both extremely sensitive organs. William W. Dawson, "The Cetacean Eye," *Cetacean Behavior: Mechanisms and Functions*, ed. Louis M. Herman (New York: John Wiley & Sons, 1980), 90.

6. Adam Summers, "Fat Heads Sink Ships," *Natural History* (September 2002): 40–41.

7. Melville, *Moby-Dick*, 327.

8. Ibid., 438.

9. Ibid., 184.

10. David K. Caldwell et al., "Behavior of the Sperm Whale, *Physeter Catodon L.*," *Whales, Dolphins, and Porpoises*, ed. Kenneth S. Norris (Berkeley: University of California Press, 1966), 690.

11. Melville, *Moby-Dick*, 179.

12. Ibid., 179–80.

13. Ibid., 183, 64.

14. A passage from Milton's work appeared as an epigraph to *Frankenstein*.

15. Bertram F. Mallee, Louis J. Moses, and Dare A. Baldwin, *Intentions and Intentionality: Foundations of Social Cognition* (Boston: MIT Press, 2001), 1.

16. Glover M. Allen, *Monographs on the Natural History of New England: The Whalebone Whales of New England* (Boston: Boston Society for Natural History, 1916), 198.

17. Amy R. Knowlton and Scott D. Kraus, "Mortality and Serious Injury of Northern Right Whales (*Eubalaena Glacialis*) in the Western North Atlantic Ocean," *Journal of Cetacean Restoration Management* 2 (2001): 193. The frequency of collisions increased from 1950 to 1970 along with the number and speed of ships at sea, according to David W. Laist et al., "Collisions between Ships and Whales," *Marine Mammal Science* 17, no. 1 (January 2001): 35–75. The incidence of collisions between boats has also been a major concern ever since the highly visible sinking of the HMS *Victoria* at the end of the nineteenth century, an event discussed in the epilogue. Also, as recently as April 2012, debris was discovered south of San Diego from a state-of-the-art yacht pulverized into pieces only two to three inches long, presumably by a larger craft. The incident certainly speaks to the helpless situation of sea creatures enduring a similar blow, with the yacht described as "looking like it had gone through a blender." "Three Dead, One Missing in Yacht Race Accident," *New York Times*, April 29, 2012.

18. Glover M. Allen, *Monographs on the Natural History of New England: The Whalebone Whales of New England* (Boston: Boston Society for Natural History, 1916), 198.

19. Ibid.

20. Ibid.

21. Philip Armstrong, *What Animals Mean in the Fiction of Modernity* (New York: Routledge, 2008), 106.

22. Allen, 198–99.

23. Caldwell, 707.

24. The Armstrong claim I contest here is that "the shock attending this incident results largely from the challenge the whale's apparent agency poses to the complacent pursuit of profits via the labor of industrial capitalism" (118). He appears to be doing what the antebellum readers were doing, only in the inverse, by casting the whale here as heroically retaliating against the forces of capitalism bent on killing

and commodifying him. However irresistible the argument both ethically and theoretically, it breaks down under the hard glare of nature science, the research from which is conspicuously absent in Armstrong's work. Such science, as shown, indicates the real likelihood that the whale was not inclined by behavior or anatomy to attack ships, but that Chase and the larger romantic culture were eager to make him appear so in his original casting in that role.

25. "In the metropolitan centers, away from the realities of the industry, such accounts were received with skepticism and mockery," Armstrong notes (119). There were indeed skeptics of Chase, whom I treat later, but they were hardly so influential as to stop the tide of popular demand for stories of whales capable of sinking ships, rather than mere boats, at will. Nor did any widespread skepticism against such agency gain traction to the extent that it could have ruined the popular reception of *Moby-Dick*, despite Melville's anticipation of backlash in "The Affidavit" chapter, which vehemently argues, based on Chase, for the plausibility of whales being able to destroy ships.

26. Thomas Nickerson, Owen Chase, and Others, *The Loss of the Ship "Essex," Sunk by a Whale*, ed. Nathaniel Philbrick and Thomas Philbrick (New York: Penguin, 2000), 30, hereafter *Loss*.

27. *Loss*, 26.

28. Obed Macy, *The History of Nantucket* (Boston: Hilliard, Gray, and Co., 1835), 242.

29. *Loss*, 24.

30. Armstrong, 102.

31. Robert Zoellner, *The Salt-Sea Mastodon: A Reading of "Moby-Dick"* (Berkeley: University of California Press, 1973), 266.

32. Caldwell, 690.

33. Louie Psihoyos, discussion with author, December 2011, Boulder, CO.

34. Jay Parini, *The Passages of H. M.: A Novel of Herman Melville* (New York: Random House, 2010), 90.

35. D. Graham Burnett, *The Sounding of the Whale: Science and Cetaceans in the Twentieth Century* (Chicago: University of Chicago Press, 2012), 317.

36. *Loss*, 30.

37. Ibid., 29–30.

38. Olmsted, 145.

39. "Decidedly Incredulous," *The Whalemen's Shipping List and Merchants' Transcript* 9, no. 38 (November 18, 1851): 2.

40. Thomas Heffernan, *Stove by a Whale: Owen Chase and the "Essex"* (Middletown, CT: Wesleyan University Press, 1981), 112.

41. Quoted in Heffernan, 111.

42. Nathaniel Philbrick, *In the Heart of the Sea: The Tragedy of the Whaleship "Essex"* (New York: Penguin, 2000), 255.

43. Caldwell, 692.

44. Henry T. Cheever, *The Whale and His Captors* (New York: Harper Brothers, 1850), 216. Hester Blum also uses the qualifier *seemingly* to project skepticism regarding Chase's account; she calls it a "seemingly premeditated attack by a sperm whale." "Melville and Oceanic Studies," *The New Cambridge Companion to Herman Melville*, ed. Robert S. Levine (New York: Cambridge University Press, 2014), 28–29.

45. Chase's influence is visible in such powerful cultural histories as George Cotkin's *Dive Deeper: Journeys with Moby-Dick* (New York: Oxford University Press, 2012), particularly in how the creature's malicious intent is presumed in the claim that "never before had it been reported that a whale had purposefully rammed a ship" (87).

46. Dolin appears to be following Philbrick's assertion that after the collision "the creature's tail continued to work up and down, pushing the 238-ton ship backward." Philbrick, *In the Heart of the Sea*, 83.

47. *Loss*, 26.

48. Melville, *Moby-Dick*, 316.

49. Clement Cleveland Sawtell, *The Ship "Ann Alexander" of New Bedford, 1805–1851* (New Bedford, MA: Marine Historical Association, 1962), 70–79.

50. Quoted in Sawtell, 9.

51. Davis Wasgatt Clark, *Travel and Adventure: Comprising Some of the Most Striking Narratives on Record* (Cincinnati: Swormstedt and Poe, 1856), 263–64.

52. Willis Abbot, *American Merchant Ships and Sailors* (New Bedford, MA: Applewood Books, 2009), 130.

53. Sawtell, 79.

54. Ibid., 82.

55. Caldwell, 691. While flight is the whale's usual reaction to danger, when the whale does resort to fighting, usually only under extreme circumstances, it will use its teeth as weapons far more frequently than its head as a battering ram. For more on the teeth as the whale's primary means of assault, see Frederick Debell Bennett, *Narrative of a Whaling Voyage around the Globe from the Year 1833 to 1836* (London: Richard Bentley, 1840), 176, 217; Charles Melville Scammon, *The Marine Animals of the Northwestern Coast of North America* (San Francisco: John H. Carmany, 1874), 82; James Temple Brown, *The Whale Fishery: Whalemen, Vessels, Apparatus and Methods* (New York: U.S. Commercial Fish and Fisheries, 1887), 261; Joshua Fillebrown Beane, *From the Forecastle to Cabin* (New York: Editor Publishing Company, 1905), 338; William John Hopkins, *She Blows! And Sparm at That!* (New York: Houghton Mifflin, 1922), 338; Robert Ferguson, *Harpooner: A Four-Year Voyage on the Barque "Kathleen," 1880–1884*, ed. L. D. Stair (Philadelphia: University of Pennsylvania Press, 1936), 41, 79; John Atkins Cook, *Pursuing the Whale* (New York: Houghton Mifflin, 1926), 9; and Clifford Warren Ashley, *The Yankee Whaler* (Garden City, NY: Halcyon House, 1942), 82.

56. Beale, 183.

57. Bennett, 220.

58. Melville, *Moby-Dick*, 163–64.

59. Barbara Ehrenreich, "The Animal Cure," *Harper's*, June 2012, 14.

60. *Loss*, 193–94.

61. The lack of an accurate historical record on the *Essex* is due in large part to the penetration of misinformation, beginning with Chase's *Narrative*, into academic research. For example, Chase is the single source behind Hester Blum's assertion that "the ship's captain shot his own cabin boy" in "Melville and Oceanic Studies," *The New Cambridge Companion to Herman Melville*, ed. Robert S. Levine (New York: Cambridge University Press, 2014), 29.

62. David Dowling, "How the Creator of *Jaws* Became the Shark's Greatest Defender," *Narratively*, August 2014.

INDEX

Illustrations following page 100 are indicated in *italics*, by the sequence number of the page on which they appear.

with, 4–5, 11, 48–49; U.S. government complicity in, 42; whaling industry culpability in, 16, 111–15. *See also* lottery

Carey, Matthew, 39–40

Carlisle, Henry, 30, 31, 109, 117–18, 125–26, 157

Chappel, Thomas, 18, 20, 124

Charles Carroll, 45–47

Charles Island, 3

Chase, Helen Winslow, 35

Chase, Owen: as basis for Ahab, 8, 120–21, 128–31, 139–40; as basis for Nehemiah, 128–31; as basis for Starbuck, 134–36; Coffin shooting and, 14, 17, 23–24, 28–29; critiques of, 156–57; descent into madness, 31–32, 109–11, 139, 168–69; *Essex* survival plan and, 3–5, 12, 33, 34, 47–49, 126–27; evasion of culpability in, 8, 30, 31, 110–11, 114–15, 120, 132, 134–35, 139–40, 160, 165, 168; family life and upbringing, 108, 137–38; financial loss in *Essex* disaster, 37–38, *100:5;* leadership/decision making of, 14, 45, 47–50, 56, 115, 124–28, 132, 139; legacy/moral assessment of, 7, 47–48, 102–3, 118–19; *Narrative* ghostwriting and, 33–41; on Nickerson, 25, *100:9;* Quaker doctrine as influence on, 135–37; Romanticism influence on, 144–45; whale agency and, 165; whaling career, 44–45, 47–48, 52, 120, 166. See also *Narrative of the Most Extraordinary and Distressing Shipwreck of the Whale-Ship Essex* (Chase)

Chase, Phoebe B., 110

Chase, Winnifred, 135

Cheever, Henry T., 158

Claggart, John, 104, 165

Clarel (Melville), 8, 33, 46, 105–7, 117, 128–31

Clark, Davis W., 162

Cobb, Sylvanus, 57–58

Coffin, Owen, 7, 10, 12–16, 18, 21–23, *100:2*

Coffin, William, 34, 37, 72

Coffin, William, Jr., 34–35, 72

Cohn, Jan, 67

Cole, Isaac, 23, 27–28

Coleridge, Samuel Taylor, 79, 92

Confidence-Man, The (Melville), 106–7

Conrad, Joseph, 23

Cook, James (Captain Cook), 89, 102, 180n23

Costa Concordia, 75–77

Crane, Stephen, 145

Crèvecoeur, J. Hector St. John de, 100, 103, 137–38

Darrow, Clarence, 72

Davis, Lance E., 38, 44–45

Davoll, Edward S., 139

DeBlois, John, 146–47, 160–62, 165

Derrick, Thomas, 78

"Desultory Sketches from a Seaman's Log" (Nickerson memoir), 17, 54–56, 60, 64–67, 87

Diana, 134

Dolin, Eric Jay, 141–42, 158–59

Douglass, Frederick, 93

Ducie Island, 11, 46, 64–65, 157

Dudley, Tom, 113–14

Dunlap, Walter B., 58

Eagle, 124

Easter Island, 11–12, 51–52

economy: African American whaling labor, 29; animal agency

as threat to capitalism, 149–50, 187–88nn24–25; cannibalism as class ritual, 27; cannibalism as free market metaphor, 45; capitalism as Chase theme, 41–43; capitalist compensatory ambition, 127–28, 136–37; Nantucket class structure, 100–102; New Bedford commercial environment, 52, 80; whaleboat laborer personal ambition and, 43–44; whaling financial investment/profits/income, 37–38, 45–46, 94–96

Ehrenreich, Barbara, 165

Elizabeth Island, 64–65

Emerson, Ralph Waldo: account of Melville whaling expedition, 9–10; human vulnerability/humility in, 88; on Nantucket, 102, 118; Pollard relationship with, 10, 32–33, 98–99, 166; transcendentalism of, 95

Essex: account of sinking, 1–4, 122–26, 148–58; Chase mainland voyage plan, 4–5, 12, 33, 34, 47–49, 109; crew member list, *100:5*; Easter Island destination, 11–12, 51–52; Henderson Island rescue, 5, 50–51; international coverage of sinking, 134; Marquesas/Tahiti as rejected destinations, 12, 22, 34, 38–39, 47–49, 106, 109, 128; Pollard lifeboat whale attack, 49–50; rescue of lifeboats, 124–25; sketches of, *100:1–3*; *Two Brothers* shipwreck and, 83, 85–93, 95, 97

Everett, Edward, 63, 177n1

Fanning Island, 82–83

Fern, Fanny, 177n1

Finch, Ann, 55–56

flash papers, 69, 178n25

Flores Island, 158–59

Frankenstein (Shelley), 89, 144–45, 149, 165

Gardner, Eben, 78, 81, 84–88, 96–97, 158, 180n21

ghostwriting, 33–41, 53–62, 72, 172n7

Gilley, William B., 39

Globe, 34

gothic fiction literary genre, 42

"Great Glacial Deluge and Its Impending Recurrence, The" (Lewis), 72–74

Hamilton, 114

"Happy Failure, The" (Melville), 107

Hawaiian Islands, 49, 83

Hawthorne, Nathaniel, 30, 106

Hayes, Kevin J., 173n16

Heffernan, Thomas, 34, 40, 51, 128, 130–31, 134–35, 137, 157, 180n21

Henderson Island, 4–5, 8, 11, 20, 46, 50–51, *100:2*

Hendricks, Obed, 127

History of Nantucket (Macy), 34, 79–80, 150

Holder Borden, 113–14

Hudson River painters, 145

hurricanes, 49

Hussey, Christopher, 116

Hussey, Cyrus, 34

Hysco, 124

Indian, 125

Ishmael (*Moby-Dick* character), 9, 18, 20, 143–44

Jackson, Shirley, 30

Jane Eyre (Brontë), 35

Jaws (Benchley film), 169

Jenkins, Henry, 120–21

129–30, 133, 142–43, 155–57, 159, 164–65; whalemen's gambling impulse in, 80; whaling advocacy in, 41. *See also individual characters*—Ahab; Ishmael

Moby-Dick 2010 (film), 154

moral and religious issues: absence of scapegoating and, 29–30; African American sacrificial roles, 28–29; Ahab and death pledge, 14; cannibalism as moral failure, 16, 20, 103–4; Chase and alignment with Christian values, 18, 20, 25, 31, 41, 134–35; Coffin's sacrificial role, 7, 10, 13–15, 18, 21–23; Cole's sacrificial role, 27; divine providence in Chappel, 20–21; hyperactive agency detection and, 165; Jonah figure in whaling, 19, 117, 130, 149; lottery as moral failure, 23–24; Melville's engagement with, 14, 20–21, 106–7; moral self-sacrifice as cannibalism paradigm, 26; Nantucket Quakers, 21, 98–99, 101, 103–4, 106, 115–16; Nantucket shame culture, 16, 100–103, 113; Oedipal/ psychological *Essex* symbolism, 12; religious allegory in Melville, 18–20; sailors' absence of religious piety, 135; scapegoating of Pollard, 15–18, 107–8; whale as divine retribution, 18–20, 144–45, 149–50

Mutiny on Board the Whaleship Globe (Lay and Hussey), 34

Nantucket: bird's eye sketch of, *100:8*; Chase legacy/reputation and, 102–3, 118–19, 130, 133; class structure, 100–102; Emerson-Pollard meeting, 10, 105–6, 109; *Essex* last voyage from, 1–2; and *Essex* tragedy moral culpability, 16, 30, 111–15; *History of Nantucket* shipwreck accounts, 79–80; as international whaling port, 101–2, 116–18, 133–34; Lewis and betrayal as concern on, 59; Nantucket Quakers, 21, 98–99, 101, 103–4, 106, 115–16, 135–37, 173n25, 182n11; New Bedford compared with, 52, 80, 101–2; Nickerson as tourist host, 54, 57, 59, 61; Pollard legacy/reputation and, 10, 15–18, 79–80, 111–18; shame culture, 16, 100–103, 113–14, 118–19; social role of Pollard as night watchman, 7–8, 17, 98–106, 118; *Two Brothers* voyage and, 111–12, 167–68

Narrative of Arthur Gordon Pym (Poe), 34–35, 42

Narrative of a Whaling Voyage around the Globe (Bennett), 164–65

Narrative of the Most Extraordinary and Distressing Shipwreck of the Whale-Ship Essex (Chase): account of Coffin shooting in, 13–15, 23–24; African American sailors in, 29; anticipative horror in, 42; effect on other accounts, 133–34; ghostwriting of, 6, 31, 33–41; Melville's view of, 32–33, 111; publication and writing of, 5–7, 31, 39–40, 41, *100:4*, 165–66; as revenge narrative, 139–40; vengeful whale theme in, 150–56, 159, 163–64; whaling advocacy in, 41–43. *See also* Chase, Owen

Native Americans, 116

Natural History of the Sperm Whale (Beale), 141

nautical fiction literary genre, 57–58

New American Practical Navigator (Bowditch), 45–46

New Bedford, 52, 80, 101–2, 129

New York Ledger, 6, 17, 40, 53, 56–67

whaling: captain's role, 2, 37–38, 42–46, 75–77, 79–80; Chase *Narrative* defense of, 41–43, 94; *Essex* tragedy moral culpability, 16, 111–15; *Essex* whaling expedition, 3–4; financial investment/profits in, 37–38, 45–46; gambling impulse in, 44–45, 80, 91–92; marine insurance, 113–14, 123, 131–32; mutinies, 22, 36, 42, 44; Nantucket as international port, 101–2, 116–18; "Nantucket sleigh ride" experience, *100:9;* Native American tutelage in, 116; navigation issues, 45–46, 75, 83; Nickerson portrayal of, 94–96; obsessive whale pursuit theme, 8, 130; personal ambition in, 43–44; sperm whales, 3, 9, 116, 125–28, 141–44, 186n3, 186n5; training and career advancement, 137–38; vengeful whale theme, 9, 18–20, 42, 82, *100:10,* 126, 129–32, 134–35, 141–58; virtue/honor in, 47–48; whale-ship collisions and accidents, 145–48, 187n17

Wheelock, Julia, 70–71

Whipple, A. B. C., 107–9

Whitehead, Hal, 157–58

Whitman, Walt, 36

Wilkes, Charles, 91, 167

Wilson, Harriet, 38

Winslow, 9–10, 45–47

Worth, Benjamin, 28

Yankee Whalers in the South Seas (Whipple), 107–8

Zoellner, Robert, 151